Henry Onderdonk, William Henry De Hart

History of the First Reformed Dutch Church of Jamaica, L.I.

Henry Onderdonk, William Henry De Hart

History of the First Reformed Dutch Church of Jamaica, L.I.

ISBN/EAN: 9783337261184

Printed in Europe, USA, Canada, Australia, Japan

Cover: Foto ©Lupo / pixelio.de

More available books at **www.hansebooks.com**

HISTORY

OF THE

First Reformed Dutch Church

OF JAMAICA, L. I.,

BY

HENRY ONDERDONK, JR.,

A. B. UNIVERSITY OF CAMBRIDGE;
A. M. COLUMBIA COLLEGE.

WITH AN APPENDIX

BY

REV. WM. H. DeHART,

The Pastor.

PUBLISHED BY
THE CONSISTORY.
1884.

PASTOR
WILLIAM HENRY DeHART.

Elders: *Deacons:*
ISAAC SNEDEKER, THOMAS H. FREDERICKS,
JOHN A. HEGEMAN, DAVID BAYLIS,
SAMUEL G. COZINE, JOHN HENDRICKSON,
FRANCIS F. GULICK, DITMARS ELDERT.

Treasurer:
ISAAC AMBERMAN.

Chorister: *Organist:*
WILLIAM FORMAN WYCKOFF, MARTHA ELLEN PHRANER.

Sexton:
BENJAMIN F. EVERITT.

CHARLES WELLING,
Printer,
JAMAICA, L. I.

PREFACE.

This History is compiled from such of the Church documents as have survived the ravages of time and carelessness of man. The Deacons had an alms-chest in which they kept not only the money but the books, memoranda and loose papers belonging to the Church. Besides these, the Journals of the Cœtus and Conferentie, and the Acts and Proceedings of the General and Particular Synods, published in 1859, have been consulted, as well as the manuscript minutes of the Classes of New York and Long Island. All these afford scanty materials, but they are supplemented by letters sent before 1772 to the Classis of Amsterdam and since, about 1845, returned to our General Synod.

At the building of the first church, 1717, a book was purchased in which were entered fully and clearly the names of contributors and the allotment of seats; but thereafter the entries were few and far between, so that for years we have no account of the proceedings of the congregation. This prevents our giving a continuous record and makes our History rather a Book of Chronicles. Many transactions, doubtless, were not reduced to writing, and we may suppose that nine-tenths of the writings have been lost, or destroyed, as not worth preserving.

The Consistory in early times do not appear to have kept a record of their proceedings; and in later times we have only one or two odd volumes.

There are no records of marriages before 1802. The entries of baptisms seem regular from 1702 to 1742; thence onward there are interruptions till 1785. There is not a single entry during the Revolutionary War. In the other Dutch Churches of Queens county the baptisms are recorded with seeming regularity from 1741 to the present time.

For the latter part of our History we have made free use of newspaper notices of the less important incidents of our Church and Sunday School.

HISTORY

OF THE

First Reformed Dutch Church

OF JAMAICA, L. I.

THE organization of the Reformed Dutch Church of Jamaica is veiled in obscurity. It was probably by or before 1702, for the record of the first baptism is dated June 1, of that year. But the Dutch had gradually been emigrating from Kings county into the western part of Queens county long before this date; for in 1695 twenty-two Dutchmen (to escape an enforced assessment) had joined with their English townsmen in a "free gift" to the Rev. Geo. Phillips, Presbyterian minister of Jamaica, promising to pay quarterly as follows :

	d.		d.
John Hansen[Bergen]	12	Peter Hendrickse	7
Hendrick Lot	12	Johannes Williamsen	4
Dowe Jansen	6	John Snedeker	5
Garret Lubertsen	8	David Loisee	6
Jacob Jansen	6	John Brewer	5
Endert Lucas	12	John Oakey	10
John Cockefer	12	Jan Monfort	7
Hendrick Aresen	6	Gerret Jansen	6
Stephen Coevert	5	Gerret Clasen	10
Theodorus Polhemus	12	Hendrick [illegible]	10
John Lambertse	6	Hendrick Hegeman	10

But when by law and town vote* the Dutch were taxed for the building of the Presbyterian Church in 1699, they, or some of them, refused to pay; and the matter was referred to John Coe, judge, and Samuel Edsall† and Content Titus, justices; and this is their award:

"WHEREAS, there have been several differences had, moven, and depending within the town of Jamaica, concerning the building a meeting-house or church within said town; and also the accounts, demands and charges thereunto appertaining, which, with all controversies anyway relating thereto, being, this 15th of April, 1701, mutually referred to us by the parties on behalf of themselves and others concerned; we, hearing both parties, do give our award as follows:

"That William Creed and Robert Reade, and all those of the west of Jamaica, that is, the Dutchmen, viz: *Frederick Hendricksen, John Oakey, Hendrick Lott, Theodorus Polhemus, and Eldert Lucas,* who have not perfectly and wholly paid their rates assessed for building the church or meeting-house, shall pay their parts unpaid within two weeks, and acquit each other of all former controversies; and we desire that they may amicably agree and live in love together."—*Town Records,* II, 360.

"Know all men by these presents, that we, Daniel Whitehead, Joseph Smith, Edward Burroughs, and Jonas Wood, Esquires, have received, this 28th of April, 1701, of William Creed, Robert Reade, and all of the *Dutchmen* living westward of the town of Jamaica, full satisfaction and payment for building of the church lately built in said town. Therefore we discharge and acquit them and their heirs forever, according to the award."

The Dutch were soon settled at Springfield; and Foster's Meadow even in 1657. There were also scattered settlements on the north side, extending along through Newtown, Flushing, Black Stump, Success, Little Neck, Great Neck, Cow Neck, Cedar Swamp and Wolver Hollow, and a few at a later date got as far east as Huntington.

The Dutch having relations and friends in Kings county, at first went thither for worship, marriages, and christenings. It was a long and tedious ride; but sometimes Dutch min-

---

* On the passage of the Church Building Act, they laid aside the prosecution of building according to the town vote, and took hold of said act, by virtue of which the church was built and distress made on Churchmen, Quakers and Baptists, people of the *Dutch congregation,* etc., promiscuously for payment of the rates. *Documentary History.*

† Edsall came from England in 1648; and intermarried with the Dutch families.

isters from Kings county and New York came out to Jamaica* and held services in the Court house or stone church, which being town property, was probably open to all comers.

About the time of the organization of the church the Minister of Kings county, Wilhelmus Lupardus, had died, and the people there were divided in the choice of a successor. A part of the congregation made a call on Bernardus Freeman, pastor of Schenectady. After some hesitation and considerable negotiation he accepted the call and removed to Flatbush. Meanwhile the other party had applied to the Classis of Amsterdam for a minister, and they sent over Vincentius Antonides, who arrived in Flatbush Jan. 1, 1706; so that there were two ministers on hand where only one was wanted. Hence arose an angry struggle for the possession of the church property, which lasted through nine troublous years.

Lord Cornbury claimed the privilege of tolerating ministers. Here follows his license to Domine Freeman:

COMMISSION TO MR. FREEMAN TO BE MINISTER OF KINGS CO.

By His Excellency Edward Viscount Cornbury, Captain General and Governor-in-chief of the Province of New York, New Jersey, &c., &c.

To *Mr. Bernardus Freeman, greeting:*

You are hereby licensed, tolerated and allowed to be minister of the Dutch congregation at New Utrecht, Flatbush, Brooklyn and Bushwick, and to have and exercise the free liberty and use of your religion according to the laws in such case made and provided, for and during so long a time as to me shall seem meet; and all persons are hereby required to take notice hereof accordingly.

Given under my hand and seal at Fort Anne, in New York, December 26, 1705.

CORNBURY. { SEAL. }

The church of Jamaica caught the factious spirit from

---

* 1661. Some of the inhabitants of Jamaica earnestly petitioned Governor Stuyvesant that he would send one of the Dutch ministers of New Amsterdam to preach for them and baptize their children. In compliance with this request he sent Rev. Samuel Drisius, who could preach in Dutch, French or English, as occasion required, to Jamaica on Saturday, January 8th, and on the next day he preached two sermons and baptized eight children and two women.—*Dutch MSS.*, IX, 486.

Kings county and took the side of Domine Freeman against Antonides, as may be seen by the following petition:

PETITION OF THE ELDERS OF DOMINE FREEMAN'S CONGREGATION.

To the Hon. Richard Ingoldsby, Esq., Lieut. Gov. and Commander-in-chief of the Province of New York, New Jersey, &c.

The most humble petition of Dorus Polhemus, John Hansen[Bergen], Christian Snedeker and John Snedeker, Elders of the Dutch congregation of Queens Co. Showeth:

WHEREAS, Mr. Freeman by orders from our late Governor, the Lord Cornbury, was to be minister of this congregation—and none else; which also was confirmed by the Lord Lovelace, according to which we Your Honor's petitioners were chosen and constituted elders of the church and now continue to be so.

Nevertheless Mr. Antonides being very well apprised hereof, but minding to make a division and disturbance in the church here (as we are told he has done in Kings Co.) has lately, as we are informed, taken upon himself in concert with some few others to make choice of other elders of the said congregation and does design to publish them as such at the church or[Presbyterian] meeting house at Jamaica to-morrow and also then to preach to the said congregation, for the doing of which, as we humbly conceive, he has no manner of power or authority from Your Honor. We therefore humbly pray for the preventing of the ill consequences which such practices by him will inevitably produce, that Your Honor will be pleased, as has been usual, to order that no Dutch minister shall preach or exercise his ministerial function in this county besides Mr. Freeman, till further orders from Your Honor; and Your Honor's petitioners shall ever pray.

THEODORUS POLHEMUS.
JOHN HANSEN.†
Sep. 19, 1709. JAN SNEDEKER.

1711. *February 4.*—Col Heathcote writes that "the Church of England,* at Jamaica, is of late very much strengthened by a violent division, which hath for a considerable time been raging among the Dutch in some of the neighboring towns concerning their minister, of whom they have two, and their heats being grown to that degree that there is now no

---

* The Episcopal church of Jamaica, the oldest on the Island, was started about the same time with the Dutch Church. The first rector, Patrick Gordon, took sick at Jamaica the day before he designed to preach, and died eight days after. He was buried July 28, 1702.

† 1684—John Hansen, John Tunesen and Jerome Rapelye buy land of the Indians at Rockaway. 1685—Jamaica allows John Hansen to set up a corn and fulling mill on Foster's river.

STONE CHURCH.

Erected by the town of Jamaica 1699, in which the Dutch Congregation occasionally worshipped before 1710.

hopes of a reconciliation, many of those people have joined Mr. Poyer's church."

1714. *December 27.*—The people of Kings and Queens counties, having got tired of disputing about the claims of the rival ministers, at length agreed to forget all past animosities, provide two parsonages at Flatbush, and unite in support of both, as may be seen by the following document:

SUBSTANCE OF AN AGREEMENT WITH DOMINES ANTONIDES AND FREEMAN, DONE AT FLATLANDS DEC. 27, 1714.

The undersigned for the churches of Flatbush, Brooklyn, Flatlands, New Utrecht, Bushwick and New Jamaica, agree to pay (in New York money) half-yearly, to Domines Antonides and Freeman for preaching as follows:

Flatbush	£40	New Utrecht	£34*
Brooklyn	40	New Jamaica	40
Flatlands	30		

They also agree to furnish the domines with firewood to be brought to their doors, and to keep in repair their dwellings and garden fences.

The domines agree to perform all the duties of their office, to preach twice a day on Sundays†. The sacraments to be administered by both ministers in their turn as follows: Bushwick, Brooklyn and Flatbush together as the first; Flatlands, Gravesend and New Utrecht together as the second, and New Jamaica by itself.

In drawing lots it was decided that Flatlands should supply the wood the first year, Brooklyn the second year, Bushwick the third, Flatbush the fourth, New Utrecht the fifth, and New Jamaica the sixth year.

The preaching turns to be as follows:
1st. Bushwick and New Utrecht. 2d. Flatbush and New Jamaica.‡ 3d. Brooklyn and Flatlands.

(Signed.)
CORNELIUS SEBRING.   JOHN TERHUNEN.
JERONIMUS REMSEN.   GARRET HANSEN.
PETER STRYKER.   PETER CORTELYOU.
JOHN VANDERVEER.   THEODORUS POLHEMUS.
JOHANNES SCHENCK.   CORNELIUS VAN BRUNT.
J. VAN ZANDT.   THEODORUS VAN WYCK.§

---

* 1715, Jan. 15. New Utrecht let Gravesend have and pay for a third of the preaching.

† Sunday, not Sabbath, is the word mostly used in the old Dutch records. In the Heidelberg catechism the translator has substituted Lords Day for Sondag, the Dutch word for Sunday.

‡ The origin of the name Jamaica is in dispute. It may have been so named from Jamaica in the West Indies, which was captured from Spain May 10, 1655. Hence often called New Jamaica.

§ His ancestor, Cornelius Barentz Van Wyck, from Wyck, in Holland, was settled in Flatbush in 1660.

Subscription lists for both ministers were now put in circulation. Two of which (containing mostly Flushing and Foster's Meadow names) have been preserved and are here printed :*

JAMAICA, QUEENS Co., Jan. 10, 1715.

We the underwritten of the Nether Dutch Ref. church in Queens Co. on the Island Nassau promise to pay yearly to the Consistory and their successors for the maintenance of both the ministers as their salary. I promise truly and honestly to pay without guile or trickery the half thereof in 6 months and the other half at the end of the year, as signed with my hand.

	s.	d.		s.	d.
Marten Wiltse	10		Frans Masten	6	
Johannes Van Wyck	12		Barent Bloem	10	
Adriaen Onderdonck	7		Peter Huf	9	
Teunis Snedeker	8		John Haviland	3	
Derick De Moet	6		Jan Montfoort	10	
Jurian Haff	6		Peter Montfort	5	
Joseph Van Klef	8		Theodorus Van Wyck	13	
Margrietie Ganon	5		Cornelius Wiltse	3	
Wyntie Wright	3		Cornelius Hoogelzend	9	
John Marston	3		Tuenes Coevert	5	
Anthony Glean	3		Jan Dorlandt	2	
Thomas Eckisen	6		Stephen Ryder	12	
Johannes Noerstraent	6		Lourens Hof	8	
Direk Brinckerhoff	13		Rem Adreanse	6	
Abm. Schenck	5		Jan Boutse	4	
Anna Haptonstell	1	6	John Van Leuwe	8	
Pieter Montfort	9		Adam Smith	8	

	s.	d.		s.	d.
Abm. Dela Montanye	6		Haen Jaensen	20	
Karel Dorlandt	6		Jan Hagewout	10	
Johannes Demot	8		Cornelius Barns	6	
Christeyan Snedeker	20		Hendrick Acten	6	
Willem Gritman	6		Johannes Coerten	14	
Thos. Hendrickson	5		Jaen Baerisen	12	
Jaen Hendrickson	15		Benjamin Hegeman	14	
Johannes Eldersen	12		Aerent V. Noerstraen	15	
Hendrick Hendricksen	6		Jem Bortes	7	
Willem Jaense	20		Hendrick Doesenburgh	16	

---

* The spelling of names varies greatly. We mostly follow the original. Thus we have Haff, Hoff, Huff; Cockefer, Kockevaer; Nostrand, Noorstrant, etc. Some are written in Dutch and some in English, as Jan, Hance or Johannes for John; Jores or Joris for George; Magiel for Michael.

	s. d.		s. d.
Hendrick Baerisen	10	Antonie Demoet	15
Jan Bortus	10	Maegiel Demoet	15
Jonathan Shaw	4 10	Jaen Remsen	10
Nath'l Monse	5	Rem Remsen	18
Jacop Pietersen	6	Andries Onderdonck	18
Hendrick Brooher	22	Elbert Monfort	14
Jaen Doesbuerch	6	Stevie Jaense	12
After Burtus	7	Jores Springsteen	6
Jaen Lenden	6	Magdalena Baird	12

Peace being now restored to pastors and people the Dutch congregation became desirous of having a house of worship nearer home. The consistory accordingly drew up and presented to the people the following proposals:

THE ARTICLES OF THE CHURCH MADE APRIL 29, 1715.

We the Consistory of New Jamaica in Queens Co. on the Island Nassau, composed of the elders and deacons of the Reformed Nether Dutch congregation throughout the whole of Queens Co. are unanimously resolved on a proposition to the congregation to build a church unto the glory of the true God and our Lord Jesus Christ to honor his name.

God hath richly blessed us and enabled us to build houses for our families; but we are also bound to show our gratitude to God by building a house for the Lord and for the family of God; for all that we have and possess is given us by a good God; and that we may induce him to grant us greater blessings we out of our own means ought from motives of piety to build a house to the glory and honor of his name, for thus saith the Lord: "in all places where I record my name I will come unto thee and bless thee." We are therefore assured that whoever giveth to the Lord for the building of His house the Lord will bless him with rich returns.

We are therefore resolved to further the building of a house for the Dutch congregation; and to prove the love of God's children not only in word but in very deed, we propose to the good-hearted brethren and sisters, the following conditions in order that every one may be regulated by them:

1. Those who are not able to give money toward the building of the church, but are inclined to work certain days to the building thereof, this service shall be received the same as money subscribed.

2. If it should ultimately be found that there is not a sufficient sum subscribed for building a house for the Lord (which we hope may not be the case), then the subscribers shall not be bound to pay what they have subscribed; because the failure of the good design is not to be attributed to them, but to those unwilling to give.

3. It shall be the privilege of the congregation to choose superintendents of the building into whose hands the money subscribed shall be lodged.

4. The congregation shall choose 2 men to whom the superintendents shall render an account of the receipts and expenditures when the church is finished.

5. The congregation shall choose church-masters [Kerk-meesters] for the first time to regulate the seats in the church.

6. The highest subscriber shall have the privilege of choosing the first seat for himself and wife.

7. Those who subscribe an equal sum shall decide by lot which shall have the first choice, that there may be no misunderstanding or dispute.

8. Further, the holders of seats shall be obliged to pay the expense at any time necessary to keep the building in good repair, so that God's house fall not into decay, which business shall be directed and ordered by the church-masters.

9. Finally it is understood that those who give no money, but their labor, or who give a little, shall have the same right by lot in the wages of their day's work at an appointed price.

This signing is attested the 29th of April, 1715:

	£ s.		£ s.
Adriause, Rem	2	Ditmarsen, Douwe	5
Atten, Hendrick	1	Dorland, Ante	2 10
Bas, Abm.	1	Dorland, Gerret.	3
Beekman, Wm.	5	Doesenburgh, Hendrick	1 10
Berrien, Peter	5	Demott, Johannes	2 4
Bergen, Jan Hansen	3	Demott, Magiel	1 10
Bergen, Johannes, Jr	2 10	Drack, Johannes	10
Bergen, Tunis	2	Forest, Johannes	3
Berrien, Nicholas	4	Glien, Antony	1 10
Blaw, Jan	1	Gennon, Margrietle	1
Burtis, James	1 10	Gerretsen, Peter	2 10
Blom, Simon	2	Golder, Wm	1 10
Bras, Hendrick	1 10	Hegeman, Adrian	2
Barentse, Johannes	1	Hardenberg, Jan	4
Brinckerhoff, Gerret	4	Hof, Jurien	1 10
Brinckerhoff, Altie, widow	3	Hof, Laurens	3
Brinckerhoff, Jores	8	Hof, Peter	3
Brinckerhoff, Derick	6	Hoegeland, Cornelius	3
Carpenter, Sarah	6	Hagewout, Jan	1
Cornell, Peter	1	Hegeman, Hend'k	4
Covert, Tunis	1	Hegeman, Joseph	1
Crankhyd, Jacobus	6	Hegeman, Benj	2
Demott, Antony	4	Jansen, Stephen	1
Demott, Derick	2	Jansen, Harmen	6 10

FIRST REFORMED DUTCH CHURCH.

	£ s.		£ s.
Kip, Jesse	3 10	Ryder, Stephen	5
Lott, Johannes	2	Schenck, Abm	2 10
Lott, Abm	3	Snedeker, Christian	8
Loise, Jan	1	Snedeker, Tunis	2 10
Lambertse, Nicholas	6	Springsteen, Derick	3
Luyster, Peter	8	Springsteen, Casper	2
Luyster, Cornelius	5	Springsteen, Jost	1
Marsten, Frans	1 10	Snedeker, Jan	2 10
Marsten, Jan	6	Stevense, Stephen	3
Monfort, Jan	5	Teller, Benj *	1
Monfort, Peter	3	Van Nostrand, Aaron	3
Nostrand, Rem	1	Van Leuwen, Dina	2 10
Nostrand, Peter	3	Van Leuwen, Johannes	2
Onderdonck, Adrian	2 10	Van Derbilt, Jacob	2
Onderdonck, Andries	2 10	Van Hoek, Isaac	1
Polhemus, Theodorus	5	Van Kleef, Joseph	2
Probasco, Jan	3	Van Lettingen Gerret	5
Remsen, Abm	4	Van Nostrand, Johannes	2 10
Remsen, Rem	2 10	Van Wicklen, Gerret	3 10
Remsen, Jores	2 10	Van Wyck, Theodorus	8
Remsen, Jan	2 10	Van Wyck, Johannes	8
Remsen, Jacob	3	Wilsen, Martin	3
Ryder, Albert	1	Willemsen, Johannes	1 10
Ryder, Jurian	2		

The after following have promised to give toward the building of our Dutch church as follows:

	£ s.		£ s.
Amberman, Paulus	1	Hoff, Jacob	10
Bras, Jan	1	Jansen, Wm	1 10
Blom, Barent	3	Kolyer, Catharina, widow	10
Cockefer, Jan†	3	Loise, Jacobus	1
Douwe, Aletta, widow	5	Lukasen, Eldert	4
Elsall, Janetie	2	Monfort, Elbert	2
Elderse, Hendrick	2	Rapelye, Jores	3 15
Fin, The widow [Anatie]	2 10	Ricke, Abm	2
Haviland, Sarah	10	Wilsen, Cornelis	1 10
Hendricksen, Jan	1 7½		

---

* Adriana, wife of Benj. Taylor, from L. I., joined the Dutch Church in N. Y., 1741.

† 1761, Nov. 24.—Died, at Jamaica, last week, John Cockefer who was born so long ago that for many years past he has forgot his age. He often said he was a soldier in the Fort at New York, in Gov. Leisler's time (who was here during the civil war in 1689) and had been a man grown several years before he enlisted and that when a young man he had often shot quails and squirrels on or near Pot baker's hill, in John street, New York, which was then a wilderness. (He and his wife Tryntie owned a house and farm of 150 acres, at the village of Springfield.—*Weyman's N. Y. Gazette.*

1715, Nov. 18   We the underwritten promise by these to pay for the building of our church the sums hereunder set:

	£ s.		£ s.
Adriansen, Rem	1	Jansen, Wm	2 4
Aten, Hend'k	5 6	Lettingen, Gerret	1
Antony, Elizabeth	1	Lott, Johannes	1
Baird, Magdalen*	11	Luyster, Peter	8
Boorem, Johannes	1	Luyster, Cornelis	1 10
Bloodgood, Wm	2	Lott, Abm	1
Barensen, Cornelis	1	Marsten, Jan	6
Barensen, Hend'k	1	Monfort, Elbert	10
Blom, Simon	10	Monfort, Jan	2
Bras, Hend'k	11	Monfort, Peter, Jr.	10
Bras, Jan	6	Montanye, Abm	10
Berrien, Clas	16	Onderdonck, Adrian	11
Berrien, Peter	1	Onderdonck, Andries	10
×Boog, Hester	11	Polhemus, Johannes	1 5
Bergen, Peter	1	Polhemus, Tunis	1 5
Brinckerhoff, Derick	2	Probasco, Jan	1
Brinckerhoff, Jores	15	Rapelye, Jores	10
Cockefer, Jan	1	Remsen, Rem	10
Demott, Magiel	10	Remsen, Jacob	1
Demott, Antony	1	Remsen, Abm	2
Ditmarsen, Do we	2	Remsen, Jores	10
Demott, Derick	8	Ryder, Jurian	10
Dorland, Gerret	1	Ryder, Stephen	1 10
Dorland, Ante	11	Robertson, Maria	11
Forhiesen, Johannes	10	Schenck, Abm	10
Gennon, Margrietie †	6	Springsteen, Casper	2
Gerritsen, Peter	10	Smith, Alida	11
Hendricksen, Thos	6	Snedeker, Tunis	1
Hendricksen, Jan	1 7½	Snedeker, Jan	10
Hardenberg, Jan	1	Snedeker, Jan	1
Hegeman, Hend'k	1	Vanderbilt, Jacob	1
Hof, Jurian	8	Van Nostrand, Johannes	10
Hogeland, Cornelius	1	Van Leuwen, Dina	10
Hof, Peter	1	Van Wicklen, Gerret	11
Hof, Jacob	10	Van Wyck, Theodorus	2
Jansen, Harmen	2	Wilsen, Martin	1
		Willemsen, Johannes	10

The first church stood nearer the road than the present one. A lot was bought (May 13, 1715) at the nominal price

* Widow Magdalen Kip, 1704, married Alexander Baird, a young Scotchman. In 1705 he was schoolmaster at Foster's Meadow. In 1712 he was Sheriff of Queens Co. [Magdalen Van Vleck]

† Margretie, wife of Jean Guenon, a Frenchman, lived in Flushing in 1680. She died 1722, leaving children: John Jeremiah, born 1671; Hannah, who married Joseph Hedger and Susanna, who married a Louereer.

× Hester Van Vleck, Half-sister of Magdalen

of 5 shillings. The deed, written on parchment, (but not recorded) reads as follows :

THIS INDENTURE, made the 13th day of May in the first year of the reign of our sovereign Lord George, by the grace of God over Great Britain, France and Ireland King, Defender of the faith, &c., and in the year of our blessed Lord and Saviour Jesus Christ 1715, BETWEEN Benj. Woolsey of Oysterbay in Queens Co. on L. I., within the Province of New York, Gent. and Abigail his wife of the one part, and Nicholas Berrien of Newtown, in the Co. aforesaid, Gent., and Abraham Schenck of Flushing, in the same county, Gent, on the other part; WHEREAS Daniel Whitehead, Esq., late of Jamaica in Queens Co. aforesaid, did by his last will and testament dated the 13th day of Nov'r *anno domini* 1703, give and devise unto his daughter Mary Burroughs, then the widow and relict of Thomas Burroughs late of the city of New York, merchant, and her heirs and assigns forever, a certain lot of land situate and being in the town of Jamaica aforesaid, containing about two acres lying next to the lot which did formerly belong to Henry Filkin, now in the possession of the executors of Samuel Denton dec'd; of which said two acres of land the said Daniel Whitehead, died, seized; and whereas the said Mary Burroughs, (who afterwards intermarried with Wm. Urquhart, rector of Jamaica aforesaid, deceased) died intestate, leaving no other children behind her but two daughters, to wit, the said Abigail Woolsey, wife of said Benjamin, and Mary Burroughs a minor, by which her death and the testamentary disposition aforesaid, the said two acres of land became the right of the said Abigail and Mary as her lawful descendants, and by representation; now this INDENTURE WITNESSETH that the said Benj. Woolsey and Abigail his wife, for and in consideration of the sum of 5 shillings lawful money of New York to them in hand paid at and before the ensealing and delivery of these presents by the said Nicholas Berrien and Abraham Schenck the receipt whereof they do hereby acknowledge, and thereof and of every part and parcel thereof do fully, clearly and absolutely acquit, exonerate and discharge the said Nicholas Berrien and Abraham Schenck, their and every of their executors and administrators by these presents and for other good and lawful considerations them thereunto moving, for the use, intent and purpose hereafter mentioned, have granted, bargained, sold, aliened, enfeoffed and confirmed and by these presents they, the said Benj. Woolsey and Abigail his wife do grant, bargain, sell, alien, enfeoff and confirm unto them the said Nicholas Berrien and Abraham Schenck and their heirs and assigns forever a small tract of land, part of the said above recited two acres of land situate in the town of Jamaica aforesaid, beginning at the N. E. corner of the said two acres of land and to run southerly along the land late in the possession of Samuel Denton aforesaid 5 English rods, thence forming a right angle westerly 5 rods, thence in the same manner northerly 5 rods and thence easterly the same length to the first station, to be bounded easterly by the land lately belonging to the said Samuel Denton, northerly by the main street in Jamaica, southerly and westerly by the rest of the said two acres of land; and all and singular rights, easments, priviledges and hereditaments with the appurtenances to the same in any ways appertaining, and also the reversion and reversions, remainder and remainders, right, estate, title, interest, possession, benefit, claim and demand whatsoever of them the said Benj. Woolsey and Abigail his wife or either of them, of, in or to, all and singular the above granted small tract of land and premises with the appurtenances: To HAVE AND TO HOLD the said above granted small tract of land and premises with the appurtenances unto them the said Nicholas Berrien and Abraham Schenck and their heirs and assigns forever, to the use, intent and purpose hereafter mentioned, and for and to no other use, intent or purpose whatsoever: That is to say, to the intent and purpose that the said Nicholas Berrien and Abraham Schenck and every their heirs and assigns shall at all times hereafter permit and suffer the congregation of the Nether Dutch Reformed Church in Queens Co. abovesaid, or such other person or persons as by them or the major part of them shall be nominated and appointed, to erect and build for the sole use and benefit of the said congregation and their successors forever a church or public edifice for the worship of Almighty God, and further to the intent that the said Nicholas Berrien and Abraham Schenck and either of them and all and every of their or either of their heirs and assigns shall at all time and times hereafter, when required, assign, release and make over unto the said congregation of the Nether Dutch Reformed church in Queens Co. or body politique incorporated representing them, or any such succeeding congregation, or to any other person or persons as by them or their successors shall be for that end nominated and appointed, all the said small tract of land above mentioned to be hereby granted, with all edifices thereon, rights and privileges aforesaid with the appurtenances to the same belonging to the use and purpose aforesaid, by such instruments and conveyances in the law at the cost of the said grantees as by their counsel learned in the law shall be devised. And the said Benj. Woolsey for himself and his heirs, executors and administrators doth hereby covenant, promise, grant and agree to clear the tract of land and premises from all manner of incumbrances whatsoever, and that he the said Benj. and Abigail his said wife are or one of them is the sole owner or owners of the said small tract of land and premises and have in them, him or herself full power and lawful authority to grant and convey away the same in fee simple as above said. And further that the said Mary Burroughs the minor or her heirs or assigns shall within the space of six months next after her arrival at the age of 21 years, execute unto the said Nicholas Berrien and Abraham Schenck or such other person or persons as by the congregation abovesaid or their successors shall be nominated or appointed, (but at their proper charge) a release or other instrument in the law as by their counsel shall be advised, for the further vesting or sure making of the said tract of land and premises unto them the said Nicholas and Abraham or such other person or persons as shall be nominated and appointed as aforesaid to the use, intent and purposes above mentioned. And lastly that he the said Benj. Woolsey and his heirs the same above hereby granted small tract of land and premises with the appurtenances unto the said Nicholas Berrien and Abraham Schenck and their heirs and assigns forever to the use aforesaid, against all manner of persons lawfully claiming the same or any part, parcel or member thereof, shall and will warrant and by these presents forever defend. In testimony whereof the said parties to these present indentures have hereunto interchangeably put their hands and seals the day and year above herein first written.

BENJAMIN WOOLSEY. { SEAL. }   ABIGAIL WOOLSEY. { SEAL. }

Sealed and delivered in the presence of us:

GABRIEL LUFF,
S. CLOWES.

Memorandum, That full and peaceable possession and seizen of and in the small tract of land and other the premises within written with the appurtenances was delivered by the within named Benj. Woolsey* and Abigail his wife to the within named Nicholas Berrien and Abraham Schenck to the use and behoof within limited according to the tenor, intent and effect of this present writing this 22d day of June anno Domini 1715, in the presence of the witnesses hereunder written:

S. CLOWES,
GABRIEL LUFF.

ALLOTMENT OF SEATS.

1716, June 15. We the Nether Dutch congregation of Queens County, on the Island of Nassau are gathered and met in our new church at Jamaica in order, according to the 5th article thereof made, to value and carry into effect our right and to choose church-masters for the first time. So we chose Jan Snedeker, Joris Remsen, Pieter Montfort and Rem Remsen in order to see that the sitting places of the men and women shall be regulated and appointed after the highest subscription according to our 6th and 7th articles; and the seats which overrun, when the builders [i. e. subscribers] shall have their own, shall be disposed of according to right reason and equity. And further if our church at any time shall have need of repairs, then those that have free seats shall pay equally to the repair thereof; and when any of the builders or owners of said church shall die, then their next heirs shall enter into

---

* Benj. Woolsey a Christian gentleman and Presbyterian divine was born in Jamaica in 1687. He officiated at Southold 16 years and then retired to his wife's estate at Dosoris preaching gratuitously till his death in 1756.—Gabriel Luff was an inn holder. Samuel Clowes who drew up this deed was a lawyer, and land surveyor. He came to Jamaica in 1702 and died here 1760.

possession. Further if any of the owners and builders shall remove out of the county then they may sell or make over their seats to any one of said church within the time of 6 months after removal, or otherwise they shall totally forfeit their right. Lastly, the right of an election of 2 new church masters every year shall remain to the congregation, and always 2 of the old ones shall remain in their places.

The church was eight sided or an octagon with a steep roof from the centre of which rose a cupola with a bell cast at Amsterdam. Instead of pews it had 14 long benches for the men and 13 for the women. Bench No. 1 was called "de Heere bank" or magistrates' bench reserved for dignitaries or men in office. Nos. 2 and 3 had each 7 sittings. Two shorter benches had each 4 sittings. The women sat apart, 8 or 10 on a bench. In later times they had rush bottomed chairs with the initials of their names marked on the back. Pews were introduced long afterward.

There were 253 sittings sold (132 for the men and 121 for the women) besides the free seats. After the choice of sittings by the subscribers the following places were appointed and sold by the church masters: bench No. 13 to Alexander Baird, Tunis and Johannes Polhemus, Johannes Boerum, Molly Robertsen, Jacob Remsen, Peter Ditmarsen, Barbara Freest, Sarah Carpenter and Elizabeth Antony. Cornelius Van Wyck; Hendrick, Jan and Cornelius Cornelise also bought sittings. Two sittings on bench No. 3 were set apart for the two "Madams" (juffrouwes) or wives of the two ministers.

The pulpit was high, eight sided, and ascended by 6 steps with a banister. It was surmounted by a sounding board to reflect the preacher's voice throughout the church. On the wall back of the pulpit were two pegs for the minister's hat and overcoat. A wooden tablet or Psalm board was suspended conspicuously, inscribed with "PSALM" and "PAUSE." In it were groves in which could be slidden moveable blocks with figures thereon to indicate to the congregation the psalm and part thereof to be sung at the opening services.

The Psalms with musical notes were bound up in a thick 16mo volume, with the Articles of faith, the Canons of the

Synod of Dort, the Liturgy and Chatechism. It also contained the Decalogue, Nunc Dimittis, Magnificat, Benedictus, Lord's Prayer, Creed and a short prayer before sermon, all set to music. It was the ambition of young ladies to have this gilt edged book (the covers protected with ornamental silver corner plates and clasps) hanging from the arm by a silver chain, as they went to church.

For Sunday collections the deacons had little silk bags [sacjes] attached to the end of a black rod 4 or 5 feet long. These hung from 2 pegs on the wall by the deacons' seat. These bags were superseded by pewter plates and these again by baskets as now in use.*

The space under and before the pulpit between the elders' and deacons' seats where stood the Lord's Table was railed-off, and was sometimes called the altar. In Dutch it was also called *doophuisje* or baptistery, because the minister stood there to christen children.

For a century the church was not heated; but the women had foot stoves and thin haired men often wore woollen caps or wigs. There were no horse sheds. The horses must have been tied under tavern sheds or to trees and fences along the highway. For years it was usual for the men to take a drink (and in winter warm themslves) in the taverns before divine service. The inn keeper was usually paid to have his best room open on Sunday mornings for the women to sit awhile, rest and converse till church time. In winter they could here replenish their foot stoves with hickory coals from a blazing fire.

People came to church on horse back or in their farm wagons washed and cleaned up for Sunday use. The harness was often made of tow yarn. Some well-to-do people had a one horse chair with or without a top. It was not till about 1820 that one horse wagons were coming into use, and still

---

* As wampum was found in the old alms chest, it is supposed contributions were anciently made in that currency. In latter times each grown person was expected to put in a cent, a younger person a half cent. There was a great accumulation of coppers which had to be sold at a discount.

later that covered two horse wagons and the present light buggy were driven to church instead of the heavy farm wagons.

In 1717 a church masters' book was bought for 8 shillings. In it were entered the articles for building the church, the names of subscribers, the buyers and sellers of sittings, etc. The following expenditures are noted:

		£.	s.	d.
1717. Oct. 16.	To Gerret Dorlant for the seal* [het seel] of the church..........		20	
	For lead.........		15	16
	" a bell		8	
	" plank		1	5
	To Abm. Lot for carting the plank............		3	
	For soldering the lead on the church.........		1	10
	" cleaning the church........		5	
	" carting the lead........		6	
	More............	3	5	6
	More, expenses		5	6
	More, for paint......		4	
	More, 18 guldens and 11 stuivers †			
	More, to the carpenter and smith, 18 guldens..			
	At the ferry, 2 gulden and 10 stuivers			
	More, 42 gulden to Lot and 3 gulden to the smith............			
	More, 5 gulden			
	More, 6 gulden for the knob [de Knope] ‡ and 2 s. to Pieter Haff........			
1719. June 18.	Joel Borres § for tarring [het picken] the steeple........		12	
	Rec. for 2 ropes 12s., for plank 8s. 3d., for nails 2s. 7d.			
1720. June 25.	To Thos. Antony for painting the church	15	10	
	Gave to the poor......		13	
	Gerret Dorrelant for whitewashing and cleaning the church		12	
	Gave to the poor.....		12	

---

* As the recorders were unlettered men, they often misspelled names and corrupted their Dutch by introducing English words. Thus SKLE may mean ceiling and PICKEN the iron rod of the vane. The ceiling of the church was of boards, leaving a space of many feet between it and the peak of the roof. There was an inner passage to the belfry [TOORKN]. The bell-rope hung down in the centre of the church.

† 20 stuivers or pennies make a gulden or florin, worth, as is said 41 or 42 cents.

‡ This gilded nob adorned the under centre of the sounding board. It is yet preserved.]

§ Joel Burroughs was a silversmith living in Jamaica.

			£	s.	d.
1729, Oct. 15.	For soldering the lead of the steeple and painting the columns		1	16	6
1730, Nov. 10.	Tuenes Covert for making the fence [heyning]			7	
1735, July 26.	Wm. Stead, carpenter, by order of church masters			5	
1736, July 30.	Lent from the deacons' chest, to pay church expenses			4	
	More, there is a bell to be sold				
	To Cornelius Ryersen for glazing			3	
	4 pounds lead sold for 1s. 10d.				
1737, Aug. 13.	For cleaning the church			1	3
1738, June 15.	" " "			1	3
Aug.	" " "			1	3
Oct. 3.	To Isaac Lot for labor at the church			3	

A FEW OF THE TRANSFERS OF SITTINGS.

1717, Alexr. Baird to Dr. Wm. Beekman.
1719, Jan Blauw to Tice Laning.
 "   Thos. Ecker to Peter Monfort.
1720, Wm. Beekman to Johannes V. Solingen.
1721, Jan Drake, fell to the church.
 "   Molly Robertson to Abm. Monfort.
1723, Matys Laning to Barent Blom.
1724, Johannes V. Solen to Johannes Coerten.
 "   The corner behind the elders to Aaron Van Nostrand.
 "   The corner behind the deacons to Joris Bennet.
1727, Wm. Bloodgood to Theodorus Van Wyck, Jr.
 "   Anatie Fin, fell to the church.
1728, Margaret Genong to Stephen Ryder.
1729, Sara Carpenter to Abm. Montanye.
1731, Casper Springsteen to Wm. Molenaar.
1733, Besse Stillwell to Jan Simeson.
 "   Christian Lupardus to Jan Wyckoff.
 "   Douwe Ditmars to Wm. Van Duyne.
1736, Maria Smith to Styntie Humphreys.*
1736, Adam Smith to Jan Van Arsdalen.
1737, Barbara Freest to Tunis Covert, her son.
 "   Hendrick Dosenborg † to Jos. Golder.
1738, Gerrit Dorland to Samuel Grix.

---

* 1732, March 27.—Last week Elizabeth Wiltse the wife of William Humphreys, of Hempstead, was brought to bed of a daughter, which child's grandfather hath a grandmother yet living, being of that age that she can say: "Grandson, send me your granddaughter, that I may have the pleasure to see of my issue one of the fifth generation." The child was baptized in the Jamaica church, June 4.—*N. Y. Gazette.*

† He in 1663 received 25s. for killing a wolf at Foster's Meadow.

1838 Benj. Taylor to Isaac Van Hook.
1740 Jacob Haff to Lucas Bergen.
1741, Peter Gerritsen to Abm. Probasco.
1742, Johannes Van Wyck, † fell to the church.
1742, Antony Glean, ‡ fell to the church.
1743, Jan Hegeman to Phillip Ried.
1744, Albert Ryder to Jos Oldfield.
1746, Adrian Onderdonek to Isaac Onderdonck.
1748, Derick Brinckerhoff ‖ to Derick Amberman.
1749, Jan Vorhesen to John Lewkur, (Luqueer.)
1750 Marten Wiltse to Andris Stockholm
1753 Isaac Van Hook to Jan Jansen. §
1774, Molly Sherlock ¶ to Jores Van Brunt.

CHURCH MASTERS OR WARDENS.

1716 Jan Snedeker, Peter Monfort,
Joris Remsen, Rem Remsen.
1717 Abm. Lot, Joris Rapelye.
1718 Barent Bloom, Elbert Monfort.
1719 Jesse Kip, Garret Dorlant.—£11. 16s. 6d. in the alms chest.
1720 Cornelius Hogelant, Andries Onderdonck. *
1721 Nicholas Berrien, Paulos Amerman.
1722 Johannes Nostrand, Tennis Snedeker.
1723 John Schenck, Joseph Hegeman.
1724 Johannes Van Lewen, Adrian Onderdonck.
1725 Jan Prooasco, Abm. Brinckerhoff.—9s. in chest.

---

† 1727, May 16. Adam Smith is fined 20 shillings for scandalizing Justice Johannes Van Wyck.—1750 Sept. 28.—The account of John Van Wyck. Sheriff of Queens County for receiving lodging and victualling sixty-three French and Spanish prisoners of war, from June 11th, 1748, to July 10th; and for transporting them from Flushing to New York, July 14th, was £94,4.—*Ass. Journal,* 2 : 300.

‡ 1667, Nov. 20.—Antony Glean, drummer of His Royal Highness' garrison of Fort James sells his title to a home lot (formerly Wm. Compton's of Gravesend) for one cow and 400 of good merchantable bran two sd.—1715 Aug. 12. Antony Glean, blacksmith, of Flushing, desires to administer on the estate of Jas. Bettersby, schoolmaster, who owes him for lodging and funeral expenses. He left some goods and chattels, but no relatives.

‖ 1747, Nov. 16.—Derick Brinckerhoff offers for sale, a very good plantation of two hundred and forty acres, on the road from Flushing to Jamaica, three miles from Flushing town landing, and two miles from Jamaica. The house has two rooms on the floor, with a banto and kitchen thereto annexed, a new barn, cedar shingled, wagon house sheephouse, a good orchard of two hundred and fifty trees of divers sorts of fruits, pretty garden spot—all in stone fence. A spot of ground in the rear produces forty loads of hay.—*Postboy.* He was moving to Dutchess Co.

§ He was great grandfather of Martin G. Johnsen, and came from Flatbush 1744.

¶ She was widow of Wm. Sherlock, schoolmaster.

* He was grand son of Adrian Andrewse Onderdonck who was living in Flatbush in 1672, and great grandfather of the two Bishops, Henry U. and Benj. T. Onderdonk.

1726 Peter Monfort, Theodorus Van Wyck, Jr.
17 gulden and 10 stuivers in chest.
1727 Isaac Amerman, Peter Luyster,—£2 19s. in chest.
1728 Frans Mnrston, Cornelius Wiltse.—£2, 19s. in chest.
1729 Tunis Covert, Tunis Brinckerhoff.—£4, 19s. in chest.
1730 Abm. Schenck, Cornelius Van Wyck,—£2, 13s. 6d, in chest.
1731 Wm. Golder, Abm. Rike.—£1, 7s. in chest.
1732 Jan Lefferts, Jeronimus Rapelye.—£1, 7s. in chest.
1733 Jurian Ryder, Daniel Rapelye.
1734 Cornelius Ryerse, Dirck Brinckerhoff.—£2, 12s. in chest.
1735 Wm. Van Duyn, Douw Ditmars.
1736 Antony Demott, Elbert Hogelant.—19s. 9d. in chest.
1737 Abm. Polhemus, Rem Remsen.—£5, 5s. 4d.
1738 Adrian Onderdonck, Rem Monfoort—£3, 19s. 4d. in chest.
1739 Abm. Lent, Isaac Van Hook,—7s, 5d. in chest.
1740 Derick Wortman, Martin Wiltse.—8s. in chest.

Hardly ten years had passed since the erection of the church before the people of Queens County wished to withdraw from Kings County and have a pastor to themselves, as we see by the following proposition:

To the Members and Elders of the Church in Kings Co.:

1727, June 7. We Douwe Ditmars, Dirk Brinckerhoff, Theodorus Van Wyck and Nicholas Berrien ruling elders of the church of Jesus Christ at Jamaica having taken greatly to heart the state of our church over which we are placed as overseers, conclude it would be more advantageous for us to have the entire services of a Pastor to ourselves. To this end we propose that both the present ministers may remain in Kings Co. and we be freed from them so that we may call a preacher for Jamaica. Our reasons are:

1. Because we through the blessing of God feel able to maintain a minister.

2. In our opinion our congregation should be fed every Sabbath day with God's word.

3. The members of our congregation dwelling 20 or 25 miles apart from each other, makes it necessary that God's word should be preached in more places than one in our county.

4. Provision should be made for catechising the children and larger persons.

5. Visiting the congregation from house to house for spiritual purposes and consoling the sick could be better attended to.

6. As we reside among Quakers, * Anabaptists and others it is more

---

* The Baptists kept up a meeting at Oyster Bay. The more emotional became Separate Anabaptists or New Lights. Friends were then numerous and influential. Their traveling

necessary for our congregation to have a watchman or shepherd of their own to keep the flock together.

7. Our children are apt to intermarry with the English, whereby they are in danger of becoming estranged from the nether Dutch worship and used to that of other churches. While their fathers yet live they should willingly for the benefit of the lives of their children provide for them a Netherland preacher so as to keep them steadfast in following the example of their fathers from generation to generation, in the support of the Netherland church.

We hope, worthy brethren, that our arguments may so fall on your venerable body as to give satisfaction and that you will be willing to take unto yourselves the services of both the present preachers, and allow us to call a minister for ourselves, which will tend to the extension of the Reformed Divine service among us. Our intention is the welfare of the church; and we therefore write with the expectation of a friendly answer.

This petition had no result, for in the call of 1730 we find the two ministers spoken of as yet to preach in Jamaica till their death.

1728, June 14. The writings of the church were given to Stephen Ryder for safe-keeping.

1739, Aug. 29. Authorized call for a minister, sent to the care of the Rev. Domines De La Moraisiere, Vos, Bakker and Noordtbeek of the classis of Amsterdam.

As in general through God's never fully praised goodness, under the blessed reign of His Princely Majesty of Great Britain, George the 2d, the Word of the Lord now has its free course in this remotely situated country of the northern part of America, and the Nether Dutch Reformed congregations are very much augmented and have spread themselves far and wide; so we have also particular reason to thank the Lord for his goodness to us here planted in a healthy climate and dwelling at 40 degrees of latitude, in the county of Queens, on the Island Nassau and Colony of New York, as we have an especial growth of the congregation around us.

At last on the 20th of August 1739 there was a great church gathering in the church at Jamaica composed of the Consistory and a great number of members, after that on the 16th of the same month previously on the Lord's day it was openly published from the pulpit by one of our preachers that such a general church gathering would be held for the

---

preachers, many coming from Great Britain, were eloquent and held meetings in every part of Queens Co. and gained many converts. The names of Francis Bloodgood and Cors. Van Wyck, Jr. in 1744 and Wm. Van Wyck and his son John in 1758 and John Rider in 1764 are mentioned in Friends' Records.

purpose of this weighty matter, inviting the members of the congregation to appear at the appointed place on that day with the Consistory.

In this great church gathering (after calling on the name of the Lord and mature deliberation) they agreed in love and peace and have decided and determined to call a minister out of Holland; and the then ruling Consistory were charged and authorized to promote this wholesome work and to go round (each in his own neighborhood) to the members of the congregation to ask of each help and consent, so that our congregation might be provided and supplied with a sufficient orthodox and pious Reformed Nether Dutch preacher or minister out of Holland, according to the direction and order of the High Reverend Classis of Amsterdam, after the same church constitution, orders and church government or discipline according to the decree of the Synod of Dort *— holden in the years 1618 and 1619. This was done and after the going around to all and each individually, there was not only a satisfactory consent but a content-giving encouragement and a pressing charge for promoting the work, with the addition of what each might be able to bring thereto, pledged with their signatures.—

These necessary subscriptions being obtained the work is at once made practicable; and we the underwritten, being the Consistory authorized and empowered to forward the business, and first of all to dispatch and transmit an authorized call through our Rev. pastors and ministers Domine Vincentius Antonides and Domine Bernardus Freeman (named at our request) to the care of the very Rev. Domines De La Moraisiere,

---

* The Synod of Dort in Holland was composed of delegates from the Netherland churches, also from neighboring countries especially Switzerland, parts of Germany and Transylvania. The king of Great Britain James I, who had urged the calling of the synod sent to it with the approval of the archbishop of Canterbury six of his clergy who took an active part in the proceedings, agreed to the canons, acquiesced in the condemnation of Arminianism and affixed their signatures and official titles thereto as follows:

GEORGE, Bishop of Landaff.

JOHN DAVENANT, Presbyter. Doctor and Public Professor of Sacred Theology in the University of Cambridge and President of Queen's College.

SAMUEL WARD, Presbyter, S. T. D., Archdeacon of Taunton and Regent of Sydney College in the University of Cambridge.

THOMAS GOOD, Presbyter, S. T. D., Præcentor of St. Paul's Cathedral church, London.

WALTER BALCANQUAL of the church of Scotland, Presbyter S. T. B.

Dr. Joseph Hall (afterwards bishop of Exeter and Norwich in succession) preached a conciliatory sermon to the Synod from Eccles vii, 16; but being forced to retire from ill health, King James sent Thos. Good chaplain to the archbishop of Canterbury in his stead.—£10 sterling per day was allowed by the Dutch to the English commissioners that they might live in a style suitable to the dignity of the church they represented; and £200 was given them to bear their charges on their return home and a gold medal of good value to each, representing the sitting of the Synod. They also visited several Dutch cities.—They were complimented by the President of the Synod with " an acknowledgement of the excellency of the constitution of the church of England and that the Dutch regretted that the convenience of their own State did not admit of the same system of subordination." (See Lingard's England and Fuller's church History.)

The King of France, Louis XIII forbid his Protestant clergy attending this Synod, but they ratified the Acts at the Synod of Alez 1619. The Ref. Dutch Church in common with the church of England yet retains the Athanasian creed.

Vos, Bakker and Nordbeck preachers at Amsterdam. So we the underwritten elders and deacons of the 4 united congregations of Jamaica, Hempstead (Success), Oysterbay (Wolver Hollow) and Newtown take the liberty to beseech your Reverences earnestly, and authorize you by these presents fully to call in our behalf an orthodox, sufficient and edifying Nether Dutch Reformed pastor and minister, a person of whose learning and piety and other laudable virtues you are satisfactorily assured (and with full qualifications to send us) to preach the word of the Lord, pure, plain and powerful, with thorough and familiar catechising to exercise those disposed to learn, in the treating of the Heidelberg catechism, to administer the Holy Sacraments faithfully according to Christ's institution, to exercise christian discipline in conjunction with the overseers of the congregation diligently and prudently, to visit the sick, and further to do all things in a christian and peaceable way as the office of a faithful servant of Christ Jesus according to God's word and as the good order of the church requires, after the way of the Synod of Dort in the year 1618, 1619, and as is usual in the Nether Dutch Reformed churches in this land.

Besides with mutual respect we make it known to you that our congregations by and around here have many residents who are free thinkers, Quakers and Anabaptists who moreover are without God's service, whereto our pastor must needs watch to look after the congregations so that the Lord Jesus Christ may triumph in his person, honor and love. Whereto gifts, earnest preaching, zealous application, appropriate catechising and further, to edify with a Godly life are necessary. So also your Reverences are requested to give heed that his gifts of speech are clear and intelligible so that the whole congregation may be edified, and that many members may have a desire to fill up the church.

But under this head we must make a more particular description of the service required according to the constitution of our congregation:

1. The called minister must preach at 4 different places viz.: Jamaica, Hempstead (Success), Oysterbay (Wolver Hollow) and Newtown.

2. He shall for himself choose his place of residence. If he chooses that of Jamaica, he must understand that the church of Newtown is 1¼ Dutch miles from his residence, the church of (Success in) Hempstead 2 miles and the church of (Wolver Hollow in) Oysterbay 4 miles.

3. The preaching turns on each Lord's day shall go round, beginning at Jamaica, and so through each congregation, till the turn comes round again to Jamaica.

4. When the turn of going round comes to Jamaica at the time when it is the turn for the preaching of our present ministers, he shall then perform service in Oysterbay or Hempstead, as it shall seem best; or the 2 encountering domines may both be present at Jamaica to hear each other for their own edification, but with consent of the Consistory thereunto consulted.

5. In consideration of these continual changes of preaching places lying far off from one another the congregation wish to find a person who is sound and strong in body so as to endure the fatigue of serving the congregations; and then the limitation of his age is fixed, that he shall not exceed 35 years.

6. He shall in the best way he can, go to the places where the preaching turn shall be.

7. He shall preach twice every Lord's day, and in the afternoon shall handle the subject of catechism according to the Heidelberg catechism; and with advice of his Consistory shall catechise.

8. In the 3 Winter months he shall preach but once on the Lord's day, as also on Christmas, on the 1st and 2d days of the New year, and Ascension day as also on the 2 days of Paas (Easter) and Pinxter (Whitsunday). *

At least 6 months in the year shall his Reverence catechise each week that part of the congregation where he preaches on Sunday, at such time and place as shall best suit him, but with advice of the Consistory.

10. Four times a year shall the Lord's Supper go round (the churches) by turns. Where the service of the Lord's Supper shall be, there shall as often in the week be made a visitation of the members, and there shall the Friday's preparatory service and the Sunday afternoon's thanksgiving sermon be given.

For an encouragement to accept this call, the person called will be recompensed as follows:

I. A salary of £80, New York money, yearly during his service with us, which is, 640 guilders. We doubt not, if his Reverence's gifts edify the congregation, that his salary would be raised up to £100; and on the death of our present ministers it shall by the courtesy of the congregation continue.

II. These sums shall be paid to his Reverence by the elders or deacons or their order, each half year, the just half promptly.

III. The salary shall begin with his first preaching before his congregations, but his Reverence shall at once at his coming and first preaching here receive a half year's salary being £40.

IV. For the cost of his coming over it is provided that his Reverence may be unconcerned. Thereto £40 are set over, so that he shall be held

---

* Though the church inculcated the observance of Christmas, Paas (Easter) and Pinxter (Whitsuntide) yet with the negro slaves it was high holiday. They roamed about the neighborhood, calling at every house for a drink, and late at night returned home reeling, noisy, and quarrelsome, disobedient to the mistress and sulky to the master. The good housewife usually made a keeler full of doughnuts for Christmas, and gave 2 or 3 with a mug of cider to every caller. It required another day or two to get the negroes in working order. No wonder our ancestors dreaded the recurrence of holy days whose observance and significance were perverted to licentiousness little worse perhaps than the parading, target shooting and hog guessing of our modern Thanksgiving day.

free from his congregation in traveling to his congregation hither, in case that £10 shall not equal the cost.

V. A suitable dwelling for a preacher shall be built for his Reverence at his coming and after the choice of residence shall be made by him, either by the church of Jamaica or by the church of Hempstead, or between the two, having by it some land sufficient for a suitable orchard and pasture ground for 2 cows and a horse.

VI. Also his Reverence shall be provided with sufficient fire-wood for Winter and Summer and to be brought before his door.

VII. Also shall his Reverence at his coming be presented with an able horse with his equipments. Yet thereafter shall he always provide himself with a horse in order to perform his duties everywhere in the congregation, as they shall be required.—It shall depend on the courtesy of his congregation to provide their minister with horses.

VIII. Also entertainment and charges shall be provided for the time whenever he preaches or does any service in another congregation where he does not dwell.

All which extraordinary advantages for the use and support of this temporal life should in some measure make the person called willing to accept, in that Long Island is above measure fruitful in all sorts of the means of living, but especially are we hoping that the person called through the grace of the Holy Spirit will be prevailed on to give up himself and his fatherland in order to do service here to the church of Jesus.

Very Revd. Domines and fathers Moraisiere, Vos, Bakker and Noordbeek, we pray you for Christ's sake to do this service for us and our congregation, to send us soon a minister, as is above expressed. The Jehovah shall provide this, to find a person sooner or later, and so with full church qualifications to send us. We shall be thankful to your Reverences our life long for your pains and labor; and we will ratify all this as if we in person had done there what you have done for us, and the person sent to us shall be received in honor and love by us; and thereupon we subscribe this authorized instrument affectionately with our hands and remain with respect and esteem your Reverences' servants and brothers in the Lord. Amen.

Signed for greater faith in presence of our present ministers.

Deacons:	TUNIS COVERT,	*Elders:*	PETER BERRIEN,
	JOOST SPRINGSTEEN,		JOHANNES VAN WYCK,
	FRANCIS MARSTON,		ABRAM LOT,
	ABRAHAM MONFOORT,		CORNELIS REYERSE,
	JACOBUS MONFOORT,		SYMEN LOYSE,
			ADRIAEN ONDERDONCK.

After calling on the Holy name of the Lord we the underwritten ministers have with our eyes seen the signing of the above written elders and deacons this 26th of Jan. 1731.

BARNARDUS FREEMAN,
VINCENTIUS ANTONIDES.

SALARY FOR THE MINISTER TO BE CALLED RAISED TO £100.

These proceedings have we the present ruling elders according to our office ordered from a sense of duty, not without consultation with many intelligent and well meaning members and also with hearty approval of both our present ministers, to undertake for another going round and soliciting a new subscription from the respective members for increasing the salary to £100 a year for the preacher to be called, and so on the old footing by and according to the foregoing friendly agreement and resolution, that all 4 united congregations should have like service so that the unity of love should not be weakened, in that each should freely out of a christian love contribute something to God's service.

This is a cause that concerns us all and the welfare of the congregation which we all with one heart and zeal in unity of love must promote. We all are therefore pledged. The necessity of the cause demands it. Oh that we unanimously might join hands with one another and without any selfish aim seek the welfare of the congregations and provide that at the death of our ministers, who both are come to old age, the congregations which are now so sweetly united may not, by being without any teacher, be split up and the members themselves be as scattered sheep who have no shepherd.

We underwritten who have with our hands written or caused to be written, promise then for this proposal and request of the Consistory above mentioned, yearly and each year so long as the called minister shall be in actual service with us to pay over and above the foregoing (with our signatures pledged for the filling up of the salary of £100 for the called minister) such sums in cash as with our name is expressed.— The Lord grant prosperity and success to this our work.

BARNARDUS FREEMAN,
VINCENTIUS ANTONIDES, } Witnesses.

Additions to former subscriptions, to raise £100 for two ministers, Aug. 20 1730. The other lists are lost.

	s.	d.		s.	d.
Minne Schenck	6	8	Andries Onderdonck	5	
Cornelius Polhemus	7	8	Andries Onderdonck	6	
Adriaen Onderdonck	7		Jacobus Monfoort	9	8
Marten Wiltse	3	9	Eida Monfoort	3	8
Martyn Wiltse Jr.	3	9	Theodorus Van Wyck	4	
Daniel Hegeman	5		Abraham Monfoort	4	
Jan Vanderbilt	5		Roelof Schenck	6	8

Proposition of the Consistories of the 4 united congregations of Jamaica, Flushing, Hempstead, Oysterbay and Newtown to the subordinate members of the same and all well meaning christians:

It is known how on the 20th of August 1730 a great general church gathering was held in the church at Jamaica, composed of the Consistory and a great number of the members; and how they in this great church gathering after calling on the name of the Lord and after mature deliberation in love and peace agreed and resolved to call a preacher out of Holland in such a way and terms which by one another were fixed on and established, viz.: that each of the 4 united congregations should have like service; that the preacher called should have £80 for salary, and that the members each according to his ability should out of a true christian love contribute and bring something thereto; and the then governing Consistory were authorized and commanded to go round and enquire what each would be willing to bring. So it has been done. Each has by his signature promised and declared what he is willing to bring freely to the above named design. In pursuance of this determination and resolution the then ruling Consistory after obtaining the signatures had dispatched an authorized call to the domines preachers in the very Reverend classis of Amsterdam (mentioned in the authorized letter). And these domines according to their letter have used all diligence and means to find a suitable preacher, but they have not yet met with any one inclined to accept the call and they declare their hearts' grief that they cannot accomplish their desire of doing the congregations a service and complain of being very much distressed with this commission; and they write that beside the burdensomeness of the call and the weight of the service on account of the distance of the places which must be served, and especially the smallness of the salary,—these all hold them back. This last objection we especially take into consideration, as in the authorized letter is also mentioned, that the salary (if the preacher called with his endowments should give edification to the congregations) should well mount up to £100, and order that we should establish the salary from £89, to £100, so that we may advance with some moderation to the relieving of his service without much prejudice of the congregations.

1732, Sept. 9. The Dutch people of Oysterbay met and agreed to go on with the building of a church and appointed Adrian Hegeman, Jurian Haff, Jacob Van Nostrand and Barent Van Wyck a building committee who bought of Edmond Wright for £6, an acre of ground at Wolver Hollow on the road from Jericho to Matinecock. They met in the new church April 25, 1734, and chose Peter Luyster and Cornelius Hoogland church masters to arrange the sittings. The record of baptisms does not begin till Oct. 24, 1741, after the settlement of Goetschius.

FIRST REFORMED DUTCH CHURCH.

SUBSCRIBERS' NAMES.

Name	£	s.	Name	£	s.
Albertson, Nicholas	1	5	Onderdonck, Andries	1	5
Amerman, Johannis	2	5	Polhemus, Cornelius	2	5
Bennet, Jeromus	2	5	Ruland, Jan	2	5
Brinckerhoff, Abm	2	5	Ryerse, Cornelius	1	5
Couwenhoven, Jan	4	10	Remsen, Isaac	2	5
Cashyou (Cashow), Johannes	2	5	Reyder, Steven	2	10
Durland, Jan	2	5	Remsen, Jan	1	5
Ditmarse, Douwe	4	10	Snedeker, Gerret	2	10
Garretsen, Abm	4	10	Symense, Johannis	2	5
Haff, Jacob	4	10	Symense, Frederick	2	5
Haff, Jurian*	5	10	Symense, Mouris	2	5
Haff, Jan	2	5	Snedeker, Gerret	2	5
Hardenberg, Hendrickus	2	5	Schenck, Minne	2	5
Hegeman, Petrus	4	10	Schenck, Roelof	1	5
Hoogland, Cornelius	2	5	Van Nostrand, Jacob	2	5
Hoogland, William	2	5	Van Nostrand, Albert	2	5
Janse, Steven	4	10	Van Wyck, Barent	5	15
Koole, Barent	3	5	Van Vores, Lucas	2	5
Loyse, Simon	8		Van Vores, Abm	2	5
Luyster, Peter†	6	15	Van Vores, Willem	2	5
Lickquier, Jan	2	5	Voorhis, Daniel	2	5
Monfoort, Jacobus	6	15	Van Wyck, Theodorus	2	5
Millear, Jost	2	5	Van Wyck, Theodorus	2	5
Monfoort, Eidae	2	5	Van Wyck, Johannes	1	5
Monfoort, Jacobus	2	5	Walters, William	2	5
Monfoort, Peter	2	5	Woertman, Jan	3	5
Noorstrant, Daniel	2	5	Wiltse, Martin	1	5
Onderdonck, Adriaen	2	5	Wiltse, Martin Jr.	1	5

The Building Committee of the Reformed Dutch Church, Success, April 14, 1731, were Aaron Van Nostrand, Martin Wiltsie, Theodorus Van Wyck, Antony De Mott, Michael De Mott, Andries Onderdonck and Cornelius Van Wyck. The congregation met in the new church, Aug. 14, 1732, and chose Cornelius Ryersen and Adrian Onderdonck church masters.‡

---

* Uriah or Jurian Haff of Flushing bought land in 1721 near Sucksoos' wigwam.

† Peter Luyster of Flushing for £100 bought 82 acres of land of Dickinson, near Little Plains.

‡ In 1731 Martin Wiltse for 25 shillings sold to Adrian Onderdonck and Cornelius Ryersen a half acre of ground at Success Pond for a church for the Reformed Dutch Congregation of Hempstead to worship Almighty God in. His name was cut on the corner stone.

SUBSCRIBERS' NAMES.

Name	£	s.	Name	£	s.
Adriance, Sarah	1		Montanye, Abm	2	5
Brinckerhoff, Derrick	2	5	Nostrant, Johannis	2	5
Bergen, Hans	2	5	Onderdonck, Andries	6	15
Bloom, Barent	2	5	Onderdonck, Adrian	6	15
Barentse, Hendrick	2	5	Polhemus, Cornelius	7	
Barentse, Jan	2	5	Probasco, Jan	2	5
Cornell, Thomas	2	5	Ryder, Stephen	3	
Covert, Tunis	1	5	Ryerson, Cornelius	2	5
Ditmars, Dowe	4	10	Ryersen, Martin	1	5
Ditmars, Dowe, Jr.	2	5	Remsen, Rem	1	5
Ditmars, Abm	2	5	Remsen, Dirk	1	5
De Mott, Antony	3	10	Smith, James	2	5
De Mott, Magiel	2	5	Schenck, Minne	6	15
Dorlandt, Garret	2	5	Schenck, Roelof	6	15
Golder, Joseph	2	5	Schenck, Abm	2	5
Halstead, Joseph	2	5	Stringham, Thomas	1	
Hegeman, Jacobus	3	10	Snedeker, Isaac	1	5
Hegeman, Adrian	1	5	Snedeker, Garret	1	
Hegeman, Peter	2	5	Thorne, Richard	2	5
Hegeman, Barentie	1		Thorne, Joseph	1	
Hegeman, Jan	2	5	Vanderbilt, Jacob	3	5
Hendrickson, Isaac	1		Vanderbilt, Jan	2	5
Hoff, Peter	2	5	Van Wyck, Cornelius	6	15
Jansen, Harmen	4		Van Wyck, Theodorus	4	10
Lott, Abm	1	5	Van Wyck, Theodorus, Jr.	6	15
Luyster, Pieter	2	5	Van Wyck, Johannis	4	10
Loose, Simon	2	5	Van Nostrant, Jan	2	5
Monfort, Abm	6	15	Van Nostrant, Aaron	3	10
Monfort, Ida	4	10	Van Nostrant, Wm	1	5
Monfort, Jacobus	3	5	Wiltse, Martin	2	5
Mitchel, Robert	1	8	Wiltse Martin,*	3	5
Monfort, Peter	2	5	Wiltse, Cornelius	2	5
Marston, Francis	1	10	May 26, 1731	173	16

The Dutch people of Newtown met Dec. 2, 1731 at the house of Samuel Fish, Jr., and resolved in peace and love to build a church 50 by 40 feet on a lot 70 by 60 feet given by Peter Berrien. On May 27, 1732, £277 12s. being subscribed they appointed Abm. Remsen, Isaac Bragaw, Joris Rapelye, Abm. Lent, Nicholas Berrien and Abm. Brinckerhoff, a building committee. Aug. 30, 1735 the church was finished, and the seats allotted March 9, 1736. Thos. Skill-

* Martin Wiltse's son-in-law.

FIRST REFORMED DUTCH CHURCH.

man, Peter Berrien and Petrus Schenck were elected church Masters, June 26.

SUBSCRIBERS' NAMES.

Name	£. s.	Name	£. s.
Berrien, Nicholas	12	Remsen, Jeromus	2 15
Berrien, Peter	9	Remsen, Abraham	5
Berrien, Cornelius	2	Remsen, Rem	2
Berrien, Cornelius, Jr	2 6	Remsen, Abraham, Jr	2
Bragaw, Isaac	8 10	Riker, Andries and Janetie	2 10
Bragaw, Bergoon	4 8	Riker, John	2 6
Bloom, Bernardus	1 15	Riker, Abraham, Jr	4 10
Brinckerhoff, Antie	10	Riker, Abraham	3
Brinckerhoff, Abm	8 10	Schenck, Petrus	6 10
Brinckerhoff, Tuenis	6	Skillman, Thomas	5
Brinckerhoff, Isaac	6 10	Skillman, Jacob	2 15
Brinckerhoff, Hendrick	5	Schoon, Joost	1
Brinckerhoff, John	4 5	Springsteen, Casparus	2
Cornell, Peter	3	Springsteen, Maria	4
Cornell, Hendrick	2	Springsteen, David	2
Culver, Johannes	2 10	Van Alst, Johannes	6
Debevoise, John	4 13	Van Alst, Andries	4
Fish, Capt. Samuel	6	Van Alst, Joris	3 10
Fish, Samuel, Jr	2	Vandervoort, Paulus	2
Gaucel, Judith	2	Van Duyn, Wm	5 15
Gilbert, Aaron	2 15	Vanderbeek, Stoffel	4 15
Hazard, Capt. Thos	2	Van Zandt, Bernardus	3 10
Hazard, Judge James	1 10	Wyckoff, John	7 5
Lent, Abraham	8 10	FROM ABROAD.	
Luyster, Peter	6 10	Brinckerhoff, Justice	3
Luyster, Elbert	6	Cornell, Johannes	2
Miller, Wm	2	Letten, Nicholas	2
Parcell, John	1 11	Lott, Abraham	1
Parcell, John (of the island)	3 15	Nostrand, Johannes	1 5
Parcell, Nicholas	3 15	Rapelye, Jeromus	4
Rapelye, Daniel	9	Ryder, Justice	3
Rapelye, Joris	8 10	Schenck, Abraham	1 5
Rapelye, Cornelius	4	Van Ditmars, Dow	3
Rapelye, Daniel, Jr	3 .10	Van Ditmars, Dow, Jr	2
Rapelye, Abraham	3 8	Van Ditmars, Abraham	2

CEMETERIES.

In early times farmers often interred their dead on their farms and put up at their graves a rough flat stone with the initials of the name, and year of decease rudely cut thereon. We do not know that any were buried under the church, as was not unusual in Kings County.

There were cemeteries in the village, at West Jamaica on land now of John B. Napier, at Blackstump, at Springfield and at Foster's Meadow.

1737, Feb. 14. The undersigned proprietors of the Burying place at Foster's Meadow, agree to keep up our proportion of the fence.

Alburtis, Jas., John; Auten, Hendrick; Barns, Cornelius, John, Henry; B erum, Johannes; De Mott, Moychi, Michel, Antony; * Durye, Daniel for Harmon Johnson; Everit, George, Richard; Hagewout, Jan; Hegeman, John; Hendrickson, Thos., Hendrick, Henry in place of John; Johnson, Wm., Abm.; Montanye, Abm.; Oakley, Thos. for his father deceased; Remsen, Rem for his mother (Elizabeth); Reyerse, Cornelius; Seaman, Giles for Hendrick Onderdonck †; Snedeker, Garret, Isaac for his mother; Van Nostrand, Aaron, Jacob, Fred'k., Albert.

THOS. STRINGHAM,
JOHN VAN NOSTRAND, } Witnesses.

1738, April 27. The Cetus or assembly of Dutch ministers met in New York and without transacting any important business adjourned. It did not meet again till 9 years after when letters of approbation were received from Holland. The churches and ministers meantime must have been nearly independent of each other, and discipline very feeble. Hence the origin of those religious dissensions that so long prevailed and interrupted the progress of the Dutch churches on the Island. Every case of discipline had to be laid before the classis of Amsterdam for final adjudication; and their replies were often very slow in reaching this country.

---

* Antony and Michael De Mott, Frenchmen, came from Esopus to Foster's Meadow.—Annatle daughter of Peter Janse Schol and Margretie Provoost married (1680) Hendrick Gillisen de Mandeville.

† He died May, 1749. In his will he says: "I commit my soul immortal to God that gave it, my Saviour and Redeemer, my body to be buried where it shall please my executors; to my daughter Letitia wife of Giles Seaman I give my moveables, my houses and lands in Hempstead and meadows in Jamaica; to Samuel Peters my servant whom I have brought up from a child, £10 and my saddle."

FIRST REFORMED DUTCH CHURCH.

A MINISTER TO BE CALLED.

1739, July 23. We the present ruling Elders have had a meeting at Flatbush and have agreed with Domine Van Basten * to perform service in the 4 Dutch churches of Queens Co. and that we shall give him £75 a year. Now the christian congregation is asked what each one is willing to give or by his signature to promise.

The above subscription paper with 49 Newtown names attached, pledging in all £16, 3s. 6d., was once among the papers of the church at Newtown, but has now disappeared. We know of no other.

1740, May 3. The church put out £50 to Peter Haff, of Flushing on a bond endorsed by Isaac Bloom, blacksmith, of Jamaica.—About the same time there was a bond of Mordecai Lester and John Treadwell for £106, 15s.

A PASTOR.

1741. After waiting 9 tedious years and having made several unsuccessful efforts to procure a pastor from Holland the Consistory made a call on Johannes Henricus Goetschius † of Pennsylvania. Domines Dorstius and T. J. Frelinghuysen had qualified him, though it was insisted they had no right to do so; and Domine Freeman with the assent of Antonides openly laid hands upon him and instituted him, April 19, in the congregation of Jamaica, with these words: "Lo, I am with you always, even to the end of the world."

A PARSONAGE BOUGHT.

1741, Sep. 4. Thos. Smith of Jamaica for £185 sold 10 acres of land with the buildings thereon to Abm. Lent, John Wyckoff, Abm. Polhemus, Abm. Schenck, Adrian Onderdonck, Cors. Ryerson, Jacobus Monfort, and Cors. Hoog-

---

* An obscurity hangs over this name, if indeed it be a name, which I cannot clear up. It might mean " a minister from Boston."

† Nov. 21, 1741. Received from John Hegeman with permission of the Consistory out of the chest £5, 10s. which is to be returned on demand, as this attests.

JOHANNES HENRICUS GOETSCHIUS,
V. D. M. in Jamaica.

land, agents and trustees appointed by the 4 Dutch Reformed congregations of Queens Co. The site is now occupied by Aaron A. Degrauw. It was then bounded south by the Main street, west by Samuel Dean, north by Dean and Amos Smith and east by Amos Smith. *Q. Co. Records, D.* 80.

PARSONAGE REPAIRED.

1742, April 17. We the Consistory of the 4 united congregations of the Nether Dutch Reformed Churches of Newtown, Jamaica, Hempstead and Oysterbay have met; and we the deacons with consent of the elders have made over the sum of £162, 13s. 7d. to the 8 authorized persons of the 4 above named congregations in order to further repair the Domine's dwelling, in compliance with the requirements of the call. According to the foregoing agreement and when that is accomplished, then shall the 8 above named persons return the overshot of the money to the 4 above named Consistories, to Newtown its 4th part to its deacons, to Jamaica its 4th part to its deacons; to Hempstead its 4th part to its deacons; to Oysterbay its 4th part to its deacons.

We the underwritten promise to fulfil the above named agreement:
Witnesses:

HANS BERGEN,
MOSES VAN NOERSTRAND,

ABRAHAM LENT,
ADRIAEN ONDERDONCK,
CORNELIS REVERSE,
JACOBUS MONFOORT,
ABRAHAM POLHEMIUS,*
JAN WYCKOFF,
CORNELIUS HOOGLAND.

We appoint Jan Hegeman as our treasurer.

1742. August 22.—Domine Goetschius preached a sermon at Newtown, on the Unknown God,† which gave great offence. This interrupted his ministry, and was the beginning of a long and painful series of dissensions in the churches of Queens County.‡ The quarrel raged six years

---

* Polheym is the original spelling; but it was Latinized, as many other Dutch names were.

† This sermon was reprinted in Dutch, in Holland, Michigan, in 1871. It was also translated by Rev. John Y. De Baun and printed in the *Banner of Truth* in 1867.

‡ Rev. Thomas Colgan, the English missionary (1744), thus writes: "The several churches belonging to my cure, as those of Jamaica, Newtown and Flushing, are in a peaceable and growing state, whilst other separate assemblies in this parish are in the utmost confusion. Independency, which has been triumphant in Jamaica for forty years past is now, by the providence of God, in a faint and declining condition."

ere it could be brought to a settlement before any ecclesiastical assembly in this country. It was not till April 26, 1748, that the Cetus (having been approved by the Classis of Amsterdam) took up the affairs of Queens County, required Goetschius to submit to their authority, and then promoted his call to Hackensack.

1746, Oct. 9. A deacons' book is made. The deacons agreed that no money is to be paid out without the consent of all. £6, 18s. 6d. now in the alms-chest.

TITLE PAGE OF GOETSCHIUS' SERMON.

The unknown God, or a short and plain advice how many who have the name of living in all their duties and piety, honor and serve a God whom they neither know nor love; shown in a truthful explanation and application of Acts xvii; 23: "For as I passed by, and beheld your devotions, I found an altar with this inscription: TO THE UNKNOWN GOD. Whom therefore ye ignorantly worship, him declare I unto you."— Preached the 22d of August 1742 in the church of Newtown, by John Henry Goetschius preacher there.

Here follows the introduction by Frelinghuysen.

To the reader health and salvation.

God-seeking souls to whom the promise is fulfilled. "They all shall know the Lord."

This church-discourse on Acts xvii :23, composed and delivered by the Reverend and very learned Domine John Henry Goetschius, pastor at Jamaica, on Long Island, we have read through with satisfaction and found nothing therein repugnant to the received doctrine of the Reformed Nether Dutch church nor with the formularies of unity, but on the contrary we perceive that the explanation is well made according to the force of the original tongue in conformity with the aim of the Spirit, and the application is distinctive, pathetic and right earnest. Wherefore we fear not to recommend it as useful to pious christians: "Prove all things," following the faithful of Berea who were more noble than those of Thessalonica, searching daily the scriptures. We call to mind the earnest zeal and fidelity with the well grounded and solid learning of this our young brother, the more as we intimately knew his Reverence, having often met him in our house, so that we love him as a son, his Reverence being as a young Timothy and not as a brother highly esteemed, since we thereby know that his ministry is blessed, and we present him a well proven seeker of God as a laborer who is not ashamed, and rightly dividing the word and giving to each his appointed part.

It causes us no wonder that his Reverence meets opposition and contradiction, so that he may in some measure say: "There is a great door opened to me and there are many opposers," insomuch that his enemies have already shut one church up on him (the usual way of those who are driven by the spirit of antichrist); but his Reverence can preach as well in barns or under the pure sky as in the church, as divers of his brethren in this land have done already before him. Also his Reverence is decried as an enthusiast, an old thread-bare slander against faithful ministers who for inward piety urge the necessity of being born again from water and Spirit and for a pious life and conversation in and through the Spirit. But what most strengthens the hands of the wicked is that a meeting of ministers with their respective Consistories is now being held deliberating on the lawfulness of his ordination and other charges against him wherein it is decided that these gentlemen cannot see that his ordination was lawful, etc. But it don't amount to much what their high Reverences can see or not see. But this is not the time nor the place to discuss that. Otherwise I am prepared and willing to prove not only the orthodoxy of his Reverence but also the lawfulness of his ordination, the more, as the Rev. Domine Dorsius is thereto competent. We therefore pass this over to his Reverence. Yet it seems something strange that so long as father Freeman lived, Domine Goetschius was a lawful minister, for that reverend man had not only endorsed his call but also inducted Domine Goetschius in the church at Jamaica with these words: "I am with you always to the end of the world." Shortly after his death they disturbed the congregation. Meantime may our partner in suffering console himself with this saying of God; all instruments directed against you shall not prosper. The Lord shed more blessings and lustre on his Reverence's ministry and instruction which he imparts in the languages and theology to the pious and gifted youth in order to prepare them as young Nazarites for the ministry.

T. J. FRIELINGHUYSEN.

New Jersey, Jan. 12, 1743.

We extract from the long, able and readable sermon of Domine Goetschius some of the more pungent passages that gave offence and made the old folks cry out: "Shall this young stripling come here and tell us that we have so long served an unknown God?"

"Worthy and beloved hearers. My only desire is that I may be enabled, through Divine aid, to unfold this notable text, so suitable to the circumstances of the present times, so plain and intelligible; and so to press it upon heart and conscience that many who are yet destitute of an experimental knowledge and worship of God, may be convicted and have their real state of soul laid open to their view." * * *

"O that the conduct of this faithful teacher, who spared no trouble, might shame so many easy and lazy ministers, etc., whom we may well compare to oxen."

"St. Paul did not look at these idolatrous things at Athens from motives of a sinful curiosity, merely to gratify his senses with these heathen fables, as many gospel ministers who are so much taken with such things. It was not with a design that he might with such stuff embellish his sermons, and so only please or tickle the ears of his hearers."

"How much more noble is our Apostle than many nowadays who come to the church! He findeth something in an Heathen church that is profitable for the soul, going but once and beholding, whereas now many go often, and that too, to a Christian church, but what do they take home with them?"

"How desirable that we had such preachers as St. Paul in these times."

"If this faithful Apostle was to come into our New Netherland and pass through our city and country searching closely, would not also his spirit be stirred within him? For he certainly would find many devotions, temples, houses of worship, excellent congregations, respectable Consistories, etc. He would find altars enough, viz: religious persons, both preachers and church-members, exhibiting many specious evidences of zeal, knowledge, labor and duties, etc., having yet a desire to draw near to God (Isa. 56.2). Seek God daily after their manner, speaking of and hearing his word, are baptized, partakers of the Lord's Supper, observe a particular religious and moral conduct, know how to speak much of the church and church affairs, prophesy, knowing languages and sciences, remove mountains, give over their all to the poor and their bodies to be burned. Yea, so much that if one did not look into their conduct with an enlightened eye he would be captivated, yea surprised at its mighty glittering appearance which in reality is only a great name and a shining formality. But then if the Apostle should cast his eye on the inscription which puts such persons and virtues in the balances of the Sanctuary, oh! how soon would he inscribe TEKEL on their foreheads! and the inscription of the Athenian altar on their religious devotions and exercises. How plain would it appear that with many persons their devotions and altars were not dedicated to the honor of the true God but rather to strange Gods, viz: to self-honor, self-love, self-praise and self-profit."

"And although with some there is an appearance of seriousness, as if they wish to do something for the service of the true God, yet this inscription is on them: *'To the unknown God.'* But do you ask who these are? I answer they are so many ignorant persons, living under a rich or abundant administration of the means of Grace, and at the same time are more stupid than an ox or an ass, for one knoweth his owner and the other his master's crib. There are so many that are easy and secure, and from their youth have been settled on their lees, who live on securely without any serious concern about their immortal souls, willing to risk their souls on a vain, groundless hope and lifeless worship, for an eternal world. They are so many stiff-necked and hardened persons, 'brass and iron,' as the prophet calls them, who will not be moved, neither by the lovely voice of the Gospel nor by the thundering curses of Sinai's law, but walk after the imaginations of their evil hearts. Their neck is an iron sinew, their brow brass."

"They are so many wicked, ungodly and profane with seared consciences. They are so many mocking, despising, caviling, Epicureans and opposers of that real and sovereign work of grace, regeneration and conversion, who cannot desist day nor night from rejecting and speaking scornfully of an experimental knowledge and worship of God and of them that do rightfully know and worship him in truth. They force on many people their old, rotten and abominable customary worship. There are yet others easily discerned who have nothing but a mere outward, literal knowledge of some points only touching the way of Truth, or a mere moral and external Godliness, name and morality; or a lukewarm approbation of the way of conversion and regeneration, of experimental knowledge and service of God and thus are only yea-brethren; or performing a great number of outward duties and devotions, viz: frequenting the church, partaking of the Lord's Supper, praying, weeping, bowing, singing, inquiring after salvation. All such are destitute of a true foundation in their souls, and neither experimentally know God nor cordially worship him, because they have never been truly serious, never in reality feared, chosen, loved, obeyed, forsaken all and followed God."

"He that rightly knoweth God glorifies him in public as well as in private, confesses him before men, tells what God has done for his soul. On the contrary the 'letter-knower' is generally ashamed to speak of the state of his soul, or he holds them that do it for hypocrites and thinks that he is a good Christian in his heart though his mouth never expresses anything of it, and thus he is ashamed of Christ and his Word before men."

"The letter-knower, that is, he who has only a literal knowledge of God, is dissatisfied or unconcerned under the adverse dispensations of God's providence, and seeks help wholly from the world and sometimes he thinks he does God's service when he can afflict the true worshippers of God and destroy the Lord's inheritance."

"Oh if all of you, great and small, young and old, rich and poor, men and women, would but prove yourselves aright, how soon would the mass of you conclude that all your devotion and worshipping of God hitherto performed has been dedicated to an Unknown God! Hear then ye infatuated and wandering sinners who neither know nor feel these works and exercises of grace, and consequently have never known nor worshipped God in spirit or in truth. Ye are the most miserable and unhappy creatures on earth. All your worship, prayers and sacrifices are an abomination to the Lord and cannot please him. All your thoughts, resolutions and ways are sin. Your best works are sinful, how much more then your evil works! How intolerable will it be for you when God for all these things shall bring you into judgment! What benefit will ye then derive from your formal lifeless worship?" "Know this ye that forget God, ye unconverted, ye ignorant, ye wicked, ye hardened in heart, ye formal Christians, hear, lest God tear you in pieces and there be none to deliver."

We have, of course, omitted the pathetic and tender, and best portions of this sermon.

PROCLAMATION, NEWTOWN, SEP. 27, 1748.

By order of the Reverend church Consistory of the Nether Dutch Reformed congregation of Newtown it was announced that it has appeared to the Consistory that the classis of Amsterdam in their letter of June 6, 1746, have written to the Consistory of Kingston that they "will not annul the ordination of Domine* Fryemoet there (in Dec. 1744) but hold it for lawful; yet that the anxiety of the scrupulous members as to the lawfulness of the Holy Baptism administered by him before his ordination is not ungrounded; and that those children must be considered as not having yet received that holy sacrament, which the sooner the better ought to be piously administered to them."

Upon which the Reverend Church Consistory of Newtown conclude that since it is the same case with Domine Goetschius (who has no more been a lawfully called and ordained minister than Fryemoet was formerly); as a consequence the Reverend Classis of Amsterdam also declare as unlawful the baptisms hitherto performed by Domine Goetschius, and on this account, the scrupulous members of the congregation would do well to receive this seasonable advice of the Reverend church Consistory and hereafter arrange it to their own contentment and for the best interests of their children, although it is not of vital consequence whether the baptism be performed by a lawful or unlawful minister, but only that the children be accepted in God's covenant of grace and be incorporated in the Christian church and be distinguished from the children of unbelievers.

Wherefore then those who are desirous to have the holy baptism administered to their children are requested to appear before the pulpit and hear the form thereof read and respond thereto.

The undernamed parents assenting to this, thereupon Domine Henricus Boel preacher of New York has for this purpose been earnestly requested to baptize the following children : * * * *

(*Names omitted.*)

---

* From early times the Dutch used to call their pastor "Domine," a word of respect and endearment, equivalent to "Mr." or "Master," and should not be confounded with "Dominie," the Scotch for "schoolmaster," which word has crept into our vocabulary from Scott's Novel of Guy Mannering.

We have not been able to find any ecclesiastical records in Queens County, that shed light on the history of the churches from 1742 to 1748, the period of Goetschius' troubles. After his exclusion from the church at Newtown, he may have remained in Queens County, waiting the course of events, teaching students, and performing religious services as he had opportunity. A statement had been made affecting his moral character. To counteract this he procured, October 16, 1744, ample testimonials of his good standing, and January 13, 1746, an affidavit made before Justice Andries Onderdonck that his accuser had (Dec. 1 1743) retracted the charge, was signed by Abm. Lott, John Van Arsdalen, Johannes Kolver, Bernardus Van Zandt, Jacobus Monfort and Adrian Onderdonck.

CERTIFICATE OF GOETSCHIUS' CHARACTER.

To all persons to whom these presents shall or may come.

Know ye that I have been personally acquainted with the Rev. John Henry Goetschius now a minister to the Dutch churches in Queens Co. some years past. During the whole time, so far as I have had any knowledge of him he has conducted himself not only as becomes a Christian, but also a faithful minister of the gospel of our Lord Jesus Christ; and I therefore, commend him to the great Head of the Church, and pray that he may be made eminently serviceable in promoting the interests of religion in any part of the Master's vineyard where he may be employed.

As witness my hand in Dosoris in Queens County, this 16th of October 1744.   BENJAMIN WOOLSEY, V. D. M.

And we also the minister and elders of the Presbyterian congregation of Jamaica do certify the same, as above written, as witness our hand.

DAVID BOSTWICK, V. D. M.
SAMUEL SMITH, Justice of the Peace.
ELIAS BAYLIS,
SAMUEL SMITH, Jr.

He added to these an able defense, written by himself, which, with all the other documents, was sent to the Classis of Amsterdam, who were satisfied with his explanations, but advised that he be released from Queens county, and sent to another field of labor. The gist of the charges against

Goetschius, were the irregularity of his ordination and that of his Consistories, his pulpit declarations and private conversations, his sitting in judgment on the piety of other ministers and professors, etc. *

It was during these troubles (in 1745 and 1747) that Whitefield visited and preached on Long Island, and produced such revivals.

1748, April 26.—Goetschius exhibited in Cetus a letter from the classis of Amsterdam to him, saying: 1. That he should be released from the congregations of Queens county and they from him. 2. That he should be recognized as a candidate in the Netherlandish church and should be taken in hand in his pious undertaking. Whereupon the Cetus recognized and received him, on his certifying a willingness to become subordinate.—In September he received a call from Hackensack, and Cetus gave him a written testimonial as a minister.

After Goetschius had removed from the scene of action, it yet required all the prudence of Cetus to reconcile the angry differences in the four congregations. In order to give some idea of their delicate and wearisome labors to bring about peace and unity in the churches, it will be necessary to give extracts from the journal of Cetus and the church book of Jamaica.

1748, September 27.—A committee deputed by Jamaica, Success and Newtown appeared before Cetus who promise to assist them in every proper way, to consider the affairs of the congregations, and write to the dissentients at Success and Jamaica, recommending the choosing of a Consistory from among those who had once been in office, and then for the opponents of Goetschius to join the Cetus as the others had done.

1748, September 29.—The Jamaica church book says: The New York Ring, † after long and fruitless labors to

---

* These documents have been translated into English and are now deposited in the Gardner Sage Library, New Brunswick.

† This Ring or circle was an assembly of ministers from New York, Long Island, and Poughkeepsie. It was subordinate to the Cetus. The records, I suppose, are lost.

unite the separatists with the others, resolved, for the good of the congregation, to choose a Consistory by means of the remaining members at Jamaica; and Domine Ritzema, who had charge of the churches of Cetus in Queens county, was thereto commissioned; and in his presence were chosen (December 26) for elders, Tunis Covert, Elbert Hoogeland and Jost Durye;* for deacons, Jeromus Rapelye, Rem Nostrand and Claas Latten. A protest against the last was handed in by the dissentients. The others were ordained (February 1, 1749) by Domine Ritzema in presence of the congregation.

Domine Arondeus (being countenanced by Domine Boel one of the Collegiate ministers in New York and an opponent of the Cetus) presided at the election of another Consistory at Jamaica and confirmed them in office the same day, which the Cetus declared unlawful.

Sep. 30.—Cetus write to the Classis of Amsterdam that "Domine Boel on Aug. 16, caused a new Consistory to be chosen by some persons at Newtown (for they who formerly were dissatisfied with Goetschius still corresponded with Boel only) and to ordain them the same day; particularly that he (Sept. 28) baptized anew 4 or 5 children who had already been baptized by Goetschius; and Cornelius Rapelye an elder said that Boel told him he did it by order of the Classis of Amsterdam." †

1748, Dec. 6.—The outgoing deacons Simon Nortwick, Daniel Durye and Rem Monfort accounted to the new deacons, Isaac Van Hook, Aaron Van Nostrand, Ares Remsen and Elbert Adriance and found in the alms chest £6, 5s, 4d. Dec. 12, Jan Hegeman delivered to them the alms-chest containing a bond of £116 and money £11 7s, 3d.—Dec. 12,

---

* 1775, Oct. 16,—Jacob Duryee and Albert Terhunen, Executors, offer for sale the homestead of Jost Duryea, near Old Neck, at Jamaica South, containing seventy two acres, on which is a gristmill of one pair of stones, mill-house, bolting-house. Also a fine healthy negro boy ten years old.

† The strife between the friends of Van Sinderen and Arondeus in Kings county was still more violent than any act in Queens county. One Sunday in Oct. 1748, the lock of the church door in Flatbush was broken off by violence and possession of the church for Divine worship was thus obtained by Arondeus' party. On Sunday, Jan. 21, 1750, the lock of the church door at Flatlands was broken off; and an Elder and deacons in opposition to Van Sinderen's Consistory led Domine Arondeus into the pulpit there.

Rem Monfort and Daniel Durye are chosen church-masters; and an accounting made by Isaac Van Hook and Derick Woertman. 10s, 11d, was found in the alms chest.

1749, Sep. 12.—The young man Thos. Romeyn appeared before Cetus and requested to be recommended to the Classis of Amsterdam in order that if found qualified by his studies under Domine Goetschius he may be admitted to the holy ministry. He is put off for the present.

1749, September 14.—Peter Luyster and John Cosjou (Cashow) from Oyster Bay, are received as members of Cetus, and report that Goetschius had revisited their congregation. Cetus decided that Goetschius is not competent to choose and ordain a Consistory there, and that he must abstain from doing any ministerial services there; but the dissentients may choose from their own party one elder and deacon to be added to the three of each already chosen by Goetschius, and to be ordained by a minister of the Cetus, so that thus the whole Consistory may become legitimate and the two parties united for the welfare and continuance of the congregation.

Cetus had written conciliatory letters to the dissentients; and on November 7, 1749, Justus Durye and Elbert Hoogeland, elders from Jamaica appeared in Cetus, and report that they had received a letter from Cetus, but the dissentients would not take it, saying that they had a minister and Consistory of their own and had nothing to do with Cetus. Johannes Colver, elder from Newtown, reports that he had given the letter to the dissentients, who read it and desired a copy. Andries Onderdonck, from Success,* reports that he had given the letter to the dissentients, who approved of it, and hoped it would work well.

Jacobus Monfort, Cornelius Hoogland, and Simon Losie, from Oyster Bay, for the one party promise to submit to Cetus, and bring about the same with their friends, and say the reason they did not submit before was the non-payment

---

* Dr. John Onderdonk father of the two bishops was baptized in the Dutch church at Success, Dec. 8, 1764.

of Goetschius' salary, and the calumnies against him as heterodox. On the other side Luyster and Cosjou promise to try to bring up the arrears of salary, and to give a caution to their friends against accusing him of heterodoxy.

1749, November 9.—A letter was read from Lanrens Haff, of Oyster Bay, not a member of the church, slandering the Cetus who declared that he should not be received into any Dutch Church until he repented and that the Presbyterian minister should be cautioned against receiving him, till he had made satisfaction to Cetus.

1749, November 14.—Cetus resolve that Arondeus (the troubler of our Israel) must be stopped from preaching in Queens county, and exclaim: "How sad is the condition of the Church of God on Long Island, in all the congregations of both counties! and, alas! growing worse and worse."

1750, September 11.—Simon Losey and Cornelius Hoogland from Oysterbay appeared in Cetus. 1. Inquiring whether they and their associates ordained by Goetschius, were not recognized as a lawful Consistory. 2. Signifying their inclination to come under the Cetus upon condition that they should have liberty to get the assistance of a preacher of the Cetus so long as the union was not established through the whole county.—Domine Ritzema undertook to write to the other party a caution not to slander as unlawful the Consistory chosen by Goetschius.—Elbert Hoogland from Jamaica asks for and is granted the service of a Cetus minister.

1750, September 14.—Cetus write to the Classis of Amsterdam that "Queens county remains the longer divided, and all our efforts are fruitless."

1751, April 19.—The new deacons Cornelius Monfort and Jan Jansen received the alms-chest (containing £8, 10.7½) from Isaac Van Hook and Ares Remsen, outgoing deacons.

1751, September 11.—Letters are received in Cetus from both parties at Oyster Bay.

1752, April 14.—Jost Durye, a delegate from Jamaica, seeks counsel and aid from Cetus against Arondeus, who hinders their union by continuing to preach there.

1752, Sept. 19.—Simon Losie and Jost Durye, a committee from Oyster Bay and Jamaica, presented a paper in Cetus asking counsel and aid (against Arondeus.) Cetus declare the Consistory of Jamaica lawful, and Oyster Bay is allowed to have a new one chosen and confirmed. Both congregations are awakened to the calling of a pastor; and Domine De Ronde is named as consulent or advisory minister thereto.

1752, September 21.—Cetus write to Holland that the long-desired peace and quiet of the congregations on Long Island are not yet established, since Arondeus resists the sentence upon him, and disturbs the congregations by administering the Word and the sacrament of baptism; and is confirmed in his obstinacy by his followers.

1752.—The church book says: "Ares Remsen commenced singing, November 21. Domine Frelinghuysen preached, and Thomas Romeyn* for the first time." This was Romeyn's trial-sermon, and proved satisfactory.

1752, November 27.—The congregations of Oyster Bay and Jamaica unite in proceeding to a call, at £100 per year, on Thomas Romeyn, student of divinity, which he accepts, on condition that he go to Holland for qualification.

1753, January 9.—The new deacons, Johannes Willemse and Rem Remsen, received the alms-chest from Aaron Van Nostrand and Elbert Adriance, and found in it a bond of £135 and money £20.17.

1753, April 10.—The church book says: "Domine Van Sinderen preached and Thomas Romeyn gave his departing discourse at Jamaica." This was on the eve of his going to Holland for ordination.

1753, September 1.—Ritzema made an explanation to Cetus concerning the election and ordination of a Consistory at Jamaica, which Cetus declared lawful.

---

* Students were not then allowed to preach in church, barn, or house, unless under their preceptors, nor use any other than the Lord's Prayer before and after sermon, nor pronounce the benediction. It must also be on a week day, and without singing or ringing of the bell. The cost of preparatory examination was £8—half paid in advance by the student; the cost of the final examination (to be paid by the congregation who called the minister) was £20, New York currency.

1753, September 13.—There were now two Consistories at Jamaica. Daniel Durye, Simon Nordwick, Abm. Schenck and Aaron Van Nostrand appear in Cetus as a committee from Jamaica, and insist that their Consistory, chosen by Arondeus* (though protested against in church by the elder, Abm. Lott) is lawful and that the one chosen by Ritzema unlawful, and therefore also the call made by them on Romeyn is void, and they laid upon the table a request for redress; and if that is not granted, that then they protest against Ritzema, Frelinghuysen and Goetschius being allowed to sit on their case, on account of their partisanship. The Cetus refuse the last request as groundless. The committee then agree with the Cetus to let everything rest for the present till further advices be had from the Classis of Amsterdam.

1753, September 14.—A letter is received in Cetus from the lawful Consistory of Jamaica.

1753, September 20.—Cetus wrote to Holland that Arondeus keeps the flames of discord blazing in Queens county.

1754, April 9.—Romeyn had gone over to Holland and was now back again.

1754, July 27.—The Jamaica church book says: "Romeyn is unwell. August 9.—We yet made an offer of peace to the dissentients, but were repelled."

1754, September 18.—Two elders from Jamaica, who had united in a call on Romeyn, appear in Cetus, and request information on their matters.

1754, Sept. 19.—Daniel Durye and others present papers against those who called Romeyn, stating that they cannot conform to the scheme of Cetus for uniting the congregation unless Romeyn be given up, and another minister be called in his place. Cetus decide that things should remain as at present; the persons who called Romeyn were prevented by

---

* Johannes Arondeus was a minister in Kings county, but was invited by the dissentients to visit Queens county and perform ministerial services for them. His last baptism at Jamaica is dated April 18, 1754. He had been deposed September 12, 1753. Henceforth he disappears from public view. What became of him I know not. It is said he died in 1754.

lawful hindrances from being present here and answering the statements of the other party; and if Romeyn (who now lies in a critical condition, struggling with a dangerous fever and more likely to die than live) should be restored (which may God grant), he shall be installed over those who called him as well at Jamaica as at Oyster Bay. Liberty is granted those congregations to install Do. Romeyn, if they choose, yet not without the action of Cetus. Daniel Durye and his friends, on hearing this, replied that they could not help matters, and could only go home.

1754, October 5.—The widow (of Jeromus) Rapelye delivered the alms-chest containing a bond for £30 and £12 in money to Rem Nostrand, in presence of us Tuenis Coevert, Elbert Hogeland and Jost Durye.

1754, October 9, is the last date in the regular baptism-book till 1766, February 16, a period of nearly 12 years. A few baptisms from 1753 to 1757 were recorded on loose sheets by one of the parties.

1754, November 10.—The church book says Romeyn was inducted at Jamaica by Domine Verbryck according to order of Classis and Cetus. His first discourse was from Psalm 119 : 9 : "Wherewithal shall a young man cleanse his way?"

1755, January 1.—Abm. Lott is chosen elder in place of Tunis Covert, whose time is out; and for deacon, Jan Dorland, in place of Jeromus Rapelye, deceased. Both were ordained by Romeyn, January 12.

1755, February 12.—Cor. Hoogland and Abm. Lott, elders from Oyster Bay and Jamaica, as authorized, put Domine Romeyn in possession of the parsonage-house and land. In the last week of March Romeyn made pastoral visitation from house to house throughout all Jamaica and met with rough handling from the dissentients.

1755, April 6.—The Lord's Supper was served for the first time by Do. Romeyn. Members received: Derrick Woertman, Abm. Hendricksen and wife, Jos. Golder and wife, Rem Lott and wife, Jan Lammerse, Christoffel Emmons and wife, Evert Van Wicklen, Gertie Durye, Nicholas Van Arsdalen and wife, Jacob Lott and wife.

1755, July 27.—Romeyn gave notice of an election of church masters, and invited thereto all the heads of families of the whole congregation. August 2.—Two were chosen for Jamaica, viz: Dirk Woertman old church-master in Domine Goetschius' time, and Jos. Golder in place of Isaac Vander Hook who had gone over to the church of England. At the same time were Abm. Lott and Elbert Hoogland, elders, sent after Daniel Durye to demand the church book and the remaining church property. Yet he refused, in presence of Laurens Masten and Jan Rapelye as witnesses. That the things are done as above stated, we are witnesses: Tunis Coevert, Jost Durye, Rem Nostrand, Elbert Hoogland, Abm. Lott.

1755, September 30.—On the proposal of some ministers to change the Cetus into a regular Classis, Domines Ritzema, DeRonde, Van Sinderen, Rubell and others withdrew and united in another assembly called the Conferentie or Conference. Hence the feud was more and more embittered, and in 1756 or 1757, we find DeRonde coming into Queens county, and presiding at a meeting of a part of the congregations of Success and Oyster Bay and all of Newtown to call another minister—while Romeyn was yet lawfully settled there; which caused Romeyn to write the following Protest, in behalf of the Elders of Success:

To the worthy Brethren, the Ruling Consistory of the Congregation of Jesus Christ at New York.

ESTEEMED FELLOW BRETHREN.—We the elders of the congregation of Jesus Christ at Success having understood that Domine DeRonde your Honors' minister has assisted in the making of a call (on a minister) for a portion of Jamaica, a portion of Success and for Newtown; and since it is a part of the worthy Consistory's duty to take notice of the conduct of their minister, so we earnestly beseech your honors to prevail on his Reverence to undo this proceeding or through some means to render it fruitless, because of many forthcoming difficulties.

Our reasons are (1.) that without the concurrence of the whole Consistory no minister can perform service in our congregation, according to the 15th Article of Church Order (of the Synod of Dort); (2.) that the bond of union will hereby be rent asunder and our congregation manifestly scattered in violation of the 80th Article of Church Order. The many reasons why we cannot in this matter agree with them we shall show at a proper time and place. In conclusion wishing you salvation and blessing, subscribed by us, your Reverences' grateful and obedient servants,

Success, Jan. 24, 1757. THE ELDERS.

1755, November 9, the Lord's Supper was served for the second time; 1756, April 18, third time; November 21, fourth time. Members received:—Isaac Leffersen and wife.

1756, January 2.—Rem Nostrand delivered the alms-chest containing £46, 15s, 2d, to Jan Dorland, Christoffel Emmons and Nicholas Van Arsdalen in presence of us, Abm. Lott, Abm. Hendricksen and Derrick Wortman.

1756, June 29.—Domine Romeyn was married to Margarita Frelinghuysen. She died at Jamaica on December 23, 1757, leaving an infant, Theodore F., only 25 days old, who also was cut off by an early death at Somerville, N. J., in 1785, having served his congregation but 10 months.

1757, April 10.—I acknowledge to have received from the Elders of the congregation of Jesus Christ at Jamaica the sum of £12, 10s, in full for a half year's salary.

By me THOM. ROMEYN,
V. D. M. *ibidem*.

1757.—I Jos Golder have bought 78 pounds of nails at 10d a pound, which comes to £3, 5s, 4d, and lent that sum to the Congregation.

1757, May 3.—In our church gathering it was found good by the elders and deacons of Oysterbay and Jamaica unitedly to repair the house standing in Jamaica where Cors. Smith now dwells, for Domine Romeyn.— So we the elders and deacons of Jamaica and Oyster Bay promise as we have subscribed each to pay equally one half of the cost.

CORNELIS HOOGLAND,
NYCKLAES VAN ARSDALEN,
JAN LAMMERSE,
JOSEPH HEGEMAN,
DANIEL DURYIE,
GARRET NOORSTRANT,

HANS BERGEN,
DERRYCK WOERTMAN,
JOSEPH GOLDER,
JOOST DURYE,
(One name illegible,)
PETER LUISTER.

1757, May 23.—The Consistory of Jamaica, by Domine Romeyn, paid to the Consistory of Oyster Bay the full sum that they asked of us (for repairs of parsonage).

1757, May 23.—Jan Dorland and Christoffel Emmons delivered the alms-chest containing £43, 13s, 6d, to Jan Lammerse and Nicholas Van Arsdalen in presence of us, Jost Durye and Jos. Golder.

1757, June 5.—The Lord's Supper was served for the 5th time.

<small>1757, June 7. Ares Remse and Elbert Hogelant agreed with Peter Luyster and Daniel Voorhees of Oyster Bay to make up the Domine's house for £30, in my presence, as witness.
JOOST DURYE.*</small>

<small>1757, October 26.—The present Deacons Cors. Monfort, Johannes Willemse and Rem Remsen overlooked the alms-chest and found in it a bond and note for £100 6s, and money £13, 7s. April 24, 1767 paid out £55, 6s.</small>

1758, January 15.—Domine Romeyn gave notice from the pulpit of an election of Church Masters.—January 20.—Jan Lammerse and Jacob Lott were chosen by the congregation of Jamaica. It was resolved by Congregation and Consistory that the two oldest deacons should from year to year be Church-masters. On these conditions we Derick Wortman and Jos. Golder give over the Church-book this 20th of January, 1758.

1758, January 23.—Nicholas Van Arsdalen delivered the alms-chest containing £40, 4s, 3d, to Jan Lammerse, Jacob Lott and Isaac Leffersen in presence of us, Jost Durye, Derrick Wortman and Jos. Golder.

1758, March 26.—The Lord's Supper for the 6th time; members received:—Bernardus Ryder † and wife, Gerret Nostrand and wife.

<small>1758, June 5.—Rec'd of Mr. John Lamberson the sum of eleven shillings and three pence for the rates of the Dutch parsonage—I say received by me.   £0, 11.3   NICHOLAS SMITH, Collector.</small>

1758, October 22, the Lord's Supper the 7th time; 1759,

<small>* 1758.—We, Ares Remsen and Elbert Hogelandt, the builders have received £8 from Nicholas Van Arsdalen.—1760, January 30, received from the congregation of Jamaica £6, 8s, 9d, in full.   ELBERT HOGELANDT.</small>

<small>† 1756.—In a gust of wind, Sunday, May 16, a negro the property of Bernardus Ryder was in a boat fishing in Flushing Bay and being overset was drowned.</small>

June 17, 8th time; December 16, 9th time; 1760, June 1, 10th time.

1758, December 8.—Jan Lammerse by consent delivered the church-book and alms-chest containing £41.7 to Jacob Lott, Gerret Van Nostrand and Isaac Lefferse, church-masters, in presence of Joost Duryo and Elbert Hogelandt.

1760, January 30.—By consent of Isaac Lefferse and Jacob Lott I deliver this church-book to Gerret Van Nostrand and Jan Lammerse, church-masters.

1760, January 30.—Jacob Lott delivered the alms-chest containing £35.12 to Rem Lott, Jan Lammerse and Gerret Van Nostrand, in presence of us, Bernardus Ryder, Jan Dorland, Ares Remsen and Elbert Hogelandt.

1760, November 30.—Says the Jamaica church book: "Domine Romeyn took his departure from us. He preached from these words (Eph. 6:24): 'Grace be with all them that love our Lord Jesus Christ in sincerity. Amen.'"

1762, February 25.—The journal of Conferentie says: Queens county is excited about a minister; with what result time will show.

1763, April 28,—The church paid Rev. Abm. Keteltas* a Presbyterian minister without a charge, living in Jamaica, (who could preach in Dutch, French or English) £16 5s. as half year's salary for his services.

1764, February 1.—John Lamberson and Rem Lott paid Benj. Waldron the half of what he demanded of us, 14s, 9d.

1764, March 1.—The Consistory of the four united congregations met at the house of Rem Remsen at the "Fly" or meadow to divide the contents of the alms-chest, and have found to distribute:

	£.	s.	d.
For Success, from Rem Remsen	12	18	9
" Rem Lott	12	10	0
Interest from Rem Remsen		16	9
	£26	5	6

---

* 1799, March 18.—On Thursday last the dwelling house of the late Rev. Abm. Keteltas, at Jamaica, took fire by accident and was entirely consumed. The house was old and out of repair and of no great value, but the loss is principally felt in discommoding a large family at a season of the year not easy to procure a habitation.

1764, May 17.—Rem Lott, deacon of Jamaica, paid £12.10 to Michael Demott and Harman Hendrickson, deacons of Success church.

1764, July 2.—Jeromus Remsen and Samuel Waldron received of Rem Lott £12.10 for the Dutch congregation of Newtown.

1765, May 9.—The alms-chest was delivered to Jan Lammerse in presence of Elbert Hogeland and Bernardus Ryder*.

"1765, October 22.—The minister, Boelen, who has been called to Queens county, still fails to appear, much to our sorrow; and we, with the congregations who expected him, are much perplexed, not knowing how to quiet them."—(*Journal of Conferentie.*)

1766.—The church book says: Domine Vander Boelen, from Holland, arrived in port February 2d; on the 4th he came to Jamaica, and on the 16th he gave his introductory discourse from Ps. 34:12. He was inducted by Van Sinderen from Heb. 13:7: "Remember them which have the rule over you, who have spoken unto you the word of God." Seven children were baptized.

1766, June 1.—Boelen had his first communion. His text was from Is. 66:2. In the afternoon he gave the usual Thanksgiving sermon after the Holy Supper, from Ps. 5:12: "For thou, Lord, wilt bless the righteous."

1766, June 23.—Elbert Hogeland and Stephanus Lott are deacons.

1767, May 17.—Domine Boelen had his second communion, Martin Schenck † and wife from Fishkill with an attestation communed with us for the first time. 1768, June 19.—Boelen's third communion.

1767.—Collections received toward building or repairing

---

* 1760, April 14.—Ran away from Bernardus Ryder, Flushing a negro man Cæsar, aged twenty-five, this country born, not a right black, has a little of the yellowish cast, a pretty lusty fellow, talks good English, if frightened stutters very much, has lost one of his front teeth; had on a light-colored Devonshire kersey coat, a soldier's red jacket, breeches and hat, and a pair of old shoes. 40s. reward if taken on the Island; or £3 if taken off the Island.—*Postboy.*

† 1769, April 10.—Martin Schenck offers for sale his farm of one hundred and fifty acres, two miles from Jamaica, on the eastern road to Flushing.

A PULPIT AND SOUNDING BOARD
OF THE OLDEN TIME.

THE ALMS-CHEST.
Made of cherry wood and strapped with iron, supposed
to be at least 167 years old, and still in use.

the church and lent to Martin Schenck, March 21, 8s, 7d. April 19, 12s, 10d. May 13, 3s, 7d. May 17, £1, 1s, 10d.

1767, June 18.—Rem Remsen, outgoing deacon, rendered an account of his expenditures, delivered up the alms-chest with £45, 10s, 7d, in it, and is thanked for his faithful service.

1767, August 10.—Jan Lammerse in presence of the greater part of Consistory delivered up to Isaac Lefferse deacon, the alms-chest containing £38, 13s, 3d, consisting of a bond of £18, bills, silver and coppers. We the under-written bear witness to it with our signatures: Hermanus L. Boelen, Minister, Joost Durye, Nycklaes Van Arsdalen, Marten Schenck, Isaac Lefferse, Jacob Lott.

1767, October 7.—The Conferentie write to the Classis of Amsterdam: "Domine Boelen* still remains apart from us with his congregations. He has many of his people who would cordially unite with us, and if the minister was of one mind with them the thing could be easily brought about. We desire, therefore, that your body would take the trouble to stir up the minister with his congregations to this end †."

1768, June 19.—Communion third time. Paid for bread and wine 9s, 2d.

1768, October 23.—Domine Boelen had the communion at Newtown, Douwe‡ and Abm. Ditmars with their wives communicated for the first time.

---

* The close of Boelen's pastorate in 1772, as well as his whole life before and after, is veiled in obscurity. We know not why he left or whither he went. He officiated occasionally at Newtown from 1777 to 1780. Riker says he resided awhile at Flatlands, and finally returned with his daughter to Holland.

He was a small man, of a powerful voice, but his language was not simple enough to be easily understood by common people.

† The dissensions of the Church having continued for nearly 50 years were brought to a happy close in October, 1771, when on the conciliatory invitation of the Consistory of the Collegiate Church in New York, the Cetus and Conferentie parties met in the Garden street Church and agreed on a plan for the reunion of brethren at variance; which having been approved by the Classis of Amsterdam the Articles were (June 18, 1772) accepted and signed by Nycholas Van Arsdalen, Cornelius Hoogland, Jacob and Joris Rapelye, Elders at Jamaica, Oysterbay, Newtown and Success; Queens County, then being without a minister.

‡ 1768, September 1s.—Run away from Dow Ditmars Gd, Jamaica a negro fellow, Tony, of a yellowish complexion, speaks Dutch and English, had on a brown camblet coat and waistcoat, plush breeches and trowsers; 20s, reward. N. B.—All persons are fore-warned not to conceal or carry away said negro.

TREASURER'S ACCOUNT.

	£	s.	d.
1739, Oct. 3.—Paid Isaac Bloom for an iron window hinge for the church.................................			6
1740, Jan. 12.—Paid for sweeping the church		1	3
1741, June, 1.— " Isaac Bloom for an iron bolt on the church door...			6
Sweeping the church...........................		1	3
Half a bushel of sand for church floor.........			4
To Wm. Stead, carpenter *...................			4
" Jas. Sebrant............................			9
" John Carman			6
" Widow Stillwell			1
" the glazier or glass-maker			5
1746, Dec. 6.—For paper		1	6
1747, —Paid to two poor women.................		10	
1750, May 6.—Gave a poor woman.......................	1	0	3
1751, Apr. 19.—Gave to the elders	4	6	6
" 30.—Gave to two high dutchers for a church		18	
1752, Oct. 14.—Gave the Elders.........................	4	10	
1753, Feb. 11.—Gave to the high-dutcher		7	4
1755, —Paid Theodore Frelinghuysen for Holland.....	2		
1758, July 1.—Gave a poor man and woman....		3	6
1766, Dec. 9.—Gave Lena Stine cash for bread 2s., a shift 9s., 1½ yards durant 14s, 3d, a yard of check 2s, 10d, making up all her goods 5s.	1	13	1

Sometimes a person made over his property to another party on condition of his being supported in his old age. We don't know how it was in the case of Peter Bennewe; but give the treasurer's expenditures in his behalf.

	£	s.	d.
1747, Jan. —Paid for a pair of leather breeches		10	
—More, for making a coat, in all	2	7	2
1748, Dec. 26.—For a pair of stockings		5	9
1749, Feb. 1.—Pair of leather breeches for P. B., a poor man .		10	
" Mar. 30.—A shirt		11	3
" June 2.—Paid to Samuel Lawrence on acct. of his board		2	10
" July 11.—Lent him		1	
1750, Mar. 17.—Gave him...........................		2	

1750-1, January 5.—Received by a vendue of the estate of Peter Benaway deceased £7, 2s, 4d, for the Dutch Church. I paid out expenses £6, 9s, 5d. There remains in my hands 12s, 11d, which I have put in our church stock.   JERONEMUS RAPELYE.

---

* William Stead indicted (May 18, 1773) for an assault on Sarah Rapelye, on offering proof in mitigation is fined 10s.

FIRST REFORMED DUTCH CHURCH.

It was found May 23, 1757 by receipts that £71, 12s, 3d, was at different times paid out of the Dutch Church for Binnewe's support.

COLLECTIONS IN CHURCH.

	£	s.	d.
1767			
April 19, Paas Sunday...		8	7
" 20, " Monday...		12	10
May 13, Wednesday.....		3	7
May 17,.................	1	1	10
" " paid for bread and wine...........		13	2
Aug. 30.................		10	
Sept. 27................		11	
Oct. 25.................		6	6
Nov. 22.................		1	
Dec. 20.................		3	3
1768			
Feb. 7..................		8	6
Mar. 6..................		4	2
Paas Sunday.............		6	10
" Monday.............		2	
May 1, Sunday...........		9	
Pinkster Sunday and Monday.................		9	11
June 15, Wednesday, preaching.............		2	11
June 19, Sunday.........	1	8	6
July 17, Sunday.........		10	9½
Aug. 14, "		11	8
Sep. 11, "		9	9½
Oct. 9, "		9	10
Dec. 4,.................		3	3
1769			
Jan. 1, New Year's Day..		5	4

	£	s.	d.
Feb. 26.................		1	3
Paas Sunday and Monday		15	4
April 19, Wednesday.....		2	
April 23	1	1	0
Took out for bread & wine		8	8
May 14, Pinkster Sunday.		10	
May 15, " Monday		4	4
July 9,.................		10	1
Aug. 6..................		11	½
1770			
July 29		8	11
Aug. 26.................		8	6
Sep. 23.................		12	7
Oct. 21.................		6	
Nov. 18.................		6	8
Dec. 16.................		6	9
1771			
Jan. 1 Tuesday..........		3	11
Jan. 27.................		3	5
Feb. 24.................		3	6
Mar. 4, Monday..........		7	3
April 21................		9	6
May 12..................		9	2
June 5, Wednesday.......		2	9
June 9..................		14	2
Took out for bread & wine		13	2
July 7..................		3	7
Aug. 4..................		11	1

1769, April 29.—In presence of the greater part of Consistory who met at the house of Isaac Lefferse, there was found in the alms-chest £44, 6s, 9d.

1769, May 3.—The Consistory met and found it good to take the money in the chest for up-building (or repairing) the church; and to begin the chest anew.

1769, May 14.—Barnardus Ryder, Elbert Hogeland, Stephen Lott and Douwe Ditmars are deacons.

1769, May 29.—Paid £16, 10s, cost of making up or repairing the Domine's dwelling.

1769, August 12.—Jacob Lott and Douwe Ditmars made a reckoning and found in the alms-chest £1, 15s, 5d.

1770, June 7.—Gerret Nostrand and Stephen Lott outgoing deacons left in the alms-chest £7, 6s, 10d.

1770.—Abm Ditmars paid for bread and wine 13s, 2d. The preaching was once a month this year.

1770, April 14.—£11, 7s, was paid by Albert Hoogland to Bernardus Ryder for sashes for the church. Before this, probably, the upper half of the windows had glass, the lower part had shutters which were opened in warm weather to admit fresh air.

1771, August 12.—Douwe and Abm. Ditmars left in the alms-chest £12, 1s, 9d.

1772, June 13.—" Paid out for Domine Boelen's salary £7, 14s." This year he left.

1773, December 13.—A call it is said was made on Rynier Van Nest, who declined.

1773, September 21.—Particular Synod met in New York ; Jacob Rapelye and Abraham Hoogland present from Queens County. On the proposal of Jacob Rapelye in behalf of the vacant congregation of Queens County; the preachers of this Synod decide to preach there by turns in order of age, every four weeks, so long as they are shepherdless.—1774, September 20.—Present Peter Onderdonck and Jacob Rapelye from Queens County. The request of Queens County was renewed and agreed to in the same way as last year.

1774, October 4-7.—Rynier V. Nest, Jr., M. C.,* appeared and having given a specimen of his sermonizing, upon Zach. 13:7 withdrew ; and Sol. Froeligh, student of Theology, having been invited in and afforded an opportunity of showing his faculty for preaching by a discourse upon 1st John 5: 7, likewise withdrew. Having given satisfaction to the Reverend Synod, they were admitted to examination, Mr. V. Nest to the final and Mr Froeligh to the preparatory ; and

---

* M. C., means candidate for the ministry.

having been afterwards carefully examined by the Deputati, both in the Greek and Hebrew languages, and on the various points of Sacred Theology, they so far afforded satisfaction to the Reverend Synod that they did not in the least hesitate to admit Mr. Van Nest to the proclamation of the Holy Gospel and the administration of the Holy Sacraments, and to receive Mr. Froeligh among the Licentiates. The Moderators, were directed to furnish them with testimonials.

SOLOMON FROELIGH CALLED.

1775, April 25.—Sol. Froeligh, M. C., presented himself to Synod, exhibiting a call made upon him by the four united congregations of Jamaica, Newtown, Success and Oyster Bay, and requesting to be admitted to the final examination. After the approval of the call the time for the examination was fixed at day after to-morrow at 10 o'clock in the forenoon.—He was accordingly admitted to his examination, and after having afforded a specimen of his gift of preaching, from Proverbs xv:3, he was subsequently carefully examined both in the Hebrew, upon Psalm xxiii, and in Greek upon Philippians iii, and especially upon the prominent points of Sacred Theology, and afforded such satisfaction that without the slightest hesitation he was admitted to the proclamation of the Holy Gospel and the administration of the Sacraments; wherefore the Reverend Moderators were directed to furnish him with a suitable testimonial. The Reverend President Lambertus De Ronde, with the ministers in Kings County was appointed to solemnly install Mr. Froeligh with laying on of hands on the second Tuesday of June next.

At the session of Synod, September 19, 1775, present Solomon Froeligh and Jacob Rapelye from Jamaica. Domine De Ronde reported to the Reverend Synod that according to the order and appointment of the last held General Assembly extraordinary he was present at the installation of Domine Solomon Froeligh, taking his text from 1 Thess. v: 12, 13, after which by the laying on of hands of the Ordainer and other Reverend brethren present, the candidate was duly invested who afterwards in the afternoon gave his introductory sermon from Isaiah lxii:1; whereon may the Lord grant his blessing.*

Froeligh says that after preaching the Gospel to the four congregations of Queens County with little visible success for 15 months and amid much conflict of mind arising from their disaffection to our Independence, I fled to Jersey and narrowly escaped being taken prisoner by the British army. In this flight I lost all my cattle, furniture, books and clothing, in which consisted my little all of earthly things. I can never reflect without emotions of gratitude on the goodness of God in favoring my escape.†

Froeligh wore the cocked hat, Geneva cloak and bands for a while, but at length discarded them.—He had bought a silver watch of Major Lefferts just before the British landed on Long Island and was prevented from paying for it by his sudden flight and the continuance of the war till the peace of 1783 when he revisited the Island and made payment. There is a strange discrepancy in this story as variously told by Froeligh's friends and enemies. Tunis Hoogland of East Woods, Oyster Bay, told the Rev. William P. Kuypers that Froeligh bought the watch of Abm Schenck‡ of Great Neck before the war. After the war he returned and preached at Success when Schenck asked him for the money.

---

* After service De Ronde enquired of Rev. Abm. Keteltas; "Who is this Froeligh? What is the occupation of his father?" Keteltas replied: "His father lives in the North and is a farmer." De Ronde exclaimed: "Ah, these farmer ministers have no dignity." Keteltas replied: "I am surprised at you. This morning you told us in your sermon that it was immaterial whether a minister was son of a farmer (boor) or of a burgomaster." "I said so indeed in the pulpit," replied De Ronde, "I must say something for the ears of the people, but I think otherwise."—*Demarest's Life of Froeligh.*

† 1780, October 3,—Froeligh having accepted a call to New Millstone, Synod appointed a committee to approve the same; and thereupon in this very unusual case, to dismiss him from his former congregations on Long Island, from which having been driven by the enemy in these disturbed times he can obtain no regular ecclesiastical discharge; Synod being fully satisfied of his blameless, profitable and edifying conversation in those congregations.

‡ 1797, June 14.—$20 Reward.—Ran away from Abraham Schenck, Great Neck, a negro man, Jake, much addicted to liquor, very impertinent when intoxicated, wore a high-crowned hat, hair shortish and tied behind. He is something of a fiddler, very active, and values himself much on jumping over fences.

FIRST REFORMED (DUTCH) CHURCH,

Fronting on the Main Street, Jamaica; intended for the Congregation spread through all Queens County. Erected 1716; taken down 1833. It was of octagon shape. In front are poplar trees, and on the west an old-fashioned hay scales.

Froeligh said he hadn't any but offered back the watch. Mrs. Schenck said : Let him keep the watch. He will pay for it sometime or other. Schenck said he could live without the watch, etc., etc. At a meeting of Classis at Hackensack, 1796, in an angry moment Knypers charged Froeligh with stealing this watch. Froeligh sued him for slander and many witnesses were summoned, Major Lefferts* among others. The trial lasted three days.

1775, May 17th, was observed as a day of Fasting and Prayer by the congregations of the Reformed Protestant Dutch Churches, in this and the Province of New Jersey.— *N. Y. Journal*, on account of the Revolution.

1776, June 1.—Douwe Ditmars and Isaac Lefferts reckoned and found in the alms-chest .£22, 17s, 7d.

1776, August 27, was a day of Fasting, Humiliation and prayer appointed by the Continental Congress.

REVOLUTIONARY INCIDENTS.

In 1776, the British took possession of Long Island. Froeligh had been an ardent Whig, and in his public ministrations had often prayed the Almighty to strike the fleets of our enemies with his bolts, and sink their soldiers in the sea, so that they might not set hostile foot on our shores. Before the enemy could lay hands on him he had fled to Newtown, and lay concealed one night in the house of a Mr. Rapelye, at Hellgate, who set him over to the main.† The parsonage was occupied by the Rev. Mr. Bowden. The church was taken possession of by the soldiers, and used as a store-house for provisions. The pulpit was left, but the seats and floor were ripped up, and taken out, and used for building huts and barracks for the soldiers who lay at Jamaica

---

* 1819, May 12.—Burglary.—The house of Mr. Isaac Lefferts near Jamaica, Long Island, was broken open on the night of the 8th inst., and robbed of a small chest, containing fifteen hundred dollars in bank bills, three hundred and fifty dollars in silver, twenty eagles, a gold watch chain, key and seals, and a number of valuable papers. Two hundred dollars reward is offered for the detection of the robber and the recovery of the property. George Ellis Ryerson had broken open the late Major Lefferts' house.

† He did not flee as precipitately as is generally supposed, for he officiated at Success, October 13, 1776, six or seven weeks after the British had possession of the Island.

almost every Winter. Here, every Sunday, wagons repaired to draw the weekly allowance of rum, pork, flour and peas. The deacons' chest, with its money, was kept out of their hands, and, it is said, buried by Isaiah Doxey, in a sheep pen, and covered with litter. The people were permitted to worship in the Episcopal church occasionally. Domines Rubell* and Schoonmaker, from Kings County visited the congregations of Queens county at distant intervals, marrying, christening and performing other religious services, but there is no record preserved of any church services at Jamaica during the Revolution; but in Newtown, Success and Oyster Bay some baptisms are recorded, those churches having been only now and then occupied by soldiers.

When a British officer sent a farmer on an errand he usually gave him a pass in order to prevent his being stopped by some other official, as the following permit shows:

> JAMAICA, 29 Aug., 1776.
> Permit Isaac Bennet to pass and repass without molestation.
> WILL. ERSKINE, Brig. Gen.

Among the hardships of the British occupation was that of the farmers having their teams taken at any time to cart provisions, baggage and munitions of war for army use, as the following order shows:

> FLUSHING, 26th Sept. 1776.
> TO LUKE BERGEN:
> Press two wagons for the Service of the Light Dragoons.
> S. BIRCH, Lt. Col.

Judge Thomas Jones in his History of the Revolution, says:

"I have seen a conductor of wagons, upon a foraging party, turn fifty horses into a loyal farmer's orchard, (one

---

* When Domine Rubell preached he evinced his loyalty by the fervency of his prayers for "King George III, Queen Charlotte, the Princes and Princesses of the Royal family and the upper and lower houses of Parliament." If the minister omitted this prayer he could hardly descend from the pulpit before receiving a reprimand from some one of his hearers.

When the services of a minister could not be procured the Dutch went to gebedt, a religious meeting at private houses where they sang, read prayers and a sermon.

Isaac Lefferts, near Jamaica), where his apples were gathered and put into heaps ready for making cider, and though the farmer earnestly begged the conductor to put them into a field where the pasture was better, the request was insultingly refused, and the apples—which turned into cider, would have produced £200—were totally destroyed. Mr. Lefferts, upon remonstrating with the conductor against so extraordinary a conduct, was called a 'damned old rebel.' He had, it is true, been a Committee-man, but upon General Howe's first proclamation, in November, 1776, he came in, submitted, and renewed his oath of allegiance. What confidence could be put in the proclamations of Generals, when they were so flagrantly, unjustly and openly violated? And yet the proclamation, in consequence of which the farmers surrendered, pledged the faith and honor of the Crown that every person availing himself of it should be protected by His Majesty in his life, liberty and property."

The sufferings of the people during the armed occupation of our Island by the British were beyond description. Besides having their fat creatures and farm produce taken from them for army use, (and if paid for, it was at a price fixed by their conquerors), their wagons and teams were often impressed so that they had not animals sufficient to do their plowing and carting. Hence they raised scant crops and were straitened in provisions. They were also forced to share their scanty fare with soldiers billeted on them by British authority, and with no certainty of payment. Col. Graydon thus describes his living in a well-to-do farmer's family :

"The houses and beds of the Dutch we found clean, but their living extremely poor. A sorry wash made up of a sprinkling of bohea* and the darkest sugar, with slack-baked bread and a little butter constituted our breakfast. At our first coming, a small piece of pickled beef was occa-

---

* Bohea was the kind of tea most in use. But tea was so seldom drank even in well-to-do families that a physician ordered tea to be purchased and drank as a cordial for a sick woman. In 1844, when tea was high-priced, some farmers substituted burnt crusts of bread instead of the China herb.

sionally boiled for dinner, but to the beef which was soon consumed, succeeded clippers or clams, and our unvaried supper was supon or mush, sometimes with skimmed milk but more generally with butter-milk blended with molasses, which was kept for weeks in a churn. I found it, however, after a little use, very eatable, and supper soon became my best meal. A black boy too was generally in the room, who walked about or took post in the chimney corner with his hat on, and occasionally joined in the conversation."

"The Dutch were quiet and inoffensive. Their religious, like their other habits, were unostentatious and plain; and a silent grace before meat prévailed at table. When we were all seated our host clapped his hands together, threw his head on one side, closed his eyes, and remained mute and motionless for about a minute."

"The principal person in a Dutch village appears to be the Domine or minister; and Flatbush (1777) revered her Domine Rubell, a rotund, jolly-looking man, a follower of Luther and a Tory. At Flatlands there was also a Domine Van Sinderen, a disciple of Calvin and a Whig. He was in person as well as principles a perfect contrast to Mr. Rubell, being a lean and shrivelled little man, with silver flowing locks under his triangular sharp pointed hat, which streamed like a meteor to the troubled air, as he whisked along with great velocity in his chair through Flatbush.—*Graydon's Memoirs.*

The negroes became insubordinate and often left their masters. Here follow two advertisements:

1780, June 4.—Ran away from John Amberman a negro man, Will, thick lips and had on corduroy breeches. Two guineas reward for his recovery.

1782, June 12.—$10 Reward.—Ran away from Douwe Ditmars, a negro boy, Frank, took a pale blue cloth coat and jacket and a new castor hat. It is imagined he intends going on board some privateer.

1777, November 24.—Douwe Ditmars and John Lamberson were two of a Committee appointed by town meeting to provide fire wood and other necessary articles for the use of the hospital and guard house in Jamaica. All who have soldiers billeted* on them will be excused from contributing.

As there were no Banks of deposit, the farmers hid their money, but were often tortured till they revealed the hiding place. We give two instances out of many:

Isaac Hendrickson was tied to a bed-post and robbed.

John Williamson was robbed of £300 which was hidden under the hearth stone.

In the Fall of 1780 Derick Amberman, a miller at the lower end of Foster's Meadow, demanded pay for flour of a British officer, Crowe, quartered at John Montanye's. This so angered Crowe that he beat the miller on the head with a loaded whip, and Major Stockton ran him through with a sword. Neither was punished, though a court martial was held.

As a captain of Militia Albert Hoogland had to distrain the property of Friends who refused to do any military service or to pay for guarding the Fort at Whitestone, taking from one and another, a watch, a looking glass, linen goods, wheat, turkeys, boots, a geography, pewter plates, tongs, andirons, sauce pan, silver tea-spoons, etc.

During the latter part of the war when things became more settled, the farmers could attend to agriculture and found a ready market for their produce which was greatly needed by the officers and soldiers of the army and paid for in British gold and silver. The officers, especially, were fond of good living and would gladly pay almost any price for setting out a luxurious table.

Of course farmers were liable to have their hen-roosts robbed at night, and subject to all kinds of theft, when soldiers were in their neighborhood.

1777. September 1.—The inhabitants were expected to show their fidelity by contributing in every way to the support of the British arms, otherwise their loyalty might be

---

* When the British army was not in active service the men were distributed in such farmers' houses as had two fire-places, soldiers in the kitchen of one house and officers in the best room of another. A sergeant previously visited each house and chalked on the door the number to be taken in. Unless a bbg was hung up was at the door the soldiers would cut up the fences for fuel. An officer always had a guard pacing before his quarters.

suspected. The following Dutch names appear in a list of contributors for raising a new regiment to be called "Fanning's Corps," at the request of Governor Tryon:

Name	£	s.	Name	£	s.
Amberman, Nicholas		8	Lamberson, Tunis		8
" Derick		16	" Waters		8
" Isaac		8	" Nicholas	1	4
" Paul	2		" Simon		8
" John		8	Lefferts, Isaac	1	12
Bennet, John	1	4	" Agnes, wife of I.		8
" Cornelius		16	Losee, John		8
" Isaac		8	" Cornelius		8
Bergen, Derick		8	Lott, Stephen	1	
" Tunis		16	" John H.	2	
" John		8	" Abraham		8
" Jacob	1	8	Nostrand, John	1	
" Abraham		10	" Garret		16
" Johannes	1	4	Remsen, Aury	1	4
" Luke		16	" Jacob		16
Boerum, Aury		10	" John	1	4
Covert, Tunis		16	" Rem		16
Ditmars, Garret		8	" Daniel		16
" John		12	Ryder, Urias		8
" Isaac	1	16	" Bernardus		8
" Abraham	1	4	" Christopher		8
" Dow	3	4	Snedeker, Garret		8
" Dow, Jr	4		" Johannes	1	17½
" Mary, wid. of Dow	—	—	" Abraham		8
Duryea, John, Jr	2	8	" Rem		16
" Rulef		16	" John		10
Dorland, Garret		16	Van Brunt, John		8
Eldert, Samuel		16	" Jost	2	
" Hendrick	1	4	Van Dam, Nicholas		8
" Luke	1	17½	Van Liew, John (pond)		16
Emmons, Hendrick	1	12	" John, Sr		16
Frederick, Jonas		12	Van Nostrand, Peter		8
Golder, Wm		16	Van Arsdale, Isaac		8
" Joseph		8	" Abraham		8
Hendrickson, Isaac		8	Voorhies, John		8
" Bernardus		16	Van Wicklen, Johannes		16
" Wm		16	" Garret		8
" Hendrick		16	" Evert		16
" Abraham		10	Williamson, Mary, widow of John		8
Johnson, Martin		8	Williamson, John	2	13½
Lamberson, Bernardus		8	Wyckoff, Jacob	1	12
" John	1	4			

RESIDENCE AT FLATBUSH OF REV. BERNARDUS FREEMAN.

BIOGRAPHY OF DUTCH MINISTERS.

Bernardus Freeman* was born in Gilhuis, Holland. He was called to Schenectady (1700) at a cost of near upon £80. He also learned the Mohawk language and instructed and converted the Indians.† He was inducted in the church of New Utrecht, November, 1705, by Domine Dubois. He married an heiress Margretia Van Schaick, 1705, and died at Flatbush, August, 1743, aged 83, leaving a daughter Anna Margaretta, who married her cousin David Clarkson, son of the Secretary of the Province.

Freeman was the means of settling Frelinghuysen at the Raritans where the people (in the pastor's view) were become too lax in their notions of christian duty and indulged in horse racing and kindred amusements. When the domine tightened the reins and refused the communion to the more notorious offenders, his Consistory with the aid of the pen of Henricus Boel put forth a pamphlet entitled their "complaint," KLAGTE. Freeman having espoused the cause of Frelinghuysen, had drawn off the fire upon himself and at length (1726) was forced to issue his "defence," VERDEEDIGING. Van Santford also published a tract on these difficulties entitled SAMENSPRAAK, "a Talking-together or Conference." The misunderstanding between the Consistory and Freeman came up for adjudication before a church court at Jamaica, July 25, 1725.‡

Vincentius Antonides was born 1670 at Bergen, in the

---

* The name is variously spelled Bernhardus, Barent, Freeriman, Vreeman.

† He was appointed to preach to the Indians and instruct them in the Protestant faith in order to counteract the instruction of the French Jesuits from Canada.

‡ Freeman had printed (1721) at Amsterdam a volume of thirty sermons (containing expositions of the Lord's Prayer, Creed and Ten Commandments) entitled the "Balance of God's mercy," prefaced with an address to the beloved supporters of the church, being the respected and much beloved brethren his colleagues; the elders and deacons of the congregation of Jesus Christ at Flatbush, Brooklyn, Bushwick, New Jamaica, Flatlands, Gravesend and New Utrecht, as also to the Elders and Deacons at Schenectady and the members of the same, being my first congregation ministered unto in these regions, with the numerous and increasing members of the congregations here in each forenamed village.

He was also the author of "The mirror of self-knowledge" (1720), a small volume of moral precepts, which he translated from the ancient philosophers.

BIOGRAPHY OF DUTCH MINISTERS.

Bernardus Freeman* was born in Gilhuis, Holland. He was called to Schenectady (1700) at a cost of near upon £80. He also learned the Mohawk language and instructed and converted the Indians.† He was inducted in the church of New Utrecht, November, 1705, by Domine Dubois. He married an heiress Margretia Van Schaick, 1705, and died at Flatbush, August, 1743, aged 83, leaving a daughter Anna Margaretta, who married her cousin David Clarkson, son of the Secretary of the Province.

Freeman was the means of settling Frelinghuysen at the Raritans where the people (in the pastor's view) were become too lax in their notions of christian duty and indulged in horse racing and kindred amusements. When the domine tightened the reins and refused the communion to the more notorious offenders, his Consistory with the aid of the pen of Henricus Boel put forth a pamphlet entitled their "complaint," KLAGTE. Freeman having espoused the cause of Frelinghuysen, had drawn off the fire upon himself and at length (1726) was forced to issue his "defence," VERDEEDIGING. Van Santford also published a tract on these difficulties entitled SAMENSPRAAK, "a Talking-together or Conference." The misunderstanding between the Consistory and Freeman came up for adjudication before a church court at Jamaica, July 25, 1725.‡

Vincentius Antonides was born 1670 at Bergen, in the

---

* The name is variously spelled Bernhardus, Barent, Freerman, Vreeman.

† He was appointed to preach to the Indians and instruct them in the Protestant faith in order to counteract the instruction of the French Jesuits from Canada.

‡ Freeman had printed (1721) at Amsterdam a volume of thirty sermons (containing expositions of the Lord's Prayer, Creed and Ten Commandments) entitled the "Balance of God's mercy," prefaced with an address to the beloved supporters of the church, being the respected and much beloved brethren his colleagues; the elders and deacons of the congregation of Jesus Christ at Flatbush, Brooklyn, Bushwick, New Jamaica, Flatlands, Gravesend and New Utrecht, as also to the Elders and Deacons at Schenectady and the members of the same, being my first congregation ministered unto in these regions, with the numerous and increasing members of the congregations here in each fore-named village.

He was also the author of "The mirror of self-knowledge" (1720), a small volume of moral precepts, which he translated from the ancient philosophers.

Netherlands. He came to Flatbush 1706, and died July 18, 1714, after a lingering illness, leaving children and a good name. He was more of a formalist than the evangelical Freeman.

Thomas Romeyn was born at Pompton, N. J., March 20, 1729, and died at Fonda, October 22, 1794, and was buried under the church. He studied divinity under Goetschius and T. Frelinghuysen. In 1765 he received the degree of A. M. from Princeton College.

Ulpianus Van Sinderen born in Holland was called to succeed Antonides and to be a colleague of Arondeus, 1747; but they did not well agree. He married Cornelia Schenck (1748), who was thrown out of a chaise and fell down a bank at New Utrecht, and died a few days after, at Mr. Cortelyou's. He was declared *emeritus* in 1786 and died at Flatlands, July 23, 1796, in his eighty-ninth year, leaving children.

Johannes Casparus Rubell, born 1719, was called (1757) from Rhinebeck as colleague to Van Sinderen. He became too fond of drink and was deposed in 1784. The rest of his life he spent in preparing quack medicines, styling himself *chimicus*. He died at Flatbush, May 19, 1797, leaving posterity. He was President of General Synod, October, 1773.

Johannes Henricus Goetschius was born in Switzerland. Coming to this country with his father a minister, he studied under Rev. G. H. Dorstius, a German, who took it upon himself to ordain him, which act was disallowed by the Cetus, and caused much trouble afterwards, though he received his examinations preparatory and peremptory, preceding his induction into the church of Jamaica. He died at Hackensack, November 14, 1774, aged fifty-seven. He had three wives and sixteen children.

Martinus Schoonmaker was born at Rochester, Ulster county, 1737. Studied the languages under Goetschius and theology under Marinus. Preached at Gravesend and Harlem 1765-84; and occasionally in Queens county during the Revolution; served the combined Churches of Kings county from 1784 till his death, May 20, 1824. He married Mary

Basset at Aquackanonck, 1761. He preached only in Dutch and spoke English with hesitation. A funeral service of his at Flatbush is thus described: "In 1819 I was present at a funeral. As I entered the room I observed the coffin elevated on a table in one corner. The Domine, abstracted and grave, was seated at the upper end. All was still, a simple recognition or half-audible enquiry, as one after another arrived, was all that passed. Directly the sexton, followed by a negro, made his appearance with glasses and decanter, and wine was handed to each. Some declined, others drank a solitary glass. This ended, again the sexton appeared with pipes and tobacco. The Domine smoked his pipe and a few followed his example. When the whiffs had ceased to curl around the head of the Domine, he arose with evident feeling and in a quiet and subdued tone made a short but apparently impressive address in Dutch. A short prayer concluded the service, and then the sexton taking the lead was followed by the Domine, the doctor and the pall-bearers with white scarfs and black gloves. The corpse was taken to the church-yard, followed by a long procession of relatives, friends and neighbors. No bustle, no confusion, no indecent haste attended that funeral. No rattling of carriages, no tramping of horses, no cracking of whips to disturb the proprieties of so solemn an occasion."

Solomon Froeligh, D. D., was born near Red Hook, May 29, 1750, and died at Schraalenburgh, N. J., October 8, 1827. He studied awhile under Romeyn, and thence entered the academy at Hackensack, supporting himself by teaching school. He studied theology under Goetschius. In 1774 he received the degree of A. M. from Princeton College, and in 1811 that of S. T. P. from Queens College.[*] In 1797 he

---

[*] We, the underwritten Consistory of the Nether Dutch Reformed congregations of Queens county (after calling on the name of the Lord with our Pastor, Sol. Froeligh, have deputed our brother, Elder Jacob Rapelye, to the Particular Synod of ministers and elders, to be held at New York, the 19th of this month, for the upbuilding of our Nether Dutch Zion, to represent us there), praying that God through His Spirit may guide the worthy Synod in all matters of importance that may come before them.

Thus done at our meeting in Jamaica, September 18th, anno 1775.

JEROMUS REMSEN,
DANIEL LUYSTER,
PETER MONFORT.

was appointed professor of theology, and instructed thirty persons for the ministry. Being dissatisfied with some proceedings of the Reformed Church he seceded and organized the True Reformed Dutch Church of which a few congregations yet survive. He was suspended (1823) but persisted in preaching till August 5, 1827. He married Rachel Vanderbeek who died fifteen years before him.

CHRISTENING AND COMMUNION.

The first time a mother left home after the birth of her child was to carry it to Church to be baptized. In early times there were sponsors or witnesses (in Dutch *getuygen*) who undertook or stood for the child. They were usually relatives. In 1753-7 they were called in our records *compere* and *peet*, or godfather and godmother. The woman after whom a child was named, sometimes claimed the privilege of presenting and holding it for baptism. *

At the Lord's Supper it was the custom of the minister to invite and even urge the communicants to approach the holy table, who seemed reluctant to come. Such was then the fashion. After a long exhortation some more prominent member rose and moved. He was gradually followed by the rest. After the men had been served, then the women were in like manner exhorted. As the people came to the table they laid their offerings thereon, and standing around the table received from the minister's hands. The first Communion vessels were of pewter.

After the new Church was built in 1833 the communicants received at their seats in the body of the Church, the deacons passing the elements. Formerly the communion service was too often read hurriedly. Latterly the ceremony has been made more interesting and impressive by distinct

---

* Baptism was then performed by trine aspersion, that is, the minister dipped his fingers three times in the basin of water, and at each sprinkling repeated the name of one of the persons of the Trinity. When a young couple married they usually left off their youthful frivolity, entered on the serious business of life, became staid and sober, and had their children regularly baptised, as their parents had done before them. Sometimes English parents who did not understand a word of the Dutch formula had children baptised.

and emphatic reading and by the body of communicants rising to the recitation of the Creed

Our Dutch ancestors generally kept their religion in their hearts rather than on their lips; though with some, their conversation easily and readily ran into a religious channel. Few, probably, erected a family altar or made extemporaneous prayer in public. In some families the Bible * was read at evening by way of devotion, and on Sundays especially, the chapter from which the minister took his text. † The preaching was then expository. The preacher often announced his text and the outline of his sermon (called in Latin, *exordium remotum*) and then made the long prayer. He then took up his sermon and stuck to his text all the way through. The church had, however, provided printed prayers for such as chose to read them, in a manual corresponding to the New England Primer. It contained the alphabet, spelling lessons and easy reading. Then came the Lord's Prayer, Creed and Ten Commandments, morning and evening prayers, grace before and after meat. In every well-ordered family the children were made to learn by heart the Lord's Prayer, Creed and Decalogue. In religious matters the Dutch were not aggressive, though adhering stiffly to their own Church, they were not given to proselyting. The long internal dissensions, the scanty preaching on account of the widely scattered population and the long persistence in the use of the Dutch language in public worship must be among the the causes of our finding so many Dutch names in other religious denominations.

We have no mention of the church owning a bier or funeral pall, till December, 1839; nor of burials under the

---

* Almost every family had the Dutch folio Bible weighing from sixteen to eighteen pounds, so heavy that it could hardly be read without its being laid on a table. In it were usually recorded the births, deaths and marriages of the family.

† The Dutch Sunday was not a dull day, it was rather a festival than a fastday. It was a day of enjoyment as well as of Divine worship. The family then had a better repast, the best the house could afford. The children read in the Testament, and learned by heart the Lord's Prayer, the Creed and Ten Commandments. Having attended Church in the morning the old folks usually spent the afternoon at home, reading good books while the young men, singly or in numbers, "went to see the girls."

church, as was often the custom formerly, at the death of distinguished persons. The tolling or funeral bell could be had in any of the churches, on paying the sexton.*

CHURCH REPAIRED.

Martin Johnson, Stephen Lott, Isaac Hendrickson and William Golder were chosen to repair the church. There is no account of the expenditures, preserved. We have, only the heading of a subscription list without the names, as follows:

We the undersigned promise to pay to the builders chosen, May 28, 1785, the different sums annexed to our names; and that for sittings that shall fall to our lot.

1786, November 21.—Cornelius Monfort and Stephen Lott reckoned and found in the alms-chest £19, 15s, 4d.

1787, January 8.—Paid to the Widow Codwise £2.

1789, June 1.—Jacob Adriance and John Durye, Jr., accounted, £29, 19s, 8d, in the chest.

1791, August 5.—Elbert Hoogland and Martin Johnson accounted, £16, 10s. 6d, in the chest, and a note of Rem and Ares Remsen for £14, besides a parcel of coppers and old silver.

CALL OF MR. VAN NEST.

1785, March 10.—At an extra meeting of Classis a call†

---

*1775, July 24, Mrs. Rapelye paid five shillings each to the Dutch and Episcopal Churches for a funeral bell for her husband John.—1775, January 10, the executors of Garret Laton paid for bell and use of pall of the Episcopal church.—1775, August 26, Mrs. Ditmars paid Episcopal Church for grave, pall and bell for her husband.—1776, October 29, Abraham Ditmars paid for use of pall.—1781, October 9, Douwe Ditmars paid for pall.—1784, October 12, John Williamson paid for pall and bell.—1811, February 9, the executors of Jost Van Brunt, Sr., paid Episcopal Church for his grave twelve shillings, use of pall six shillings, funeral bell four shillings.—1815, June 4, twelve shillings was paid for John Williamson's grave in the Episcopal Church yard.

In 1749-50,—Jacob Vanderbilt and Laurens Haff paid £3, 9s, 3d, for a funeral pall (doodkleed) for the use of the congregation of Oysterbay alone and not for those of Jamaica, Newtown and Hempstead. It was to be under the control of Simon Losee and Peter Luyster. When two lay dead and unburied at the same time, the older was to have the preference in its use.

† His salary was £125 per year with a parsonage, as appears by his receipts:

October 16, 1792.—Received from the Consistory of the congregation at Jamaica the sum of £15, 12s, 6d, in full for a half years salary for the congregation.

By me RYNIER VAN NEST.

PLAN OF PEWS AND NAMES OF PEW HOLDERS IN FIRST CHURCH, 1785.

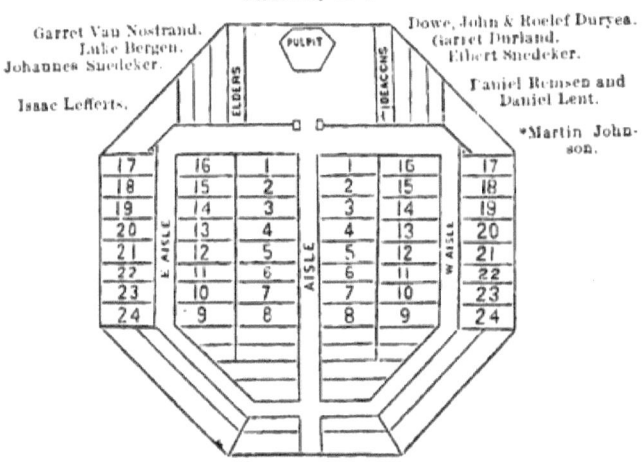

† "Fore-Singer."

1. Minister's Pew.
2. John Suydam.
3. Hendrick Eldert.
4. Isaac Lefferts.
5. Abraham Polhemus.
6. Benjamin Hegeman.
7. Isaac Hendrickson.
8. Stephen Lott.
9. Abraham Lott.
10. Elbert Adriance.
11. John Amberman.
12. Martin Johnson.
13. Johannis Wyckoff.
14. Garret Van Wicklen.
15. Hendrick Emmons.
16. Tunis Covert.
17. Casparus Springsteen.
18. William Monfort.
19. John Duryea.
20. John Suydam.
21. Abraham Suydam.
22. William Hendrickson.
23. Ares Remsen.
24. Stephen Lott.

1. Jost Van Brunt.
2. Barnet Bennet.
3. Hendrick Brinckerhoff.
4. Isaac Amberman.
5. Abraham Golder.
6. Dow Duryea.
7. Maretie Ditmars.
8. Isaac Brinckerhoff.
9. Jacobus Ryder.
10. William Golder.
11. Jacob Adriance.
12. Cornelius Monfort.
13. Johannis Remsen.
14. Maria Ditmars.
15. Abraham Ditmars.
16. Elbert Hoogland.
17. Ares Remsen.
18. Martin Schenck.
19. Johannis H. Lott.
20. Hendrick S. Lott.
21. Abraham Van Arsdalen.
22.
23. Cornelius Bennett.
24. John Williamson.

from the four united congregations of Queens, county on the Rev. Reynier Van Nest, minister at Shawangunk, was produced, dated March 7, and laid on the table for the approbation of this Reverened assembly, which call in its entirety being conformable to the sincere aim or design of the congregations and being found sufficiently formal is approved and confirmed and the Lord's blessing thereon invoked. Ordered that he be installed at Success by M. Schoonmaker.—March 25, the Rev. Reynier Van Nest* called and lately invested as preacher in the four united congregations of Queens county exhibited his dismission and satisfactory certificate from his former congregation and also a like attestation from the Rev. Classis of Kingston, by which his Reverence, in a christian and brotherly manner, is commended and given in charge to this Rev. Classis. September 20, Mr. Van Nest, having taken his seat in this Classis, he and his elder, Isaac Lefferts, have signed the articles according to the Synod's resolution of October, 1772†.

1788, June 11.—The Synod of the Reformed Dutch Church set apart this day as a day of fasting, humiliation and prayer that the members of the State Convention may be inspired with wisdom from on High, and that their decisions may perpetuate our civil and religious privileges.

1789.—Wednesday, January 28th, is to be observed as a day of humiliation, fasting and prayer, by all the Dutch and Presbyterian Churches in New York and New Jersey, that God would put a stop to the progress of the destroying insect (the Hessian fly) which is cutting off the fruits of the earth in the Middle States; for the establishment of wise, efficient, united and permanent civil government, &c.

In early times the Dutch were averse to having ministers of other denominations occupy their pulpits. In 1786, the

---

* Reynier Van Nest was born in New Jersey in 1754 near Somerville, and died there July 9, 1815. He was educated by his pastor John Frelinghuysen and called to Shawangunk in 1774 where he married his professor's widow. He preached usually in Dutch, and when (by vote of Consistory) he preached in English "he made but a poor fist of it," as people said.

† Up to 1794, the records of the Classis are in Dutch.

congregation of Success voted that no service of any other religion (that is contrary to the doctrines of the Reformed Dutch Church) should be performed in the Church without the consent and agreement of the Consistory and a majority of the true members of the Church.

In 1811, the Classis cautioned the Consistory of Oysterbay against having the services of Rev. Bradford Marcy, a Congregationalist. In 1828, a complaint was made to Classis that a Methodist Minister and a Presbyterian Missionary also had been allowed to preach in the vacant Church at Success.

UNION HALL ACADEMY.

1791, March 1.—A meeting was held in Jamaica for building an academy*. Rev. Rynier Van Nest was chairman. The following Dutch names occur in the list of subscribers:

	£	s.		£	s.
Amberman, John	2		Lamberson, Waters	3	
Bennet, Bernardus	4		Lamberson, Bernardus		10
Bogart, Cor's (Fos. Mead)	2		Lott, Hendrick	1	
Boerum, Aury	1		Snedeker Rem	1	
Dewitt, John	5		Sprong, David	5	
Ditmars, Abraham†	5		Suydam, Femetie	2	
Ditmars, Abraham Jr	5		Totten, Joseph	5	
Duryea, John	2		Van Arsdale, Abraham	2	
Duryea, Aaron	1		Van Brunt, Jost	3	
Eldert, Samuel	1		Van Dam, Richard	5	
Eldert, Hendrick	1		Van Dyne, John		10
Hendrickson, Bernardus	5		Van Lew, John	1	
Hendrickson, Hendrick	5		Van Lew, James	10	
Hendrickson, Wm	1		Van Lew, John	5	
Hoogland, Albert — three loads of timber			Van Nest, Rynier	5	
			Vanderbilt, John	2	
Johnson, Martin	5		Williamson, John	10	
Lefferts, Jacobus	1	4	Wyckoff, John	4	
Lefferts, Isaac Jr	5				

* On November 3, 1852, I became Principal of this academy, and retired from the situation of classical teacher in April, 1865, with John N. Brinckerhoff, then Principal.

JAMAICA, June 13, 1776.

† To CAPT. ABM. DITMANS, Esq.: You are hereby required and commanded to meet with the company of militia of foot under your command, completely equipped according to law, on Monday, 17th inst., at 10 o'clock in the morning, at the Green, at Beaver Pond, at Jamaica, in order to join the First Battalion of this county then and there to be mustered and exercised.   JEROMUS REMSEN, Col.

1792, Oct. 17.—It was decided to have the services in Church, half the time in English. Hitherto they had been wholly in Dutch, and hardly intelligible to the young. An English pulpit Bible had to be bought (£2, 14s.) and an English Psalm-book (6s.).* Simeon Marston (1798) and John Bremner, Jr. (1801) were in succession fore-singers in English; and Isaac Brinckerhoff from 1799 to 1805, and his son Hendrick, in Dutch, from 1806 to 1823. Their salaries varied from $2 to $8 per year. They at first sat in one end of the deacons' pew by a high-raised book-board. They used a pitch-pipe and afterwards a tuningfork, on giving out the tune. The bellringer was paid $4 a year.

CALL OF MR. COOPER.

1794, March 12.—At an extra meeting of Classis a call of the four combined congregations of Queens county, on Zacharias H. Kuypers (or Cooper, in English) was presented for approbation; after reading which the Classis found it to be regular, approved the same and resolved that it might be put in the hands of the candidate. The members of Classis could not refrain from expressing their surprise at the small and inadequate sum (£150) mentioned in the call as the annual salary promised to their minister. They wish to impress on the minds of the people the obligation of supporting the Gospel in a decent and honorable manner, and of rendering the annual incomes of their ministers proportional to the increased prices of the necessaries of life.

1794, April 29.—Rev. Z. H. Cooper, a candidate licensed by the Classis of Hackensack, having received a call from Queens county, applied for trial in order to his ordination. He produced a dismission and recommendation, and was admitted to trial. He gave a discourse from Galatians, v. i.;

---

* In 1788 Synod, with a view of introducing uniformity of English Psalmody in the Church, ordered a Psalm and Hymnbook to be compiled from Tate and Brady, Dr. Watts and a book used in the Collegiate Church, N. Y. This book with revisions and alterations to it in 1813, 1817 and 1847, was used in Church till Easter Sunday, April 9, 1871, when the present Hymnal superseded it.

and the Classis proceeded to examine him as to his skill in the original languages of the Holy Scriptures, and his acquaintance with natural and revealed religion, in all which they obtained satisfaction, as well as of his own attachment to Divine truths, and agreed to admit him to ordination for the ministry.

Classis appointed the Rev. Messrs. Van Nest, Livingston, Lowe, Stryker and Jackson to attend at Success, on the second Sabbath of July, solemnly to set him apart for the sacred ministry, with such forms as are used in this Church. Dr. Livingston or Mr. Lowe to preach the ordination sermon.

ORDINATION OF MR. COOPER.

On Sunday, July 13, the Church at Success (now Lakeville), the largest in the county, was crowded to its utmost capacity by people eager to witness the novel and interesting ceremony. Those that could not get inside the Church took seats out of their wagons to stand upon, peering in and listening at the windows, if so be, they might hear or see something.* The sermon was preached by the Rev. Dr. John H. Livingston on a text from St. Matthew, xxviii: 18, 19, 20—"And Jesus came and spoke unto them, saying, 'all power is given unto me, &c. Go ye therefore, and teach all nations,'" &c.

DIVISIONS OF THE DISCOURSE.

First—The authority and ability with which the Redeemer is invested; Second—The commission and work of the Apostles; Third—A gracious promise of support and help. In the application he addressed the candidate who is to be ordained. First—Upon the work of the Ministry; Second—Upon the encouragement and promises here given; Third—

---

* That the ceremony of ordination might be seen of all the people, it was usual to have a staging erected before the pulpit, and partly resting on the pews, whereon sat the ministers and candidate, who kneeled at the laying on of hands. This was so done at the ordination of Rev. Henry Heermance, at Manhasset, September 20, 18 6. Sometimes ordination is performed at the foot of the pulpit, and can be seen by a few only.

Upon the duty of professing people, that they must learn, become disciples, attend the ordinances, keep the commands of Christ, &c.

He then addressed the people on the duties they owe: first, to Christ; second, to themselves; and third, to their pastors. Next he addressed Van Nest, the colleague of the new pastor, the Consistory, the whole body of the people, and thus closed: "Now may it be Amen to you." Amen.*

1796, November 6.—The treasurer paid for cleaning the Church for the Communion, three shillings and nine pence; for three loaves of bread, three shillings; for a gallon of wine, ten shillings.

VAN NEST LEAVES.

1797, June 8.—At an extra session of the Classis, Mr. Van Nest produced a call from the Church of Schoharie, and gave several important reasons for accepting it, with which the Classis were fully satisfied; while they sincerely regret the removal of a brother from their body, much endeared to them by his worth and usefulness. Mr. Van Nest attending on Synod could not get his regular dismission from his congregation. As soon as it may be obtained, the president is authorized to furnish him with ample recommendations and dismission from this Board. Mr. Cooper was now sole pastor of the four congregations.

1800, September 2.—The Classis find the congregations of Queens county have delayed for several years to call an additional minister. *Resolved*, That Mr. Kuypers and an elder from each of his congregations be notified by the clerk to attend at the next extra meeting of Classis (11th inst.) to explain why such delay has happened, and to receive such direction as Classis may think proper upon the subject. September 11.—Three of the elders appeared and told Classis that as soon as they could effect the sale of the par-

---

* As it was in harvest time, Dr. Livingston improved the occasion and flattered the farmers by saying: "The harvest truly is great but the laborers are few, &c.

sonage (which is the common property of the four congregations) they would form other combinations and call another minister. Whereupon the Classis recommended to them to agree as soon as possible in the division of their common property, that the new combination may be formed, and they proceed to the call of another minister.

1801, September 1.—Elder John De Witt, from Newtown, informed Classis that at a late meeting of the Consistories of the four Churches of Queens county, it was resolved to appoint four commissioners to report to Classis the inconvenience of their present connection and request Classis to dissolve it, and unite Jamaica with Newtown, and Oysterbay with Success, for the purpose of making separate calls in those new congregations. Only one commissioner was present, and the subject was postponed 'till next session. 1802, April 20.—John De Witt and Albert Hoogland appear before Classis and say they were last year appointed by the united Consistories of Jamaica, Newtown, Success and Oysterbay, with Abm. Monfort and Daniel Bogart to request Classis to dissolve the combination of those Churches and unite Jamaica and Newtown into one, to enable them to call a separate minister. Classis enquired of Mr. Cooper who assented to the statement as true, and that Success and Oysterbay had no objection. Though Bogart and Monfort were absent, it must be from some other cause. Classis grant the request and hope the two other Churches will do, the same; but not to interfere with their present engagement to Mr. Cooper.* A call from Jamaica and Newtown on the candidate, Jacob Schoonmaker was presented and approved. September 14, Mr. Schoonmaker preached before Classis from I Peter, i: 9. He was then examined in the original languages of the Old and New Testaments, on didactic and polemic theology. Agreed that he be ordained in Newtown, on the fourth Sabbath of October, and that Rev'ds G. A. Kuypers, P. Lowe, John F. Jackson and Z. H. Kuypers with

---
* Classis ordered that preaching on the Heidelberg Catechism be recommenced in Queens county, that the children be catechised and families visited.

Elders Chas. Duryea, Robert Manley, Isaac Mead and David Waldron be a committee to attend to it. Lowe to preach the ordination sermon in English, and Jackson to preside.

At his first coming, Mr. Schoonmaker being unmarried, boarded at Mr. Snedeker's, Mr. Lott's and Mr. Conklin's. Having married Catharine Ludlow he occupied the parsonage, now owned by Jos. P. Disbrow.

1802, May 20.—Builders of the Church chosen, viz: Hendrick Hendrickson, Jost Van Brunt, Stephen Lott, Isaac Hendrickson.

1804, April 17.—The first record is made of a contribution ($2.50) to the Missionary Society.*

1801, March 31.—An act passed the Legislature for the sale by auction of the parsonage. Half the proceeds to be paid to the congregations of Oysterbay and Success to buy another for themselves, and the other half to Jamaica and Newtown. The advertisement of sale was published six weeks in a Brooklyn Newspaper. The commissioners to sell it were Abm. Polhemus, Jr., of Newtown, Abm. Ditmars, of Jamaica, Abm. Schenck, of Great Neck, and Jacob Van Wicklen, of Oysterbay. The parsonage (now belonging to Aaron A. Degranw) was sold, May 6, 1801, to Zebediah and Dorothy Story, for $2,277.50. Deed signed by Abm. (and Charity) Polhemus, heir of Abm. Polhemus, one of the original purchasers.—*Queens county records, O., p. 192.*

A PARSONAGE BOUGHT.

1805, April 13.—Isaac Clason, an India merchant of New York, for $3,000 sold to Albert Hoogland,† Johannes S. Lott, Johannes Dewitt and Rem Hegeman, as trustees of the

---

* Probably there were many collections taken up in Church for charitable purposes, of which no record was made. In 1761 the new Church at Kakiat, or New Hempstead, built by Dutch emigrants from Queens county, applied to their mother Church for aid; and in 1775, £2, 10s. was given as an alms to Kakiat or Tappan.

† 1792, Feb. 6.—Albert Hoogland, Flushing, offers for sale cheap, for no fault but only for want of employ, a negro wench, aged thirty, who understands all kinds of country housework, with her two children, a girl aged eighteen and a boy aged six.—*Daily Advertiser.*

Reformed Dutch Churches of Jamaica and Newtown, seven acres of land for a parsonage, bounded north-east by Monson Hoyt, south by John Mottley (both lands late of Edward Bardin), south-west by Isaac Clason and north by the Ferry road.—*Queens county records, X., p.* 162.

1805, March 4.—We, the subscribers promise to pay the sums annexed to our names, for buying a parsonage for the minister who now and henceforth may serve the Dutch congregations of Jamaica and Newtown.

	£.	s.		£.	s.
Rem Snedeker.	10		Isaac Brinckerhoff.	6	
Hendrick S. Lott	8		Albert Hoogland.	10	
Isaac Lefferts.	8		Isaac Hendrickson.	10	
John Wyckoff.	8		Albert Snedeker.	5	
Barnet Bennett.	8		Mary Monfort.	2	
Stephen Lott.	10		Aletta Monfort.	1	10
Hend'k Emans	6		David Sprong	2	
Johannes S. Lott.	6		Aaron Duryea.	1	10
Stephen Lott, Jr.	5	10	Jacob Conklin	4	
Barnet V. Suydam.	6		Jacobus Ryder.		
Abm. Snedeker.	1	12	Nicholas Ryder.		
John Williamson.	4		Paul Duryea.		
Abm. Lott	2		Rulef Duryea		
Jost V. Brunt	2		Garret Snedeker.		
Hend'k Hendrickson.	20		Donwe Duryea		
Rem Remsen.	4		Garret Van Wicklen.		

The other subscription papers are lost.

1810, October 31.—List of Pewholders:

No. Pew.
 1 Rem Snedeker.
   Rulef Duryea.
 4 Johannes S. Lott.
 6 Abm. Rapelye.
 8 Hendrick S. Lott.
13   ''   ''
14 Rem Snedeker.
15 Jacobus Ryder.
16 Michael Golder.
17 Jos. Hendrickson.
18 Aletta Monfort.
19 John Duryea.
22 Daniel Hitchcock.

No. Pew.
25 Jas. Hendrickson.
26 Tunis Van Brunt.
27 Abm. Hendrickson.
28 Hendrick Hendrickson.
29 Rem Snedeker.
30 Isaac Brinckerhoff.
31 Albert Hoogland, sold to Crinyonce Sutphin.
32 Johannes Lott, Jr.
33 John and Bernardus Bennet.
35 Jas. L. Rapelye.
36 Aaron Duryea.
37 Stephen Lott.

No. Pew.	No. Pew.
38 Isaac Hendrickson.	55 St. Lott.
39 Wm. Totten.	57 Wm. Hendrickson, Jr.
40 Stephen Lott.	59 Hendrick Suydam.
42 Johannes H. Eldert.	60 John Duryea.
43 John D. Suydam, deceased.	61 Aaron Duryea.
44 Minister's pew.	62 John V. Nostrand.
51 Abm. Snedeker, sold to Wilhelmus Stoothoff.	68 Rev. Jacob Schoonmaker.
	69 Bernardus Lamberson.
53 Isaac and Abm. B. Selover.	70 Albert Hoogland.
54 Johannes S. Lott, sold to Luke Covert.	71 Wm. Rhodes and Fred. Smith.
	72 Johannes Wycoff.

1812, August 26.—Chosen trustees of the Church: Rem Snedeker, Aaron Duryea, John I. Duryea, Abm. Hendrickson.

The whole expense of painting and repairing the Church was £290, 3s., 10d., which was paid in 1815.

	£	s.	d.
Jacob Sherred's* bills	172	4	3
David Lamberson	1	10	11
John Dunn		11	8
Stephen Hicks		1	8
Gold leaf		2	9
Wright & Herriman	17	1	8
Wyckoff & Van Dine		10	8
Isaac Peck, joist and planks	9	17	
Wm. Sales, "		1	3
Parcel's bill	14	9	4
Mr. Baroum	27	4	
Wm. Hendrickson, for scaffolding steeple		10	
Jonathan Jones		8	6
Crinyonee Sutphin's bill	18	18	6
	11	1	
	£290	3	10

1813, June 7.—John Rider, carpenter, laid the cornerstone of the Presbyterian church. While it was building the congregation met for worship in the Reformed Dutch Church.

1814, August 3.—The British being expected to attack New York, a part of the Militia of Queens county was ordered to Brooklyn, and the farmers were invited to cart

---

* Sherred, a painter and glazier of New York, left a legacy of $50,000, by which "Sherred Hall" was built.

timber for the construction of Fort Greene. There were one hundred and twenty loads of fascines, (twenty-five bundles each) brought from Jamaica to Brooklyn. The Rev. Jacob Schoonmaker headed the procession, Mr. Eigenbrodt and the pupils of the Academy assisted the people in cutting the fascines.

1814, September 7.—There are one thousand two hundred of General Johnson's brigade of infantry, from Kings and Queens counties, now encamped on Fort Greene, Brooklyn. The Jamaica Militia marched to Brooklyn September 2.

1811.—Statistics of the Churches of Queens county:

Jamaica .... 107 families, 56 communicants.
Newtown 79   "   76   "
Success 54   "   49   "
Oysterbay 66   "   50   "

THE CHURCH REPAIRED.

1815.—The expense of painting and repairing the church was £290, 3s., 10d., which was paid by the trustees elected August 26, 1812, viz.: Rem Snedeker, Aaron Duryea, John I. Duryea, Abm. Hendrickson, and assessed on the pews as follows:

1 Albert Hoogland	$10 50	13 Nicholas Williamson	$6 00
2 Garret Dorland	3 00	15 Hend'k S. Lott	3 00
Paul Duryea	6 00	16 Rem Snedeker	6 00
3 Williamson Ryder	3 75	17 Nicholas Ryder	7 50
Garret Dorland	3 75	18 Michael Golder	7 50
4 Albert Snedeker	4 50	20 Aletta Monfort	7 50
5 Nelly Lott	9 00	21 John I. Duryea	7 50
6 Rem Remsen	6 00	22 John D. Ditmis	7 50
7 John Bennett	6 00	23 Abm. Ditmars	7 50
8 Jacobus Lott	6 00	24 Dr. Daniel Hitchcock	7 50
9 Hend'k S. Lott	6 00	25 Bernardus Lamberson	7 50
10 Abm. V. Arsdalen	6 00	26 Tunis Van Brunt*	7 50
11 Ruth Golder	6 00	27 Barnet Bennett	7 50
12 Bernardus Bennet	6 00	28 Jas. Hendrickson	7 50

* John Rider and Luke Covert received, May 29, 1821, of Jas. Foster $33, for pew No. 26, that did belong to Tunis Van Brunt's estate.

29 Isaac and John Amberman.	$7 50	rick and John V. Wicklen	$7 50
30 Abm. Hendrickson	7 50	52 John Wyckoff	7 50
31 Hend'k Hendrickson	7 50	53 Phebe Johnson	9 00
32 Rem Snedeker	7 50	54 Derick Amberman	4 50
33 Hendrick Brinckerhoff	7 50	John Hegeman	3 00
34 Crinyonee Zutphen	7 50	55 Abm. Snedeker	7 50
35 Johannes Lott*	7 50	57 Isaac and Abm. B. Selover	7 50
36 John Bennett	7 50	58 Lucas Coevert	3 00
37 Joshua Mills	7. 50	59 John Wyckoff	4 50
38 Jas. L. Rapelyet†	7 50	60 Stephen Lott	6 00
39 Aaron Duryea	7 50	61 Aury Remsen	6 00
40 Stephen Lott	7 50	62 Wm. Hendrickson, Jr	6 00
41 Abm. I. Hendrickson	7 50	63 Abm. Lott	6 00
42 Wm. Totten	7 50	64 Rem. Suydam	3 00
43 Stephen Lott	7 50	Abm. Hegeman	3 00
44 Isaac and Jas. Lefferts	7 50	65 Wm. Willis	6 00
45 Johannes H. Eldert	7 50	66 Aaron Duryea	6 00
46 Hendrick S. Lott and Barnet V. Suydam	7 50	67 David Springsteen	6 00
47 James Van Siclen and Cor's Eldert	7 50	68 Isaac and Jas. Lefferts	9 00
		69 Wm. Stoothoff	4 50
48 Rev. Jacob Schoonmaker	— —	70 Ann Bergen	7 50
49 Tunis Covert and Catharine Covert	7 50	71 Rem Nostrant and Nath'l Nostrant	6 00
50 Hend'k Emans	7 50	72 Nicholas Wyckoff	10 50
51 Garret, Tunis, Evert, Der-			

MONEY PAID OUT.

	£	s.	d.
1787, Jan. 8.—Given to a stranger		12	
1788, June 14.—Abm. Probasco (carpenter?)	4	13	6
1791, Jan. 24,— " " "	3	7	6
" " —Isaac Rikeman		4	
" Dec. 21—Abm Probasco		17	7
1794, May 19—For expenses of Domine Cooper	3	15	
" Aug. 19—Cost of Mr. Cooper's procurance	3	17	
1795, Ap'l 21.—Gave the fore-singer and bell-ringer	3	6	
1795, May. 1.—Simeon Marston, fore-singer in English	3	4	
" Oct. 27.—Wm. P Kuypers, one Sunday's preaching	1	12	
" " —Received in exchange for the old coppers	7		3
1799, May 1,—John Amberman, bell-ringer, one year	1	12	
" " —Isaac Brinckerhoff, Dutch fore-singer	2	8	

* 1795, February 22.—Johannes and Petrus Lott offer for sale the farm of Hendrick Lott deceased, three miles west of Jamaica, on the road to the Ferry. It has a house, barn, orchard, stone well, a watering place for cattle and one hundred and fifty acres of land.

† Sold, October 29, 1825, to Nicholas Williamson and John Van Brunt.

		£	s.	d.
1800, Ap'l 27.—Phillip H. Duryea, proponent, or candidate.....	2			
1802, Jan. 3.—Sunday—Isaac Van Doren, preaching	2			
" Feb. 17.—Wednesday, and March 28, Sunday, Jacob Schoonmaker, preaching	4			
" Ap'l 19.—Mr. Cooper, for writing Schoonmaker's call.....	16			
" May 24.—Stephen Lott, for repairing the Church	50			
1804, May 1—John Bremner, Jr., English singer.............	4	4		
1805, May 14, and 1806, June 13 (Fridays).—Rev. Van Nest......	2			
1808, May 29.—To the worthy Domine Van Nest	2			
1809, Sep. 21—Cor's R. Duryea, for leveling the road by the Church	6			
1810, Feb. 27.—John D. Ditmis, for moving fence	1	15	2
1810, Mar. 7.—Hendrick Hendrickson, posts and rails for parsonage	15			
1812, Jan. 1.—For cleaning the Church	3			
1819, July 6.—Money taken out of the alms-chest, for Jack: 14 lbs. rye flour 3s.; quart of molasses 1s.; 1 lb. butter 2s.; loaf of bread 1s.; load of walnut wood £1, 4s......................	1	11	

STATE OF CHURCHES IN QUEENS COUNTY, 1813.

	Families.	Communicants.	Total.
Success............................	51	61	264
Oysterbay...........................	64	50	315
Newtown...........................	80	67	450
Jamaica	107	56	550

The salary of both pastors was made up by voluntary subscriptions. The Deacons went around to each house and collected in their respective districts. Most of these lists have been lost. We give one as a specimen of the rest.

March, 1816—Half year's salary for Schoonmaker and and Kuypers, jointly:

	£	s.		£	s.
Isaac and Jas. Lefferts.....	1	14	Peter Lott		8
Rem Snedeker....	1	6	George Lott............		6
Johannes Wyckoff.........	1	4	Nicholas Lott...........		4
Widow Mary Bennet......		12	Johannes H. Eldert.......		12
Barnet Bennet	1	4	Hendrick Emmons........		8
Phebe Suydam.............		4	Luke Emmons............		6
Barnet V. Suydam..... ...		14	James L. Rapelye........		4
Hendrick S. Lott...........	1	12	Jacobus Ryder		8
Stephen Lott, Sr...........	1	14	Henry Pullis......		8

	£	s.		£	s.
Wm. Bennett (1809)	1	3	Williamson Ryder		6
Johannes S. Lott (1809)	1	5	Theodorus Snedeker		4
Widow Nelly Lott	1	6	James Cortelyou		10
Garret Van Wicklen		8	Wm. Van Dine		16
Abm. Snedeker		4	Wilhelmus Stoothoof		16
Evert and John V. Wicklen		4	John Remsen		2
Wm. Raymond		4	Peter Williamson (1817)		4
Stephen H. Lott		6	Widow Cornelia Eldert (1809)		8
Paul Duryea		6	Widow Ida Stryker (1809)		8
Abm. Duryea		2	Dow D. Duryea (1809)		4
Abm. Hegeman		8	Rulef Duryea (1809)		12
St. W. Williamson		4	Richolas Ryder		14

1815, May 17.—Bernardus Lamberson, Nicholas Ryder, Hendrick Brinckerhoff and Barnet V. Suydam, account to Jas. Hendrickson and Jas. Van Siclen and find £59, 19s. in the chest.

1818, October 11.—Domine Froeligh preached at Newtown.

Received from the Jamaica Consistory, forty-five pounds, the full sum of a half year's salary, ending November 1, 1804; as witness my hand this second of November, 1804.

JACOB SCHOONMAKER, V. D. M.

Received from the Consistory of Jamaica, the sum of fifteen pounds in full, being my half year's salary.

ZACH. H. KUYPERS.

JAMAICA, April 21, 1818.

1819, August 12.—Thursday was a Fast day on account of the drought.

1821.—An auxiliary to the United Foreign Missionary Society was organized in the Reformed Dutch Church on the evening of January 1. Its object was to civilize and evangelize our western Indians. 150 members were obtained. The officers from the Dutch congregation were: Rev. Jacob Schoonmaker, President; John Bennet, Vice-President; Managers, Abm. and James Hendrickson, Johannes Lott.

1820, May 27.—John Bennet, and Johannes H. Eldert, Aury Remsen Jr. and George Johnson account to John

Bergen, and Wilhelmus Stoothoff, and find $129.62 in the chest.

STATE OF RELIGION AS REPORTED TO CLASSIS.

1827, April 11.—"In two sections of the congregation of Jamaica, there appears a considerable religious excitement, and an earnest seeking of the Lord. Their pastor, Rev. Jacob Schoonmaker, who has labored among them for nearly twenty-six years, feels his heart greatly encouraged and his hands strengthened. For some time back prayer-meetings and lectures in the week have been thronged, and a good number seem deeply affected. The last Sabbath when the Lord's Supper was administered the assembly was unusually large and solemn. Many appeared to be under great exercises of mind; many tears of joy and of Godly sorrow were shed; and there was an addition of ten members, making in the whole twenty-six, who have been admitted to the Church within a year. Not only have new subjects been awakened, but aged professors have experienced a new impulse in the Divine life, have had their strength renewed, and taken an active part in devotional exercises at prayer meetings."

1825, Easter, April 3.—A dreadful storm, deep snow, cold.

1825.—Simeon Marston, on the morning of April 12, fell down his well, accidentally, and instantly expired.

INCORPORATION.

1827, June 9.—The minister Jacob Schoonmaker, Hend'k S. Lott, Jas. Van Siclen, Jas. Hendrickson and John Bergen, elders; Abm. I. Hendrickson, Abm. Hegeman, John A. Ditmars and John I. Bennet, deacons, of the Reformed Dutch Church, of Jamaica, do declare that we have this day assembled in our Church and do hereby certify that we and our successors in office (according to Act of Legislature of April 5, 1813) shall be known by the name of "The First Reformed Dutch Church of Jamaica."—*Queens County Records, W., p.* 165.

PARSONAGE SOLD TO THE PASTOR.

1828, May 16.—For $2,500, Francis Duryea, President, and Abm. Remsen, Clerk, of the Consistory of Newtown;

and Jas. Hendrickson, President, and John A. Ditmars, Clerk of the Consistory of Jamaica conveyed seven acres of land, being the parsonage, to Rev. Jacob Schoonmaker.*—*Queens County Records*, X., p. 162.

1829, October 6.—The Church at Success (having twelve to twenty families) was disbanded by Classis. The members residing at Hinsdale and Foster's Meadows joined the Church at Jamaica.

1829.—General Synod unanimously appointed Thursday, January 22, as a day of Fasting, Humiliation and Prayer, on account of the sin of intemperance; and earnestly advise a total abstinence from the use of ardent spirits, except as a medicine. Ministers are requested, by example and precept, to promote the cause of temperance by the formation of societies, or other measures adapted to that end.

1829, June.—"A goodly number have been received in full communion, and considerable seriousness and seeking of God prevails."

1831, July 15.—Timothy Rhodes and George I. Lott accounted to Theodorus Snedeker and John Simonson, and found in the chest $189.74. 1832, June 16,—They accounted to Luke Covert and John I Bennet, and found in the chest $6.26.

1831, September 25.—Dr. Schoonmaker preached for the last time in the old Church at Newtown, which was taken down October 4, and the new Church dedicated, July 29, 1832.

1832.—Thursday, July 26, was set apart by the Reformed Dutch and Episcopal Churches of Jamaica and Newtown, as a Fast day on account of the cholera in New York.

1832, August 23.—Money and clothing to the amount of $150 was sent to the sufferers by cholera in New York, from the Dutch Reformed and Presbyterian Churches of Jamaica.

---

* Mr. Schoonmaker gave a mortgage for $2,500 to be without interest as long as he was pastor of the two congregations. When the Classis released him from Newtown, in 1850, that Consistory released to him their part of the mortgage. After his death, in 1851, his executors paid $1,250 to the Jamaica Consistory.

Whole yearly expenses of the church: 1829, $28.62; 1830, $44,84; 1831, $41.46; 1832, $38.32; 1835, $75.94; 1837, $75.60.

BIOGRAPHY.

Zacharias Hoffman Kuypers (or Cooper) was born at Rhinebeck, February 19, 1771, and died, unmarried, October 4, 1850. His father, Warmoldus, came from Holland to Curacoa and thence (about 1769) to New York. He had five sons, Elias, Gerardus, Zacharias, William and Peter, all ministers except Peter. Elias became an Episcopalian. Zacharias was probably educated at Hackensack Academy by Peter Wilson. It was intended he should reside in the eastern part of the county, but he preferred Jamaica, and at one time boarded with John Williamson.* He was fond of his pipe and entertained children with witch stories. From 1797 to 1802 he was sole pastor of the four churches. When visiting the distant churches he usually set out from home with horse and sulkey on Friday or Saturday, and returned on Monday or Tuesday. On these occasions he availed himself of the hospitality of the people, and also made pastoral visits. He was of a mild temper, unsuspicious, and lacked energy and worldly wisdom. He bought a farm at Jamaica which involved him in difficulties, and the Sheriff levied on his effects. In the pulpit he gave good sermons—his enemies said they were his father's. They were committed to memory and his mind, absorbed in recalling the words, was not enough at leisure to give emphasis to them, so that his delivery was monotonous and mechanical. To

---

On April 17, 1819, Classis took notice of the low state of religion in Mr. Cooper's congregations at Wolver Hollow and Success. The people complained that the pastor did not catechise and make family and religious visitations, and only preached once a month. On hearing both parties (for one denied what the other affirmed) Classis censured both pastor and people.—*Minutes of Classis, p. 295–30.*

1821, December 27.—At an extra session of Classis at Jamaica, charges were made against Mr. Kuypers; First—That he is not a man of veracity; Second—Not honest in his dealings. The witnesses were Timothy Nostrand, Eliphalet Wickes and John Bergen. After hearing the evidence, Classis vote that the charges are not substantiated, because: First—Not brought forward within the time prescribed by the Constitution; Second—Not established by the mouth of two or three witnesses to the same fact.

Cooper was dismissed from Newtown April 8, 1822; from Jamaica and Oysterbay, April 13, 1824; from Success, April 12, 1825, and went to New Jersey.

prevent distraction of mind he fixed his eyes on some distant object and allowed his arms to hang down by his sides and thus stood almost motionless. In politics he was a Federalist and had he acted in the Revolution would have been a Tory. On one occasion, just before the war of 1812 he brought his politics into the pulpit and uttered his sentiments on public affairs. Once, at Wolver Hollow, in winding up his discourse he exclaimed "our blessed Federal Government." This was too much for the hot-headed Republicans to bear; and one or two rose from their seats and left the Church. He was a great stickler for old usages and was opposed to Hopkinsianism and all innovations. He used to say: "if we begin to reform, where shall we stop?" He spent his last days with a relative in New York.

SUNDAY SCHOOL.

The precise date of starting the Sunday school is not known. John Simonson with Miss Phebe Covert and others were the first teachers. The school was held in the old octagon church.

The minute book begins July 10, 1831, with prayer by Rev. John Mulligan, Principal of Union Hall Academy, with 7 male and 7 female teachers, 28 male and 22 female scholars; and closed with singing.

School was opened with prayer by the following among other persons:

1831, July 17, by Elder Jas. Hendrickson.
 " July 24, by Rev. Mr. Schoonmaker.*
 " July 31, by Rev. Mr. Mulligan.
 " Aug. 7, by Rev. R. C. Shimeall.
 " Aug. 14, by Mr. John Amberman.
 " Aug. 21, by Rev. Mr. Schoonmaker.
 " Aug. 28, by Mr. Richard L. Schoonmaker.
 " Oct. 9, by Mr. Jeremiah Fowler.
 " Dec. 4, Reading by Mr. Cornelius Amberman.

---

* Dec. 25, 1831, the Pastor visited the school and examined the classes; and again on Feb. 19, 1832.

1832, Jan. 15, Prayer by Mr. Isaac Simonson.
1833, Ap. 7, " by Mr. Johannes Lott.
1833, Sep. 21, " by Mr. Elkanah Bartow.

Isaac Simonson seems to have become Superintendent, Dec. 16, 1832, when there were 7 teachers and 27 scholars in attendance, and 10 teachers and 86 scholars absent. Among other books Hellenbroek's Catechism was used. Simonson ended his services, Dec. 29, 1833, with 6 teachers and 15 scholars present. There are no further minutes of the school 'till June 15, 1834, when Henry Onderdonk, Jr. acted as superintendent with 8 teachers and 34 scholars present. The school was held Sunday mornings before service, in the basement of the new church; and the old octagon pulpit was removed and put up there. Aug. 3, 1834.—Dr. Schoonmaker addressed the scholars on the importance of religion and piety, hoped they would refrain from swearing and Sabbath-breaking. Oct. 5, 1834.—Mr. O. left, when there were 12 teachers and 57 scholars present and 6 teachers and 38 scholars absent.

MONEY PAID OUT.

1819, April 11.—Black Tom, for ringing the bell	$ 3 00
1821, Mar. 4.—Wood, $3; Tom, for cutting it up, .62*	3 62
" June 23.—Expense of Classis at Jamaica	6 30
" July 8, Sunday.—Rev. P. H. Duryea, sermon	1 75
" Dec. 12.—Abm. Hendrickson, load of wood	2 50
1822, Jan. 15.—Expense of Classis at Jamaica	12 50
" April 26.—Expenses of Synod and Classis	3 00
" June 15.—Expenses of the parsonage	27 36
" Nov. 17.—Wm. Puntine, 2 elbows for the stove	1 75
" " 30.—Abm. Hendrickson, load of wood and cutting it	3 50
1824, May 10.—John Bennet, singing	8 00
" Oct. 24.—Tom, for sanding the walk	38
" " —Fixing stove-pipe, and a ladder for the church	3 71
1825, May 3.—Tom, for scouring the collection plates	25
" " —A necessary house	20 25
" " —1½ gallons wine	1 50
1826, April 17.—Wm. Smith, sand for the church	05
1827, April, —1½ bushels sand	23
" June 30.—John Bergen, for a record book	2 25

* In the winter of 1820-1, as I suppose, a stove was first set up in the church.

REFORMED DUTCH CHURCH, JAMAICA.

Standing near the site of the first one. Corner stone laid July 4th, 1842; consumed by fire Nov. 19th, 1857.

FIRST REFORMED DUTCH CHURCH.

1827, Nov. —Supplies to Domine Schoonmaker	$ 4	50
" " —Jas. Hendrickson, for a seal	4	50
" " —Paid Mr. Van Hook for his labor	1	00
1829, Contribution to the Missionary Society of R. D. Church	14	22
1830, Contribution to the Missionary Society of R. D. Church	10	00
1834, May 5 and June 8.—Rev. G. J. Garretson, preaching	10	00
" " 12.—Schoonmaker's expenses in exchanging with Garretson	4	00
" Aug. 1.—John Rhodes, for making rings and staples	1	00
" Dec. 10.—Richard Brush, for wood and coal	12	66
1836, Nov. 26.—Broom, 1 lb. candles and sand in the church		58
1837, April 8.—A broom, 1½ bushels of sand		69
1839, Oct. 15.—George Crane, sexton	15	00
" Dec. 9.—Isaac Simonson, making a bier	10	00
" " 15.—Justus Noll, making a pall	2	00
1840, Feb. 6.—Squire Thos. Bradlee, singing	10	00
1841, Jan. 26.—Brush & Phraner, for candles		33
" Mar. 3–28— " " oil and candles	1	43
1842, Feb. 14.—Geo. Crane, for pine wood	4	00
" Feb. 8.—Thos. Bradlee, repairing instrument	1	50
" April —1 lb. candles		15
" Aug. 17.—Rev. J. Schoonmaker, for a church book		75
" Dec. 30.—Geo. Crane, for oil and wicks	1	12½
1843, May 21.—Geo. Crane, sawing cord nut wood	1	00
1846, May 23.—J. A. Herriman, for carpet got in 1841	4	00
1847, May 13.—Elias B. Hendrickson, sexton one year	35	00
" May 5.—Thos. Bradlee, chorister one year	30	00

1832.—NOTICE.—We are requested to mention that the annual Fair of the "Fragment Society" of the R. D. Church, will take place April 9, at one o'clock in the afternoon, and continue in the evening, at the hotel of John Hunter.—*L. I. Farmer.*

NOTICE TO BUILDERS.

1832, Mar. 20.—Sealed proposals for building by contract, the ensuing summer, in the town of Jamaica, a frame church, 82 feet in length and 62 feet in width, will be received by the Trustees of the First Reformed Dutch Church of Jamaica. Plan and specifications of the building may be known by applying to Mr. Crineyonce Sutphin, Jamaica, to whom proposals must be handed, on or before the 1st day of May ensuing.—*L. I. Farmer*, Ap. 5.

CORNER STONE.

1832.—On Wednesday, July 4th, the corner stone of a new Reformed Dutch Church was laid. The ceremony was attended by a very large concourse of people, who were addressed in a very appropriate manner by Dr.

1827, Nov. —Supplies to Domine Schoonmaker	$ 4 50
" " —Jas. Hendrickson, for a seal	4 50
" " —Paid Mr. Van Hook for his labor	1 00
1829, Contribution to the Missionary Society of R. D. Church	14 22
1830, Contribution to the Missionary Society of R. D. Church	10 00
1834, May 5 and June 8.—Rev. G. J. Garretson, preaching	10 00
" " 12.—Schoonmaker's expenses in exchanging with Garretson	4 00
" Aug. 1.—John Rhodes, for making rings and staples	1 00
" Dec. 10.—Richard Brush, for wood and coal	12 66
1836, Nov. 26.—Broom, 1 lb. candles and sand in the church	58
1837, April 8.—A broom, 1½ bushels of sand	69
1839, Oct. 15.—George Crane, sexton	15 00
" Dec. 9.—Isaac Simonson, making a bier	10 00
" " 15.—Justus Noll, making a pall	2 00
1840, Feb. 6.—Squire Thos. Bradlee, singing	10 00
1841, Jan. 26.—Brush & Phraner, for candles	33
" Mar. 3-28— " " oil and candles	1 43
1842, Feb. 14.—Geo. Crane, for pine wood	4 00
" Feb. 8.—Thos. Bradlee, repairing instrument	1 50
" April —1 lb. candles	15
" Aug. 17.—Rev. J. Schoonmaker, for a church book	75
" Dec. 30.—Geo. Crane, for oil and wicks	1 12½
1843, May 21.—Geo. Crane, sawing cord nut wood	1 00
1846, May 23.—J. A. Herriman, for carpet got in 1841	4 00
1847, May 13.—Elias B. Hendrickson, sexton one year	35 00
" May 5.—Thos. Bradlee, chorister one year	30 00

1852.—NOTICE.—We are requested to mention that the annual Fair of the "Fragment Society" of the R. D. Church, will take place April 9, at one o'clock in the afternoon, and continue in the evening, at the hotel of John Hunter.—*L. I. Farmer.*

NOTICE TO BUILDERS.

1832, Mar. 20.—Sealed proposals for building by contract, the ensuing summer, in the town of Jamaica, a frame church, 82 feet in length and 62 feet in width, will be received by the Trustees of the First Reformed Dutch Church of Jamaica. Plan and specifications of the building may be known by applying to Mr. Crineyonce Sutphin, Jamaica, to whom proposals must be handed, on or before the 1st day of May ensuing.— *L. I. Farmer,* Ap. 5.

CORNER STONE.

1832.—On Wednesday, July 4th, the corner stone of a new Reformed Dutch Church was laid. The ceremony was attended by a very large concourse of people, who were addressed in a very appropriate manner by Dr.

J. Janeway, of N. Y., and Dr. Jacob Schoonmaker, the pastor of the church. The ceremony of laying the corner stone was performed by Dr. Janeway, the introductory prayer was offered by the Rev. Eli Baldwin, D. D., and the concluding prayer by the Rev. Dr. Westbrook, both of N. Y. The age of the old church, which has been standing 117 years, and the growth of the congregation, render it necessary to erect a new building. The change will, however, no doubt occasion some regret, inasmuch as it will deprive our village of one of its most venerable and striking features.—*L. I. Farmer.*

CONTENTS OF THE CORNER STONE.

Besides the historical sketch, or memoranda of the church in the hand-writing of Dr. Schoonmaker, there were several numbers of the *Christian Intelligencer*, a copy of the Constitution of the Reformed Dutch Sunday School Union, a portrait of Rev. Dr. Livingston, a copy of the Hellenbroek Catechism, and a copy of the *Long Island Farmer.*

MEMORANDA

Of the First Reformed Dutch Church of Jamaica, (Long Island), made the 4th day of July, A. D., 1832, when the corner stone of the new or second Dutch Church was laid, viz:

The First Reformed Dutch Church, in the town of Jamaica, Long Island, was built in the years 1715 and 1716, and cost about 360 pounds or 900 dollars.

The first Trustees or Church Wardens were John Snedeker, George Remsen, Peter Monfort and Rem Remsen.

The Ministers and the time of their settlement in said Church as Pastors were:

Rev'd John Henry Goetschius in the year 1741.
Rev'd Thomas Romeyn, " " 1752.
Rev'd Hermanus L. Boelen " " 1766.
Rev'd Solomon Freeligh, " " 1775.
Rev'd Rynier Van Nest, " " 1785.
Rev'd Zacharias H. Kuypers, " " 1794.
Rev'd Jacob Schoonmaker, " " 1802.

The first named minister who was the first settled Pastor of this Church, was the grandfather of the last by his mother's side.

The present or second Dutch Church was built in the year of our Lord, 1832.

The Corner Stone was laid on the 4th of July, 1832, by the Rev'd Jacob J. Janeway, D. D., who also delivered an eloquent address on the occasion. The Minister or Pastor is the Rev'd Jacob Schoonmaker, D. D., who also delivered an appropriate address on the occasion. The Elders and Deacons, being the Trustees, at present in office, are James Hendrickson, Nicholas Ryder, Timothy Rhodes and George Johnson, Elders; Luke Covert, John I. Bennet, Abm. Hegeman, Albert Amberman, Deacons.

The Building Committee are Nicholas Wyckoff, Nicholas Williamson, Abm. Bergen, Crineyonce Sutphin, John Van Nostrand, James Van Sielen, Isaac Hendrickson and James Bogart.

The Committee to superintend the building of the Church are James Hendrickson, George Johnson and Crineyonce Sutphin.

The Builders are Charles Fosdick, Jeremiah Fowler, carpenters; and Gasper Phraner, mason; with whom the Trustees have convenanted to build the Church for the sum of 8,130 dollars; the builders to find all the materials and do all the work complete, and the congregation to cart all the materials.

The building is to be completed on or before the 15th day of January, 1833.

Jamaica, July 4th, 1832.

JACOB SCHOONMAKER,
Pastor of the Reformed Dutch Churches of
Jamaica and Newtown, Long Island.
Soli Deo Gloria.

1833, Jan. 7, was a day of Fasting and Prayer, on account of the Act of Nullification passed by the State Convention of South Carolina.

NOTICE OF DEDICATION.

1833.—We understand that the Reformed Dutch Church will be dedicated to the Worship of Almighty God, on Thursday, July 4th. The religious exercises will commence at 10 o'clock A. M. It is expected that the Rev. Dr. Milledoler, President of Rutgers College, and Professor of Theology, will deliver the dedication sermon. As this solemn occasion will occur on the day sacred to American Independence, the friends of religion and of their country in this town and vicinity, are respectfully invited to attend. The community will probably remember that the corner stone of this splendid church was laid on the last 4th of July, amidst a vast concourse of people, who manifested a deep interest in the solemn exercises on that occasion; and now that the top stone is about being laid, we pray with the Psalmist: "Peace be within its walls and prosperity within its palaces."—*L. I. Farmer*, July 3.

The new Reformed Dutch Church was dedicated to the service of the Lord, according to previous notice, on the 4th of July. The spacious house was well filled, and an appropriate discourse was delivered by the Rev. Dr. Baldwin of N. Y., President Milledoler having been prevented from attending in consequence of an injury received a few days previous by falling into an open vault in the middle aisle of the North Dutch Church, N. Y.—*Farmer*, July 10.

1833.—On Sunday, June 2, at 3 o'clock P. M., the Domine preached the last sermon in the old Church, in Dutch, which few understood. Next day they began to take it down.

The materials of the old church were sold in lots, at auction, to the amount of $240. The communion table was bought by Johannes Lott.

At the raising of the church a bountiful collation was served under a large tent by the wives of the congregation. As the timber was heavy the people had to assist the carpenters. The cost of the church was $8,442.

At the dedication a collection of $55 was taken up.

$106 was raised by the ladies of the congregation for dressing the pulpit and carpeting the altar.

Pews were sold (July 20, at 3 P. M.) to the amount of $11,000 which covered the expense of building, and additional land bought.*

The folio pulpit Bible was the gift of Rev'd Wm. Lupton Johnson, Rector of the Episcopal Church, Jamaica.†

The list of pew-holders begins from the pulpit:

Nos. 1–7—$160 to $200.	John D. Ditmis.	John Van Sielen.
Deacons' Pew.	Catalina Eldert.	John Hults.
E. W. Van Voorhis.	John N. Brinckerhoff.	Alex'r Rogers.
Henry Onderdonk, Jr.	Nicholas Amberman.	Henry Van Cott.
John C. Stoothoff.	George I. Lott.	Eldert Eldert.
Margaret Adrain.	Waite S. Everit.	John Bennet, Jr.
	Dow I. Ditmis.	William Golder.
Nos. 8–27—$85 to $12.	Willet Skidmore.	Cor's Johnson Selover.
Hendrick Van Wicklen.	John S. Lott.	Jacob Morrel.

* 1832, May 24.—Nicholas Williamson and wife Cynthia, for $642, sell to the Church a parcel of land east of the old church, containing three roods, 1 and 7-10 of a perch bounded east by Henry Van Cott.—*Queens Co. Records, C. C.*, p. 324.

† David W. Wetmore gave $40 to buy 6 linden trees, which were set out (April 11, 1834,) by Domine Schoonmaker and Elias J. Hendrickson along the front fence of the church. The western one of these and the Norway spruce trees in front of the church were so scorched by the fire of 1857 that they died.

Nathaniel Remsen.

Nos. 46-29—$120 to $20.
Phebe Duryea.
John I. Bennet.
Mrs. John Bergen.
Daniel Hendrickson.
Jacobus Ryder.
Adriana Lott.
James Van Sielen.
John Johnson.
Aury Remsen.
N. Nostrand & S. Mills.
William I. Furman.
John Bennet, Sr.
Isaac Simonson.
Abm. Hendrickson.
Bernardus Bennet.
Nathaniel Nostrand.
Peter Nostrand.
No. 28, free.

Nos. 48-66—$130 to $25.
David Baiseley.
James Bogart.
John G. Fleet.
Abm. Bergen.
James Hendrickson.
Peter & Ann Cortelyou.
Aaron Duryea.
Phebe Brinckerhoff.
Colden Bartow.
James Ditmars.
Johannes Lott.
Henry Mills.
Rem Remsen.
John B. Golder.
Melancton Carpenter.
Peter Bartow.

Hendrick Brinckerhoff.
Joseph Skirm.
Barnardus Bennet.
George Stilwell.
No. 67, free.

Nos. 87-68—$130 to $25.
Minister's pew.
John A. Ditmars.
Timothy Rhodes.
William Seaman.
Nicholas Williamson.
John S. Lott.
Abner Chichester.
Richard Brush.
Wilhelmina Lott.
Rutgers Van Brunt.
William Totten.
John Van Nostrand.
Theodorus Snedeker.
Stephen H. Lott.
Aury Remsen, Jr.
John S. Van Nostrand.
John Amberman.
William Van Sielen.
John Morrel.
Nicholas Ryder.
No. 68, free.

Nos. 88-106—$120 to $20.
Johannes Lott.
Derick Remsen.
Peter Duryea.
Oldfield Bergen.
Hend'k A. Hendrickson.
Abm. Hegeman.
Stephen I. Lott.
Luke S. Bergen.
Derick Van Wicklen.

Abm. D. Remsen.
Benjamin Rhodes.
Crinyonce Sutphin.
William L. Hendrickson.
Mrs. Sarah Van Liew.
Benjamin Hegeman.
Albert A. Amberman.
Michael Golder.
Stephen Mills.
No. 107, free.

Nos. 127-108—$85 to $12.
William Stoothoff.
Luke Covert.
Abm. Amberman.
John R. Snedeker.
Luke Eldert.
Jeromus Snedeker.
John W. Messenger.
Mrs. John Wyckoff.
Nathaniel Nostrand.
John Simonson.
Robert Allen.
Johannes Eldert.
Henry Simonson.
Isaac Snedeker.
Morris Covert.
John Rhodes.
Cornelius Amberman.
Jeffrey Smith.
Tunis D. Covert.
Stephen Henderson.
John Van Sielen.

Nos. 134-128—$100 to $200.
Elders' pew.
Nicholas Wyckoff.
Jacob Schoonmaker.
George Johnson.
Phebe Hendrickson.

1833, Sept. 4.—The Jamaica Bible Society met in the Church at 3 P. M.

1834, July 5.—Abm. Hegeman, Albert A. Amberman, John Bennet and Abm. B. Hendrickson accounted to T. Snedeker and John W. Stoothoff, $67.84 cents in the chest.

1835.—On Tuesday, Jan. 6, the Rev. Garret J. Garretson

was installed, at Newtown as associate pastor with the Rev. Jacob Schoonmaker, D. D., of the united churches of Jamaica and Newtown. Sermon by Rev. M. W. Dwight; the installing service by Rev. Dr. Schoonmaker; the charge to the pastor, by the Rev. Thos. M. Strong; to the people by Rev. Jas. Demarest. Dr. Schoonmaker has been for many years past sole pastor of these united churches, and it is hoped that this connection now formed under highly favorable circumstances will be a source of many blessings. Jan. 10th, he gave his introductory sermon in the Jamaica Church.—*Intelligencer.*

1835, Nov. 4.—The singing school of the Dutch Church is now in successful operation. There is, however, an opportunity for the enlistment of a few more pupils.

1836, Feb. 10.—SACRED MUSIC.—The closing performances of the school of singers, taught by Mr. John Murch, of Newtown, assisted by some members of the Jamaica Sacred Music Society, took place in Rev. Dr. Schoonmaker's church, yesterday afternoon, and evinced a constant improvement going on among us in this delightful science.—*Farmer.*

1836.—July 4th was celebrated in the church. Wessell S. Smith was the reader, and John Mills the orator. Dr. Schoonmaker made the opening prayer, and the exercises were closed by Rev. Mr. Crane, with prayer and benediction. The Choir sang the 712 and 930th hymn of the present Hymnal.

1837, Jan. 8.—Rev. Geo. Bourne preached on "Popery."

1838, May 20.—Rev. Dr. Brownlee preached on "The Papacy."

1838, June 8.—No preaching; the church being cleaned.

1839, Ap. 23.—John Amberman and Melancton Carpenter accounted to Isaac Simonson and Peter Lott, $115.62 in the chest.

SACRED MUSIC SOCIETY.—The regular meeting, the first Tuesday evening in April, the 7th, at 7 o'clock, at the house of Rev. Dr. Schoonmaker. Per order,

N. W. CONKLIN, Secretary.

JAMAICA, March. 23, 1840.

1840, April 11.—George Johnson, an Elder, acknowledges the receipt of $50, being a legacy to the church from Abm. Hendrickson, of Blackstump.

NEWTOWN, Dec. 19, 1840.

The Church at Jamaica to Mrs. C. Baylies Dr., for 4 years' accommodation* for Rev. Mr. Schoonmaker, at $5 per year, commencing Nov. 1836. Received payment. CATHARINE BAYLIES.

PAINTERS! PAINTERS! NOTICE.—Proposals will be received for painting the Reformed Dutch Church, in the village of Jamaica. The inside of the building to have one coat; the roof one coat; and the outside of the building two coats. The paint and oil to be furnished by the Consistory. It is to be divided into three parts: interior,—exterior with roof and steeple,—and blinds. Proposals for the workmanship of any or all of which, must be put in writing, and left with Richard Brush, previous to Saturday, 23d inst., at which time the Consistory will meet to examine and decide with respect to them. The work to be done immediately, and in the best possible manner. Any further information may be obtained by calling on Mr. Brush.

JAMAICA, Oct. 19th, 1841.

1841, Nov. 14 to 28.—Church being painted, inside and out, there was no preaching.

QUADRAGENIAN ANNIVERSARY, 1842.

On Feb. 15, at Jamaica, and 16th, at Newtown, the 40th year of Dr. Schoonmaker's ministry was commemorated in the churches by an historical address from the Rev. G. J. Garretson, which was afterwards printed.†

1842.—STATE OF RELIGION.—"Week-day evening lectures are given by the Pastor, in the basement of the church. Weekly prayer meetings are held in the four districts of the congregation. There are two Sabbath schools connected with the Union of the Dutch Church, and three with the American Union. Many, we fear, neglect the religious duty of the family altar, and the closet."—*Minutes of Consistory.*

---

* The Consistory hired a room for their minister to sit in, rest and converse with them, before going into the church on Sundays. A decanter of liquor and glasses were kept in a closet for their mutual refreshment.

† There were two other publications of Mr. Garretson, "The Christian Citizen," 1842, and a sermon on the death of A. S. Rapelye, 1847.

1842, July 24.—Afternoon, Rev. F. M. Noll preached.*

1842, Dec. 18.—Rev. Henry Heermance, as Tract Agent, preached.

> DONATION.—The widow Elizabeth Hagner has presented to the Reformed Dutch Church a valuable clock, which has been placed upon the interior of that noble edifice, upon which great improvements have recently been made.—*L. I. Farmer*, May 10, 1842.

1842.—The fourth of July was celebrated on temperance principles. The order of exercises in the Reformed Dutch Church was as follows :

Introductory music,—" Praise Ye Jehovah ! "
Prayer, by the Rev. Garret J. Garretson.
Musical prayer for our country.
Reading Declaration of Independence by H. O., Jr.
Hymn,—" Columbia, Tune Thy Voice ! "
Oration, by Wm. Betts, Esq.
Closing Anthem,—" Salvation to Our God."
Prayer and Blessing, by the Rev. James M. Macdonald.

About 200 ladies and gentlemen sat down to a dinner in the upper room of Union Hall Academy, with nought to promote hilarity but nature's beverage—sparkling, cold water. The Rev. Dr. Schoonmaker invoked the blessing ; and thanks were returned by the Rev. W. L. Johnson. The performances of the Sacred Music Society elicited the warmest approbation. The Jamaica Volunteers made an imposing military appearance, and the Flushing Band were much admired for their musical performances.

1843, Feb. 5.—Stormy. Few people out. Dr. Schoonmaker gave a lecture, standing in the altar space.

1843, June 20, Tuesday.—Classis met in church.†

At a meeting of the inhabitants of the village of Jamaica to confer upon the expediency of sending delegates, to repre-

---

* I prepared Mr. Noll for Princeton College. In 1844 he became an Episcopalian, and died on Ashwednesday, 1860, Rector of Caroline Church, Setauket, aged 69.

† The Classis of Long Island was formed from that of New York, June 1, 1813 ; and was divided into the North and South Classis, Jan. 3, 1843. The North Classis was organized in the Jamaica Church, June 20.

sent this town at the National Sabbath Convention, to meet at Baltimore on Nov. 27, 1844, Doct. Nathan Shelton was called to the chair, and James H. Reeve appointed secretary.

The following delegates were appointed to said convention, with power to fill vacancies: Rev. Jacob Schoonmaker, D. D., Rev. Jas. M. Macdonald, Rev. Matthias E. Willing, and Messrs. Walter Nichols, James Rider, John French, James Ditmars, Jr., Laurens Reeve, James H. Reeve, Ab'm Smith, and Gilbert Sayres, Esq.

Resolved, That the Rev. Messrs. Sayres, Macdonald, Schoonmaker, Johnson, and Willing be a committee to remonstrate with the Long Island Railroad Company, in relation to their Sunday train, and respectfully to urge the President and Directors of that Company, to discontinue the running of their cars on the Lord's Day; and to solicit the inhabitants of the neighboring towns to co-operate with them in lending their influence to bring about this desired result.

1844, May 13.—Jacobus Ryder and Nath'l Nostrand accounted to Nicholas Emmons and Abm. Ayres. $1.44 in the chest.

Aletta Brinckerhoff by her will (dated 1842, and proved 1846), gave $150 to the Consistory in trust, to be put at interest, and the interest to be applied for the benefit of the Reformed Dutch Church at Jamaica. She also gave $50 to the church at Manhasset.

1845.—The Reformed Dutch Churches have set apart Friday, Oct. 10, as a time for general fasting. Services in Dr. Schoonmaker's church, at 10½, forenoon.—*L. I. Farmer.*

1846, Aug. 6 and 7.—A missionary convention was held in the church. Rev. Dr. Scudder addressed the youth.

To the Rev. Jacob Schoonmaker, D. D.:

1846, June 16.—In the Board of Trustees of the Presbyterian Church, Jamaica, it was *Resolved*, That this Board, in behalf of the congregation, gratefully acknowledge the kindness of the Pastor and Consistory of the Reformed Dutch Church, in inviting us to occupy their house of worship on a portion of the Lord's Day, during the time we have been engaged in making some alterations in our own place of worship; and whilst we take this method of expressing our sincere thanks to our brethren, we would also improve the opportunity to express the hope that the present happy relations existing between the two congregations may be perpetual.

NICHOLAS S. EVERITT, Sec.   LAURENS REEVE, President.

In the Fall of 1847, Mr. Garretson with Rev. Dr. Gordon travelled six weeks in the Western States, to see what openings there might be for establishing Dutch Churches there. Their report was favorable, but never acted on.

1848, June 4.—Dr. Schoonmaker preached a Dutch sermon in Flatlands' Church, which was to be taken down.

1849, June 18.—Rev. G. J. Garretson gave his reasons for, and offered his resignation to a joint meeting of the Consistories of Jamaica and Newtown, and desired them to unite with him in an application to Classis for a dismissal. The Consistories bore testimony to his constant and unwearied exertions to further the interests of religion among them, and discharge his duties as an ambassador of Christ, and pray God to bless him and his family with all temporal and spiritual blessings.*

PARTING SERVICE.—The farewell discourse delivered at the Reformed Dutch Church by Rev. G. J. Garretson, on Sunday last, June 24, 1849, at the close of his ministry of nearly 18 years, is represented to us to have been deeply affecting to pastor and people. This highly gifted clergyman retires from his pastoral relation here with the best wishes of his flock at Jamaica, and we hope at Newtown also, for the success of his future labors wherever they may be hereafter rendered.—*L. I. Farmer.*

1849, Aug. 4.—PASTORAL CONNECTION DISSOLVED.—"The North Classis met at Newtown, to dissolve the relations of Rev. G. J. Garretson to the Dutch Churches of Newtown and Jamaica. He has left, and settled at Lodi, on a salary of $700 and parsonage. We regret very much the removal of Mr. G., who has been very successful in building

---

* Garret J. Garretson was born near Somerville, N. J., 1808; graduated at Rutger's College, 1829, and at the Theological Seminary, 1832. He served at Stuyvesant 'till 1834, when he was called to the churches of Newtown and Jamaica, as colleague of Dr. Schoonmaker. He was twice married, first to Ellen Van Liew and secondly (1839) to Catharine Rapelye.

Rev. Garret J. Garretson

up the two churches, which form a collegiate charge. Before he settled over them, some 15 years ago, we understand they were both in a sad condition, from the fact that each had the service of one man only, once a fortnight, and that now they are very flourishing. This is no disparagement to Mr. G.'s venerable colleague, whose long continuance in the above charge is *ipso facto* the testimony of all that he can desire here below. But no church with Gabriel even for a preacher could be held together now, with only one service in a fortnight. Formerly religious privileges were circumscribed, now they are abundant. Mr. G. as an acceptable minister has been duly appreciated, and his departure is much regretted. He has left with the affection of all his people clinging to him, and they know it never was misplaced. We hope he may be as useful and more happy in the charge to which he has been called."—*Flushing Journal*.

Monumental inscription in the church-yard, Newtown:

REV. GARRET J. GARRETSON,
PASTOR OF THIS CHURCH
DURING 15 YEARS OF HIS LIFE.
HAVING KEPT THE FAITH
AND FINISHED HIS COURSE,
ENTERED INTO THE JOY OF HIS LORD,
AUG. 16, 1853,
AGED 45 YEARS, 1 MO. 17 DAYS.
FOR HIM TO LIVE WAS CHRIST, TO DIE WAS GAIN.

1849, June 3 to 17.—"Our church being cleaned, we used the Presbyterian Church. After being cleaned it looked nice." M.

1849, July 13.—"The young ladies form a Sewing Society to get an organ, in addition to other improvements. The young men are to get a carpet." M.

1849.—Friday, Aug. 3, (on the recommendation of President Taylor), was observed as a day of fasting, humiliation and prayer, on account of the fearful pestilence, the cholera, in New York. Services, at 10 A. M., were held in the churches, and all the stores closed.

1849, Aug. 20.—"The ladies met to see about getting a new carpet for the church. Mrs. E. W. Van Voorhis, Misses Harriet K. Mills and M. E. Story, with Mr. John N. Brinckerhoff, went to New York and bought it." M.

1849, Sept. 16.—On Sunday morning, five Indians, of two different tribes, attended church, viz: Black Hawk, son of the famous Black Hawk, and two others of the Sac and Fox tribe, and Oceola and sister, of the Callapoohas tribe. They had been at school in Massachusetts, and were now lecturing on "Indian Customs" to raise means for further education.

1849, July 5.—A committee of the two Consistories was appointed to wait on the Rev. Dr. Schoonmaker, and obtain his views on the present state of things, and receive from him a proposition, if he had any to make. Aug. 18.—The Consistory of Newtown agreed to give up their part of the mortgage on the parsonage, $1,250, and pay the Domine half salary for life. Sep. 10.—It was agreed that the churches of Newtown and Jamaica should separate.

1849, Dec. 19, Wed.—The fair of the young ladies was held at Remsen & Hentz's hotel. We have the room for nothing, if we will pay for lighting it. It was open at 10 A. M. Books, needlework and refreshments were on sale. From the net proceeds of this fair ($397.74) an Æolian Seraphine was bought, Dec. 26, for $300, and $70 allowed for the old instrument, net cost $218.50.

RESIGNATION.

1850, April 13.—Though Dr. Schoonmaker had a host of friends, yet, perceiving that some of his people desired a change, he now being in his 73d year, prepared the way for settling a younger minister, by tendering his resignation, on condition that provision be made for his support during life. April 19, the congregation met in the church and agreed to allow him $150 per year during life; but on July 12, it was agreed to give him $750 outright.

1850, July 13.—"We observed the funeral of President Taylor, who died, July 9, by the tolling of bells and shutting up of shops and stores, from 12 to 2, P. M., and displaying of black broadcloth, and flags at half-mast."*

---

* Gov. Fish, by proclamation, recommended the clergy and people of all denominations, on the next day of public worship (July 14), to unite in earnest invocation of the continued blessings of Divine Providence upon our beloved country and its cherished institutions.

1850, July 22.—"Classis met at Newtown and separated Dr. Schoonmaker from the church. In a fortnight the congregation will meet to tax the pews to raise $700 or $800 salary for the new minister, and to appoint a committee of four persons to enquire who will do for candidates." M.

The Classis made this entry in their minutes:

"The Rev. Dr. Schoonmaker, with the concurrence of the Consistory, having applied to this Classis for a dissolution of the Pastoral connection subsisting between himself and the Reformed Dutch Church of Jamaica. It was therefore,

"*Resolved*, That the said application be granted. In doing which this Classis cannot refrain from expressing their high respect for the Reverend Father who for nearly half a century, has borne the Pastoral office with fidelity to his Master, and usefulness to the Church. And while the infirmities of growing age advise his withdrawal from the active duties of the ministry, yet we trust he may long be permitted to see the fruit of his toils, in the spiritual enlargement of that vineyard, where the dew of his youth, the energies of manhood, and the councils of age, have been untiringly bestowed."

1850, Aug. 4, Sunday.—Rev. Dr. Schoonmaker gave his farewell sermon at Jamaica, from Acts xx, 32; and administered the communion, assisted by Rev. Dr. Broadhead.

1850, Aug. 6.—The congregation met in church. Messrs. J. N. Brinckerhoff, Wm. Phraner and H. O., Jr. were appointed a committee to look out for a minister whose salary was to be $1,000 per year. Nov. 18.—Rev. John B. Alliger, on the recommendation of the Committee, was called at $950 per year. He to find his own house till a parsonage be procured, and to preach twice each Lord's Day, and lecture once in the week at some designated place. The call was not to be presented to Classis till the congregation have heard him.

1850, Dec. 2.—The congregation met in church at 4 P. M. and agreed to prosecute the call. 1851, Jan. 11.—It was agreed that the Pastor should preach mornings in the church and afternoons in the outskirts of the congregation, and give a week-day lecture. Apr. 28.—Agreed that a tax of

10 per cent. be laid on private pews and 15 per cent. on those owned by the church.

1850, Sept. 26.—Classis met in church. $14.50 was paid H. Pearsall for their dinners.

The young ladies of the Reformed Dutch Church, Jamaica, respectfully give notice that they will hold their fair in this village, at Military Hall, on Thursday, Dec. 12th (Thanksgiving Day), opening at 12 o'clock M., at which time and place the ladies will be most happy to see all their former patrons and friends. The proceeds of the fair are designed for the improvement of the music of the church.

JAMAICA, Nov. 26, 1850.

The fair was highly successful, and realized nearly $400, clear gain, toward the purchase of an organ. Now then, let them have another fair for chandeliers and lamps, and the thing will be done up completely.— *L. I. Farmer*, Dec. 17.

1850, Dec. 1, Sunday.—"Rev. J. B. Alliger* preached for us in the morning and gave general satisfaction. In the afternoon he preached at Henry Story's and in the evening at Stephen H. Lott's, the former in the eastern part of the congregation, and the latter in the western. On Monday, P. M., the people met in the church and unanimously confirmed the action of the Consistory in calling him. Classis will meet on Friday week, at Jamaica, to approve the call."

1850, Dec. 25.—" Dull Christmas, Mr. Alliger moves here to-day. He stays all night at Mr. J. N. Brinckerhoff's. He has a number of things put in his house,†—butter, tea, sugar, coffee, coal and wood. The young ladies of the Sewing Society (formed July 13, 1849,) met yesterday to see about buying an organ to improve our music."   M.

1851, Wednesday.—New Year's service in the church at 10½ A. M.

1851, Jan. 11.—"Domine Schoonmaker had a large donation party, realizing over $300 in cash. Last Sunday afternoon, Mr. Alliger preached at Springfield."

INSTALLATION.—On Tuesday morning last (Jan. 7, 1851), the Rev. Mr. Alliger was duly installed into his office as Pastor of the Reformed Dutch Church, in presence of a very large and attentive audience, composed not only of the congregation steadily worshipping there, but of

---

* John B. Alliger graduated at Rutgers College, 1835, and at the Theological Seminary, 1840. He served at the Clove 1840-44, and at Shawangunk 1843-50, when he was called to Jamaica. Alliger is a Dutch corruption of the English name Alger.

† Mr. Ainslee's house (now Benardus Hendrickson's) was hired till a new parsonage was built.

many from sister churches, who embraced this very appropriate occasion to testify the interest and kindly feelings they cherished for the prosperity and future usefulness of this ancient church. The order of exercises was as follows:

1. Prayer by the Rev. John W. Ward, of Greenpoint.
2. Anthem, sung by the choir from the 52d Chapter of Isaiah, 7 to 10th verses inclusive:

"How beautiful upon the mountains are the feet of him that bringeth good tidings, that publisheth peace; that bringeth good tidings of good, that publisheth salvation; that saith unto Zion, Thy God reigneth."

3. Prayer by the Rev. Talbot W. Chambers, of New York.
4. Singing of 154th Hymn, 2d book:
   "Let Zion's Watchmen all awake."
5. Sermon by the Rev. Dr. Jacob Broadhead of Brooklyn.
6. Installation of the Pastor by the Rev. Dr. Schoonmaker, late the Pastor.
7. Charge to the Pastor by the Rev. E. S. Porter, of Williamsburgh.
8. Charge to the Congregation by Rev. Thomas C. Strong, of Newtown, President of Classis.
9. Concluding Prayer, by Rev. Mr. Porter.
10. Singing of 153d Hymn of 2d book:
    "Come as a *Shepherd*; guard and keep,"—
11. Apostolic Benediction by the Pastor, the Rev John B. Alliger.— L. I. *Farmer*.

1851. Apr. 30.—"They are fixing the gallery in the church for the organ. It is to be up next Sunday, (May 4,) and a gentleman from the city is to be up to play on it." M.

May 1, 1851, Henry Erben sold the church a second hand organ of 20 stops, two sets of keys and pedals, for $1,200; and allowed $350 for the melodeon.

1851, March 27.—George Crane, formerly sexton of the church, died suddenly, of congestion of the brain, at the Head-of-the-Fly,* Flushing, aged 53.

1851, Aug. 25.—John A. King asked the use of the church for the Queens County Agricultural Society's address. On Oct. 2, at 12 o'clock, the church was completely filled, there being present not less than 1,500 persons, including every leading and influential man in the county, and many ladies. A voluntary on the organ, by Miss M. E. Brinckerhoff,

---

* Fly is the Dutch word for meadow or marsh.

opened the proceedings, followed by a prayer and thanksgiving from Rev. Dr. Goldsmith, to the Sovereign of the universe, whose gracious providence fertilizes the earth. An anthem and ode were sung by Thos. Bradlee and the choir. At the close of the address by Gen. John A. Dix, the thanks of the Society were tendered to the choir, and to the Consistory for the use of the church.—*N. Y. Times*.

The ladies of the Sewing Society had a fair and festival, in Union Hall Academy, on the same day with the Agricultural Fair, to raise money to pay for the new organ. $603 was taken in, being a net profit of $383.

1851, Oct. 27.—A collection is to be taken up in church in aid of the Sunday School. $76.50 was paid for $8,000 insurance on the church and $1,000 on the organ.

1851, Nov. 27.—Thanksgiving service in the church.

  1852, Jan. 18.—"Rode to church in a sleigh, 25 persons (including three girls) present. In the evening a drifting snow, and the thermometer at 10°. Though the bells rang there was no service in the other churches." M.

  1852, Jan. 30.—"They now have Tuesday evening prayer meetings at private houses; and if they come well attended the Thursday evening lectures will be given up." M.

  1852, March 4.—"At the Domine's donation party, Thursday, Messrs. Lowerre and Van Voorhis, each gave a $20 gold piece, and Mr. Cor's Amberman, three old silver dollars. He also received a pair of gold glasses from Mrs. J. N. B., some silver forks and $230 in money, and other articles." M.

1852, Apr. 11.—Collection in church to pay off incidental expenses.

1852, July 4, Sunday morning.—Rev. P. D. Williamson gave his farewell sermon, before leaving for California.

1852, Nov. 29.—"The Consistory intend to extend out the gallery four feet so as to allow the singers to stand before the organ. The front will go outside the stovepipe.*" M.

---

  * There were 3 stoves in church, two at the entrance doors and one by the pulpit. The drippings from the pipe soiled the carpet in the middle aisle.

1852, Nov. 25.—Thanksgiving Day, the Jamaica Branch Bible Society held its 36th anniversary in the church.

1852.—Died at his residence on Sat. Apr. 10, after a short illness, Rev. Jacob Schoonmaker, D. D., in the 75th year of his age. The friends of the family, and the public generally, are respectfully invited to attend his funeral at his late residence, Tuesday afternoon, at one o'clock, and at the Reformed Dutch Church, at half-past one.

The funeral of the Rev. Dr. Schoonmaker, on the 13th inst., was very numerously attended, notwithstanding the unfavorable state of the weather. After a brief prayer at the house of the deceased, by the Rev. Dr. Strong, of Flatbush, the procession commenced moving to the church about two o'clock, in the following order:

Officiating Clergy.
Attending Physicians.
BIER,
With the Rev. Drs. Goldsmith, Strong and Campbell, Messrs. Sayres, Elmendorf, P. N. Strong, Williamson and Mandeville,
as Pall Bearers.
Family and Relatives of the Deceased.
The Consistory of the Churches of Jamaica and Newtown.
The Rev'd the Clergy.
The Trustees and Principal of Union Hall Academy.
Citizens generally.

The church (pulpit and organ) was hung in black in respect to the memory of the late pastor, and as the procession entered, a dirge was appropriately played on the organ. The multitude, who had assembled to testify their affection and pay the last tribute of respect to the memory of the departed, was so great as to fill the church to its utmost capacity. A great number could obtain no seats.

The exercises at the Church were then commenced with reading part of the 11th Chapter of Hebrews, by the Rev. Mr. Alliger, the Pastor.

Prayer by the Rev. Thomas C. Strong, of Newtown.

Singing by the choir, "How blest the Righteous, when he dies."

Obituary sketch of the life and services of the deceased, by the Rev. Mr. Alliger.

An impressive discourse, by the Rev. Dr. Marselus, from Hebrews, xi. 13: "These all died in faith, etc."

Concluding prayer by the Rev. Professor Campbell of the Theological Seminary.

Hymn by the choir: "Unveil thy bosom, faithful tomb."

The audience were then invited to take a last look at the deceased, whose countenance was truly calm and placid in death. He was laid out in bands and gown. And so great was the throng at the coffin (which was placed immediately in front of the pulpit) that over an hour was consumed in this mournful ceremony. Although the day was showery yet it fortunately abated, both at the time of the moving of the procession to the church and to the village cemetery, where the remains were deposited in the family vault. After which solemnity the spectators were dismissed with the Divine Benediction by the Rev. Mr. Elmendorf, of Bedford.—*L. I. Farmer*, Apr. 27, 1852.

At a meeting of the Rector, Wardens and Vestry of Grace Church, Jamaica, held at the church, on the 13th day of April, 1852, it was unanimously

Resolved, That this Vestry has heard with grief and deep regret the painful intelligence of the death of Rev. Jacob Schoonmaker, D. D., for half a century the clergyman of the Reformed Dutch Church, in this village, whose life and services have been a practical example of the great and salutary influences of the virtues, piety and charity, which should ever adorn the character of a Minister of the Church of Christ. And that we deeply and truly sympathize with his afflicted family in this their great bereavement. And that a copy of this resolution be transmitted to them by the Clerk of the Vestry.

Testimonials of respect and condolence were also sent to the family from the trustees of Union Hall Academy.

Jacob Schoonmaker was born at Aquackanonck, N. J., May 11, 1777. He was prepared for Columbia College at the Hackensack Academy. He graduated Aug. 7, 1799, when he delivered an oration in St. Paul's Church, on "Imprisonment for Debt." He studied for the ministry under Froeligh. He died of typhoid pneumonia brought on by a cold caught at a funeral. On the day before his death the Rev. Wm. L. Johnson, D. D., called to see him, and kneeling at the bedside made an appropriate prayer, which the old Domine repeated after him word by word. He then gradually became less sensible to external objects. Among his last broken sentences were: "I have fought the good fight, I have finished my course." His breathing soon grew fainter and fainter, till he expired without a struggle or a groan.

In the course of his ministry he had married 700 couples.

1813, Apr. 23, he wrote a recommendation for a new edition of the Hellenbroek Catechism which he himself used in his classes on Saturday afternoons in the old church.

1815, Aug. 1, at the formation of the Long Island Bible Society, he was one of a committee to solicit subscriptions.

1817, May 20, he was president of the newly established Female Academy, under the care of Mrs. E. Bartlette and Miss Laura Barnum.

1820, July 12, as president he made the prayer at the laying of the corner-stone of the new Union Hall Academy.

1824, June 3, he was vice-president of the Jamaica Auxiliary Society for Meliorating the condition of the Jews.

1829, June 3, as president of General Synod he preached a sermon in the North Church, N. Y., from Romans, i: 16.

1831.—He received the degree of S. T. D., from Dickinson College.

He wore bands (*befjes*) from the first. After a while the ladies gave him a gown. Before ascending the pulpit he paused at the foot of the stairs, covered his face with his hat and made a short silent prayer.

His salary was small.* He eked it out by taking boarders for the Academy. His people were also considerate. His wood was carted and he had many presents—a bag of wheat, a ham, a pot of butter, a load of hay, &c. During his visits, especially in killing-time, many a piece of meat was quietly put in his carriage. He and his wife had a happy knack at making their wants known.

He bought land of Mrs. Stewart and became a thrifty farmer. At his death his personal property was appraised at $6,630.12, and his farm of over sixteen acres, subject to a mortgage of $1,000, was sold, in 1852, to Dr. M. J. Bailey, for $8,000.

In politics he was anti-federal. He made no pretensions to much learning, but by his courteous manners and modest bearing, he passed off well in the best society. He wrote two pieces for the Dutch Church Magazine.

He made the formal visitations, and held the service (anciently called sermon of repentance), preparatory to the

---

* At a meeting of the two Consistories at Newtown, 1816, Apr. 8, it was agreed to make an addition to his salary.

Communion, on Fridays, which was changed to Saturdays, in Mr. Alliger's time.

The expenses of Dr. Schoonmaker's funeral were assumed and paid by his friends, as follows:

Theodorus Snedeker	$5 00	Nath'l Nostrand	$ 33
Stephen N. Lott	3 00	Remsen Bennett	50
Dow S. Lott	2 00	John S. Snedeker	2 00
Peter Lott	1 00	Mary Snedeker	1 00
John S. Lott	1 00	John B. Golder	1 00
Wm. Stoothoff	1 00	Wm. H. Furman	1 00
Abm. Hegeman	1 00	Henry Story	5 00
Henry Drew	1 00	Nicholas Williamson	3 00
Ditmars Stoothoff	1 00	John Spader	5 00
Geo. Rhodes	5 00	John N. Brinckerhoff	2 00
John V. Nostrand	3 00	Henry Mills	1 00
John S. V. Nostrand	3 00	Phebe Covert	1 00
John R. Bennett	1 00	Margaret Adrain	2 00
Jacob M. Duryea	2 00	Elias Hendrickson	1 00
Jas. Lott	50	Isaac Amberman	1 00
Martin R. V. Sielen	50	Richard Brush	16 75
Stephen H. Lott	1 00	Wm. Phraner	16 75
Henry S. Lott	1 00	James S. Remsen	5 00
Garret V. Wicklen	1 00		

Inscription on a mural tablet in the church at Newtown:

"Mark the perfect man, and behold the upright; for the end of that man is peace."

Ps. 37: 37.

IN MEMORY OF

JACOB SCHOONMAKER, D. D.,

WHO FOR THE UNUSUAL PERIOD OF 48 YEARS
FAITHFULLY LABORED
IN THE PASTORATE OF THIS CHURCH.
BY HIS CONSISTENT PIETY, HIS WISDOM IN COUNCIL
AND HIS DEVOTION AS A FRIEND,
HE WON THE HIGH ESTEEM
AND UNSHAKEN CONFIDENCE OF BOTH THE
CHURCH AND THE WORLD.
BORN, MAY 11, 1777.
DIED, APRIL 10, 1852.

It is said Domine Schoonmaker was the first to introduce funeral services in the congregation, in compliance with the recommendation of Synod in 1812, that there be a sermon and Scripture lessons read, or, at least, a prayer and benediction at the grave. In early times Synod disapproved of religious ceremonies at burials as superstitious. At funerals the people either quietly took seats in the house, or stood conversing in groups outside. Wine was passed in-doors and a bottle of spirits out of doors. There being no minister or sexton, a certain responsibility and gravity rested on the company. A neighbor brought up his clean farm wagon, with straw on the bottom. The pine, cherry or black-walnut coffin was solemnly lifted by friends into the wagon and, covered with a blanket or bed-coverlet, was slowly driven to the grave where it was let down and the earth shovelled in by the friends. A plentiful repast was usually provided for friends who came from a distance.*

1852, May 3.—"Our church has been cleaned for summer, and the mourning removed. The subscription for the parsonage goes on very briskly. Rev. N. E. Smith preached for us, Sunday afternoon."
M.

1852, May 21.—"The Dutch people seem very busy talking about a parsonage. They have spoken of a number of places, but they don't seem to suit. Tunis Van Brunt has offered a lot by his house; some think of the land next the church commencing with Mr. Hendry's shop and ending with Snell's store. Some like O. P. Leech's house, at $5,500; some, Wm. J. Cogswell's, $6,000; some, Judge Henry Hagner's, $5,000; some, a lot opposite the old parsonage, $1,000; some, Dr. N. Shelton's; some, six lots on Union Hall street, east of the Academy, at $1,200. Nov. 29.—The Consistory met but could not fix on a site for the present."
M.

1852, July 20.—Wm. Phraner was appointed treasurer.

1852, Nov. 8.—Ferdinand S. Snedeker appointed sexton at $32.50 per year.

---

* The items of expenditure for Dr. Schoonmaker's funeral were:

45 yds. linen	$22 50	Shroud	3 50
8 yds. ribbon	72	Making 14 scarfs	1 63
20 yds. black ribbon	1 80	Tolling bell of three churches	3 00
8 black Italian cravats	7 25	Opening vault, &c	1 00
3 pair silk gloves	1 56	Carriage hire	8 50
Use of alapaca and linen	2 00	Other expenses	4 05
Mahogany coffin	28 00		
Silver plate	8 00	Total	$101 59
Over-coffin	5 00		

1853, May 7.—John C. Metcalf appointed chorister at $50 per year.

1853, May 25.—John A. King and wife Mary, for $2,330, sold the church, land for the present parsonage, 102 feet front and nearly 497 feet deep, containing one and 165-1000 acres.—*Queens County Records*, 109: 9.

Here follows a list of contributors:

Ri. Brush	$100 00	Isaac Amberman	5 00
Wm. Phraner	100 00	Hend'k Hendrickson	3 00
Dan. Hendrickson	100 00	Jas. A. Fleury	25 00
Theod's. Snedeker	100 00	From Schoonmaker's Mortgage	1,000 00
Isaac Simonson	10 00		
John Rhodes	25 00	Jno. Spader	100 00
Benj. Hegeman	40 00	Henry Story	100 00
Ann. Bergen	20 00	Tunis V. Brunt	100 00
Jno. N. Brinckerhoff	5 00	Jno. V. Nostrand	20 00
St. Henderson	3 00	Hend'k Suydam	50 00
Jas. A. Herriman	15 00	David Bergen	5 00
Geo. Rhodes	100 00	Daniel S. Waters	3 00
Sam. W. Lowerre	100 00	Margaret Powell	6 00
Jno. A. King	100 00	Abm. Brinckerhoff	3 00
David Baiseley	50 00	Jas. S. Remsen	20 00
Geo. C. McKee	5 00		
Ann E. V. Noyse	15 00		$2,333 00
Jno. T. Waters	5 00		

1853, Nov. 23.—"They are now collecting money for the new parsonage house which is just raised. $800 to be paid when raised; $800 when enclosed; $800 when walled; and final payment when the house is finished. It is a two-story double house, with two-story kitchen. It will cost about $6,500. It is a large but not showy house. Mr. John Spader is going around for the subscriptions, but some hold out and don't pay."* M.

1853, Nov. 17.—"Mr. Metcalf is not coming up this winter to sing. Abm. Duryea is to lead the singing hereafter." M.

1853, Nov. 24.—Thanksgiving service in church.
1854, Jan. 7.—A Sewing Society was formed.

---

* Paid by outsiders, towards the parsonage: Cornelius Duryea, $25; Abm. D. Snedeker, $5; Albert Priest, $20; Christian G. Gunther, $20.

PARSONAGE OF THE FIRST REFORMED DUTCH CHURCH,

On Fulton street, Jamaica. Erected 1853.

1854, Jan. 29.—A Youth's Missionary Society of the Reformed Dutch Church was formed, and a Constitution printed. The members were to meet the second Sabbath of each month, and pay not less than 12 cents yearly.

1854, Feb. 14.—The congregation present a silver pitcher and salver to Miss Mary E. Brinckerhoff, in recognition of her gratuitous services as organist.

<blockquote>1854, Feb. 14.—Donation party. "The Domine had a good turnout, considering the weather. House comfortably filled $200 received."
M.</blockquote>

1854, Feb. 22.—Washington's birthday. The first notable marriage in the church was that of Wm. F. Story and Mary E. Brinckerhoff. Pedro A. Andreu played on the organ. Messrs. C. Baylis and Randall were groomsmen and Misses Lib. Willets and Julia Ludlow, bridesmaids, who all proceeded directly to the railing, in front of the pulpit, where stood the celebrant, Rev. E. P. Stimpson with Rev. Mr. Alliger beside him. After the ceremony the party returned to their coaches at the west side of the church, a carpet being laid from the door to the carriages.

1854, Apr. 1, Sunday.—Rev. Dr. Baird, Secretary of the Evangelical Union, preached morning and afternoon.

<blockquote>1854, Apr. 16.—"A tedious, dull Sunday, no church at night, and but few out in the morning."
M.</blockquote>

1854, Apr. 19.—Classis met in church, discussed and negatived the change of name of the church by omission of the word "Dutch."

1854.—Friday, May 26, was a Fastday to supplicate Almighty God to avert the evils that now threaten this nation by reason of a Bill in Congress allowing slavery in the Nebraska Territory.*

1854, July 31.—The pastor's salary, from July 1, is to be $1,000 with the parsonage.

---

* The Kansas-Nebraska Bill (repealing the Missouri compromise) was passed, May 31.

1854, Sept. 28.—At the Queens County Fair, C. Lyon gave the address in the church. Voluntary on the organ by Jos. T. Duryea, invocation by Rev. P. D. Oakey, singing by the choir. The audience were dismissed with the benediction.—*L. I. Farmer.*

1854, Oct. 22, Sunday.—Mr. Alliger gave a sermon on the "Arctic,*" and the previous Providences of God in our Congregation," to a very full church. He was (by direction) to preach on the increase of ministers' salaries.

1854, Nov. 30.—Thanksgiving day. A very full church. Union meeting of Methodists, Presbyterians and Dutch. Mr. Seaman made the long prayer, Mr. Oakey preached on the duty of American citizens, and Mr. Huntting made the last prayer.

1854, Nov. 14.—$5 reward will be paid to any person giving information that will lead to the conviction of the person that broke the glass of the circular window in rear of the Reformed Dutch Church.

By order of Consistory,

WM. PHRANER.

1854.—The taxes on the parsonage, assessed at $3,500, were $24.44, viz : 30 cts. on $100, for town, &c.; 27½ cts. for school, and 9 cts. for the village.

1855, Jan. 16.—"Robert Adrain will go 'round the village to try to get money to buy a parlor carpet for the parsonage." M.

1855, Feb. 2.—"The Domine had a party last night; a great crowd; Mr. King and daughter there. Some of all denominations there. Laureus Reeve, Gilbert Sayres, Dr. Kissam and wife, and son George, Judge Fosdick, Jos. T. Duryea, &c." M.

1855, Mar. 28.—The funeral of the County Clerk, Martin I. Johnson, at 2 P. M., was the largest assemblage of persons ever gathered together in this village, on a similar occasion. The church seats 750 persons, and judging from the number standing, the audience could not have been less than 1,000. As a mark of respect to the deceased, all places of business were closed, from 1 o'clock till after the burial. The family and relations of the deceased, accompanied by the clergy and pre-

---

* The Arctic collided (Sep. 27.) with the Vesta, in a fog, on the banks of Newfoundland, and went to the bottom.

ceded by the Firemen, went in procession to the church. The services were conducted and an address delivered by the Rev. Mr. Alliger, assisted by the Rev. Dr. Johnson, of the Episcopal, and Rev. Mr. Seaman, of the Methodist Church.—*L. I. Farmer.*

1855, Apr. 9.—The Pastor is to have an eye on Brushville. A Sabbath School should be started there to secure so important a neighborhood for a Reformed Dutch Church.

1855, June 29, Friday.—All the Sunday Schools of the Dutch Reformed and Presbyterian Churches had their excursion to St. Ronan's Well, together. The line of about 65 vehicles filled, some with 30 persons each, presented a fine spectacle. At the grove, after a sumptuous entertainment, the children were pleasantly addressed by Messrs. Pardee and Bissell. At 4½ P. M. the party of about 1,000 persons left the grounds.—*L. I. Farmer.*

1855, July 10.—A subscription paper to give the pastor $200, additional salary, was circulated.

1855.—The use of the church for celebrating the Fourth of July was refused.

1855.—On Sunday, Sept. 30, there was no service in church. A fire broke out at 9.30, A. M., in the barn of Jas. R. Hendry, which, with his blacksmith shop, was consumed. Loss, $2,000, and no insurance.

1855, Nov. 8.—The Long Island Bible Society met in the church, at 2 P. M. The members of the choirs of the different churches led by Abm. Duryea, conducted the music.—*L. I. Farmer.*

1855, Nov. 18.—Collection for lamps, $41.55. M.

1855, Dec. 31.—"The lamps are up in the church and look very fine indeed. They were repaired at a cost of $40." M.

1856, April 1.—Paid for chandeliers, $60, and hanging them $26.75. Collection for chandeliers, &c., $126.77.

1856, July 4.—The teachers and children of the Sunday School of the First Reformed Dutch Church, held a fair and festival in the afternoon and evening, which was the great attraction of the day. The room (lately occupied by F. G. Crossman, opposite John A. King's,) was crowded until 10 o'clock at night. The receipts were quite equal to the expectation of the managers, and we are requested to thank the liberal of their own congregation and those of the other congregations who contributed so cheerfully, of refreshments and money, to assist a good cause and encourage the children, who were more immediately interested in the Fair.— *L. I. Farmer.*

1856, July 19.—Old silver taken from old alms chest was sold for 37 cents.

1856, Aug. 21, Thursday.—The annual excursion of the Reformed Dutch and Presbyterian Sunday Schools was to St. Ronan's Well. Sixty-four wagons were stowed with old and young. In the grove, at half-past ten, the tables were set with towers of biscuits, ham, sandwiches, pies and cakes. After the repast the company dispersed, some to drink the water of the well, others to promenade on the hillside, or bridges, some to read under the shady trees, others to gather into little companies and talk on all sorts of subjects. At half-past one, on the signal for reassembling, the great hall was full, 700 awaited the exercises, songs, addresses, &c., till 4 o'clock, when they were on their way to Jamaica.

1856, Oct. 15, Wednesday evening.—The anniversary of the Jamaica Bible Society was held in the church. Rev. T. L. Cuyler and others addressed the meeting.—*L. I. Farmer.*

1856, Dec. 31.—The Reformed Dutch Church will be open for worship, on New Year's eve, at 6½ o'clock.

1857, Apr. 2.—Most of the pew-holders request Consistory to have the church painted and fences repaired, and assess cost on the pews.

1857, May 28, Thursday.—Jos. T. Duryea delivered a lecture, in the church, on "The Philosophy and Claims of Sacred Music."

1857, June 24.—"They are now painting the church steeple. The two south windows, beside the pulpit, were walled up." "Nov. 5.—they are putting a furnace in the basement of the church, and the old stoves are to be sold." M.

1857.—The Congregation of the Reformed Dutch Church will, by invitation, occupy the Presbyterian Church for Divine worship on the morn-

ing of the first and third Sabbaths of July, and thereafter alternate Sabbaths, till the repairing and painting of their church be completed.—
L. I. Farmer.

1857.—On Sunday last, Aug. 30, the Reformed Dutch Church, of Jamaica, was opened for Divine worship after being closed several weeks for repairs, and it is a model of what a church should be; and reflects great credit on those who had the management of the renovation. It is handsomely painted within and without, the fences renewed, and the path and walks graded. Among the interior changes may be mentioned the introduction of gas with most beautiful fixtures, the graining of the pews, pulpit and organ, the painting of the walls and ceiling by a new and very effective process, in which the art of perspective has been successfully applied. The closed pulpit has been replaced by an open platform, and as appendages to it on either side are tablets painted on the wall containing in gilt letters, the Lord's Prayer, the Apostles' Creed, and the Ten Commandments.* The circumstances under which the congregation assembled suggested the following text: "The glory of Lebanon shall come unto thee, the fir tree, the pine tree, and the box together, to beautify the place of my sanctuary; and I will make the place of my feet glorious," which was happily illustrated by the pastor to a numerous audience.—L. I. Farmer.

1857, Oct. 4.—Services changed from afternoon to evening.
1857, Oct. 7.—Classis met in church. Dr. Porter preached at 10½ A. M. Religious services in the evening. The public were invited to attend. Addresses by members of Classis.

THE FIRE.

On last Thursday night, Nov. 19, about 7 o'clock, an alarm of fire was given, and it was soon ascertained that the carriage manufactory of Mr. J. R. Hendry, standing west of the Reformed Dutch Church, was in flames. The wind blew a gale from the south-west, carrying the sparks and cinders across Gov. King's lots, lying just opposite, and causing some apprehension lest the Episcopal Church might be endangered. Just before the coach factory fell, and while the fire was at its height, the wind suddenly veered to the west and carried the burning cinders in showers upon the roof of the Dutch Church. In less than thirty minutes the large and beautiful building was consumed. Two of our citizens deserve an honorable mention in connection with the efforts made to rescue the church, Messrs. Edward Hendrickson, and Foster Van Wicklen. At the risk of their own lives they ran from place to place upon

---
* The cost of these was $100. Within a modest shield, underneath, was inscribed: "Presented by His Excellency, John A. King, LL. D., Governor of the State, 1857."

the roof, succeeded several times in putting out the fire spreading underneath the shingles, dried and warped, and therefore exceedingly combustible. The efforts of the engine companies were at first crippled for want of water, and when, afterwards, water was obtained the hose was maliciously cut in several places by parties upon whose character and conduct we dare not allow ourselves to comment. The supply of water from the line formed through the building was inadequate, and at last could not be applied at the point of danger, as the cornice in front, which finally took fire was entirely out of reach. Almost all the movable articles were removed from the building without suffering damage. The fire extended west to the corner of Church street—burning "Rotten Row," and the dwelling and grocery of Mr. Hendry.

The buildings, (5 in number) which stood between Mr. Hendry's shop and dwelling, belonged to John McGrath. They were insured for their worth, $2,000. Mr. Hendry was insured on both buildings, about $2,000, two-thirds of their value. Mr. Hendry saved most of his furniture, but in a damaged state. The Reformed Dutch Church was insured for $6,000, about one-half its value. The organ was insured for $1,000, it was valued at $1,500. It was consumed with the building. In all, at different times, there were 20 buildings on fire, and had it not been for a dash of rain about the time the church was burning, the extent of the disaster would have been beyond calculation. Two of the Flushing fire companies came to the assistance of their brethren of Jamaica, and have the gratitude and good wishes of the whole community.

The prevailing impression is that the fire was the work of an incendiary.*

The loss of the church has been indeed a sore trial, under circumstances peculiarly disheartening. The building had just been repaired and painted. The walls were most tastefully frescoed, the pulpit had been improved in design and convenience, a chaste and exceedingly beautiful design in recess behind the pulpit gave completeness and finish to the decoration of the interior. The organ, a noble instrument, had just been grained anew and put in perfect order. A furnace had been placed in the basement, and on the very day of the calamity Messrs. Brush and Phraner had finished the last piece of work necessary to the full completion of the improvement on the building. Over $3,000 had been expended, and many weeks of individual labor. In a half-hour all this was destroyed.—*L. I. Farmer*, Nov. 24, 1857.

1857, Nov. 22, Sunday.—"This afternoon Mr. Alliger met with his people in the Presbyterian Church, for the first time since the fire, and

---

* At a public meeting, held on Saturday evening, Nov. 21, the trustees of the village were authorized to offer $200 reward, for the detection of the incendiary, and $200 for the discovery of the demon in human shape, who secretly and maliciously cut the hose of both engines, when the firemen had almost arrested the flames, a crime more startling and fiendlike, if possible, than that of the incendiary.

it was a solemn time. All felt and some said: 'Our holy and our beautiful house, where our fathers praised Thee, is burned up with fire; and all our pleasant things are laid waste.' The Domine was assisted by Rev. Baynard R. Hall, who read the 64th Chap. of Isaiah, and preached from Hebrews 12: 6, 7, 8: 'For whom the Lord loveth he chasteneth,' &c. He said whether the fire came by accident, or the torch of an incendiary, it did not alter its being a chastisement from the Almighty. Next Saturday afternoon a prayer meeting of the whole congregation is appointed to be held in the Methodist church; and on the following Monday a meeting will be held of the Congregation, in the Academy, to consult upon some measures for rebuilding." M.

At a special meeting of the Vestry of Grace Church, Jamaica, Nov. 23, 1857, the following preamble and resolutions were unanimously adopted:

WHEREAS, the congregation of the Reformed Dutch Church in this village has been deprived of the use of their house of worship by a disastrous conflagration;

Resolved, That we deeply sympathize with them in this severe dispensation of an over-ruling Providence.

Resolved, That the use of this church be tendered to that congregation, to be occupied on Sunday afternoons, at such hours as may be most convenient to them.

Resolved, That seats be provided for members of that congregation who may wish to attend our regular services.

JEREMIAH VALENTINE, Clerk.

1857, Nov. 27.—At a special meeting of the Consistory, at the parsonage, it was resolved that the male members of the congregation be invited to meet with the trustees, on Monday, Dec. 7, at 2 P. M., in the lecture room of Union Hall Academy, for the purpose of advising and assisting the trustees to adopt such measures as may be deemed necessary to rebuild their church edifice.

1857, Nov. 27.—The congregation are to meet, Sundays, at 2 P. M., in the Presbyterian Church. Dec. 5, Saturday.—The congregation (and professors of religion especially) are to meet in the Methodist Church, for prayer to the Great Head of the Church, that he would guide, comfort and bless his people.

1857, Dec. 28.—At a meeting of Consistory, it was resolved that their most grateful thanks are due to the trustees of the

Presbyterian Church, to the Vestry of Grace Church, and to the Wardens of the Methodist Episcopal Church, for their fraternal and christian courtesy and kindness in tendering the use of their churches to the congregation of the Reformed Dutch Church of Jamaica, who in the Providence of God have been deprived of their place of worship by fire.

1858, Jan.—Summary of the indebtedness of the church, presented to the meeting in the Academy:

Cost of parsonage lot	$2,330 00	
" House and fence	4,923 37	
		$7,253 37
Paid on account of parsonage:		
Subscriptions	$3,957 75	
Schoonmaker's mortgage	1,250 00	
		$5,207 75
Total debt on account of parsonage		$2,045 62

Debts of the congregation:	
On general account	$ 485 64
Painting the church	1,537 94
Parsonage debt	2,045 62
Total debt	$4,069 20

Unpaid pew rents, for salary	$638 70
" Assessments for painting	313 75
Making fence for railroad and Hendry	54 28
	$1,006 73

1858, Jan. 4, Monday.—"They decided by a vote of 28 to 24 to build the church on the old site." Feb. 12.—"I fear that the church will be built on the old site, as about $300 more is subscribed in favor of that site." "I feel that all hopes of getting the church in a more central place, is about lost." M.

1858, Jan. 14—Paid Howard Pearsall, for dinner to Classis, $20.

1858, Jan. 15.—The vote on salary of the pastor, as per resolution of July 31, 1854, raising it from $800 to $1,000, was rescinded.

1858, Feb. 1.—A motion of Theodorus Snedeker, seconded by Daniel Hendrickson, to build the church on the old site was lost. Agreed that subscription papers for either site be circulated. Daniel Hendrickson is to ask legal advice ; and reports (Feb. 15,) that the old site may be sold if no remonstrance be made.* The subscription papers came in with a large amount for the old site. Feb. 22.—The Consistory conclude to build on the old site.†

1858.—At a meeting of the Consistory of the Reformed Dutch Church Jamaica, held on Monday, Feb. 22, a resolution was passed to build a lecture room in Union avenue, 30 by 60 feet. The lecture room is to be built immediately for the congregation to worship in until a new church is erected. Messrs. Richard Brush, John T. Waters, Isaac Amberman, J. N. Brinckerhoff, and S. L. Spader are the Committee appointed for that purpose.‡—*L. I. Farmer*, Mar. 2, '58.

1858.—Religious Revival.—The Reformed Dutch people, being for the present without a place of worship hold meetings at private houses, at which the attendance is increasing. On Tuesday evening, at Mrs. Wm. L. Hendrickson's, Springfield; Wednesday, at Richard Brush's; Friday, at Mrs. Jas. A. Fleury's.—*L. I. Farmer*, Mar. 23.

1858, Mar. 31.—Fastday. Great awakening. Union meeting in Methodist Church. Abm. D. Snedeker and Rev'ds Alliger and Oakey spoke.

The burning of the church at Jamaica was the occasion of starting two other enterprises, one in the eastern, and the other in the western part of this extended congregation. Their history is briefly as follows :

1858, April 18.—A church was organized at Queens. The corner-stone of the new building was laid by Dr. Creed, September 28, 1858, and the church was dedicated in a most solemn and impressive manner, May 8, 1859, by Dr. A. R. Van Nest, who gave a most eloquent discourse from

---

* See deed for this land on page 15 of this book.

† July 22, H. O., Jr., sent in his protest against building on the old site: First—As not being central. Second—As surrounded by taverns ; and Third—the annoyances of Sunday and railroad travel.

‡ 1858, July 29.—John A. King, Richard Brush and Michael P. Holland, for $400, sell to the Reformed Dutch Church two lots on Union Avenue, 50 feet front and nearly 125 feet deep.—*Queens County Records*, Vol. 174, p. 142.

S. J. Young contracted to build the Consistory room for $1,412.15.

Lev. 26 : 2: "Reverence my Sanctuary." The same day, by a generous donation from D. F. Manice, the church debt was extinguished. Oct. 18.—Stephen H. Lott, George Johnson, Abm. Smith and others requested a dismissal in order to form a church at Woodhaven, which was organized Nov. 8, consisting of seventeen members; but was, after a while, disbanded by Classis.

1858, May 20.—$100 was paid for a melodeon for the Sunday School.

1858, May 30, Sunday.—The Consistory room was opened for worship. The room is large and pleasant. The congregation will worship there till the church edifice is erected, plans for which are now drawing by a skillful architect.

1858, July 31.—Sidney J. Young contracted to build the church for $14,477. Richard Brush, Wm. Phraner, John Spader, Isaac Amberman, David Baiseley,* Theodorus Snedeker, Daniel Hendrickson were appointed a committee to complete the contract and superintend the building.

1858, Aug. 3.—The congregation have agreed on a plan for a church edifice, and the building will be commenced immediately. It is to be of brick and well finished. It is to be enclosed before Nov. 1, and completed by Feb. 1, 1859.

1858, Aug. 17.—The Dutch, Presbyterian and Methodist Sunday schools (including the rural schools of the three congregations) united in a picnic to St. Ronan's Well. The farmers came in their market wagons (130) and filled them with the teachers and children. Rev. Messrs. Van Buren, Alliger and Oakey and Henry Hagner addressed the children.†

LAYING THE CORNER STONE OF THE CHURCH.

This interesting ceremony took place on Tuesday, Sept. 14, in presence of a large gathering of people. The exercises commenced with an appropriate prayer by the Rev. P. D. Oakey of the Presbyterian Church, which was followed by singing. Rev. Mr. Mandeville, of Flushing, then read a history of the church, written by H. O., Jr. The Rev. Mr. Alliger,

---

* In March, 1858, some bones of a mastodon were dug up in Baiseley's mill pond. In July, another skeleton was found in Springfield Creek, said to be 30 feet long. One tooth (black) weighed 3½ lbs. being five inches in diameter and 17 inches round. It had four prongs, the longest, 6½ inches. The crown had six projections.—*N. Y. Evening Post.*

† Expenses of Union Picnic : toll on bridge, $7.44 ; on plank road, $20 ; grove, $16 ; and other expenses equal to $114.34.

REFORMED DUTCH CHURCH, JAMAICA,

Built of brick and roofed with slate. Corner stone laid Sept. 14th, 1858, church dedicated Oct. 6, 1859.

Pastor of the church, then came forward with the box to be deposited, and stated the contents to be:

1. The articles found in the corner stone of the church recently destroyed, such as the Magazine of Reformed Dutch Church, *Christian Intelligencer*, *Episcopal Recorder*, portrait of Rev. Dr. Livingston, Hellenbroek Catechism, memorandum of the church, ministers, building committee, builders, Consistory, &c., &c.

2. A Bible, presented in behalf of the Long Island Bible Society, by the treasurer.

3. Psalm Book, gift of Isaac Rapelye.

4. Constitution of the Church.

5. Portrait of Rev. Dr. Schoonmaker, gift of William Phraner.

6. Portrait of Rev. J. B. Alliger, gift of Wm. T. Brush.

7. Portrait of His Excellency John A. King, LL. D., Governor of the State.

8. Drawing of the octagon church built, 1715, gift of Henry Onderdonk, Jr.

9. Drawing of the church recently destroyed.

10. Section of Atlantic cable, gift of R. L. Meeks.

11. Circular of the male and female departments of Union Hall Academy, with names of its officers, teachers and pupils.

12. Piece of the timber of the church built in 1715, gift of Richard Brush.

13. List of church officers.

14. List of all the churches in the village, and their pastors.

15. Village Charter and list of the Corporation.

16. Lithograph, and report of Public School.

17. Historical sketch of the church, as prepared by Henry Onderdonk, Jr.

18. Village Papers—*L. I. Farmer*, *L. I. Democrat*.

19. *Christian Intelligencer*, and the New York daily *Tribune*, *Times*, *Sun*, *News* and *Express*, of September 14.

The box was then, by Richard Brush, one of the building committee, deposited "in the name of the Triune God, Father, Son and Holy Ghost, to whom be all the praise."

Rev. Messrs. Cuyler and Van Zandt then addressed the assembly in terms suited to the occasion.

The Rev. J. M. Huntting made the closing prayer, when after singing the Doxology, the congregation was dismissed by Rev. J. W. Bouton.

The church will be ninety by sixty feet, built of brick and fire-proof, and will cost, when completed, nearly $15,000. The builders are Mr. Sidney J. Young, carpenter, and Mr. Anders Peterson, mason. The names of the building committee are Messrs. Richard Brush, John Spader, Daniel Hendrickson, William Phraner, Theodorus Snedeker, Isaac Amberman, David Baiseley and John N. Brinckerhoff.—*L. I. Farmer*, Sep. 21, 1858.

1859, Jan. 2, Sunday.—Jos. T. Duryea gave a sermon in the Consistory room to the youth of Jamaica.

1859, June 29.—Union prayer meetings were held from church to church. Sep. 28 and Nov. 30 they met in the Consistory room, at 7 o'clock in the evening.

1859, July.—The baptismal basin, now in use, was presented to the church by James Augustus Herriman.

1859 to 1863, the Consistory room was used for lectures in aid of the Jamaica Circulating Library.

On the completion of the church the following circular with a diagram of the pews, was sent to the members:

Dear Sir:—The new edifice, erected for the use of the congregation of the Reformed Dutch Church of Jamaica, will be dedicated (D. V.) to the service of Almighty God, on Thursday morning, Oct. 6, 1859, at 11 o'clock. Sermon by the Rev. Thos. E. Vermilye, D. D.,* of the Collegiate Reformed Dutch Church, of the City of New York.

The pews of said church will be sold by auction, on Wednesday, Oct. 12, between the hours of 2 and 5, in the afternoon.

Yours, &c.,

ISAAC AMBERMAN, Sec.

JAMAICA, Sept. 27, 1859.

DEDICATION.

The interesting ceremony of dedicating a house of worship to the service of Almighty God took place in this village, on Thursday last, Oct. 6. The new church edifice, erected for the use of the congregation of the First Reformed Dutch Church of Jamaica, Rev. J. B. Alliger, Pastor, is located upon the site of the old edifice, that was destroyed by fire on the evening of Nov. 19, 1857. The corner-stone of the new church was laid on the afternoon of Tuesday, Sept. 14, 1858, and in about one year thereafter the building is completed, and consecrated to the service of the Triune God. This is an elegant and imposing edifice, built of brick, sixty by ninety feet, and cost complete about $24,000. It is certainly one of the finest churches on Long Island, and there are not many, even in the City of Brooklyn, to excel it in outward appearance and internal convenience, neatness and beauty. The entrance is by a spacious vestibule, from which are doors and passageways leading to the gallery, and

---

* Dr. Vermilye was greatly pleased at the attention of the audience, and said he had never been better listened to. At the close of the services of dedication, and before the collection was taken up, Mr. Alliger requested none to leave the church, except such as did not intend to contribute.

to the audience room, the floor of which measures seventy-five by fifty-five feet. It affords us pleasure to say that most of the work was done by Jamaica mechanics. The architect and builder, Sidney J. Young; the mason work, by Anders Peterson; the painting, by Silas Carman; the upholstery (cushions), by Th. Hoffstater; the gas-fitting, by Jas. T. Lewis, all of Jamaica.

The walls are beautifully and tastefully painted in fresco, by J. Stanly D'Orsay, of New York. The elegant gas fixtures were made at the manufactory of Messrs. Donaldson, New York. The organ, which is pronounced by good judges, to be of superior tone and power, is from the manufactory of that prince of organ builders, Henry Erben, of New York.

The building was completed, in all its appointments, about one week since, and was dedicated on Thursday last. On this occasion it was filled to its utmost capacity, there being about 1,000 persons within its walls. The services were exceedingly interesting, and the large congregation present seemed to be highly pleased. The clergy present were Revs. Messrs. Alliger, Ten Eyck, Elmendorf, Hammond, West, Vermilye, Demarest, and Himrod, of the Dutch Church; P. D. Oakey and W. Phraner, of the Presbyterian Church; Wm. L. Johnson, D. D., of the Episcopal Church; J. D. Bouton, of the Methodist Church.

The opening Scriptures were read by the Rev. Wm. H. Ten Eyck, of Astoria. The prayer before the sermon was made by the Rev. Wilson Phraner, of Sing Sing, N. Y. An eloquent and appropriate sermon by the Rev. Thomas E. Vermilye, D. D., of the Collegiate Reformed Dutch Church, of New York, who also dedicated the building, the whole congregation standing. The concluding prayer by the Rev. A. Elmendorf, of Brooklyn, and the benediction by the Rev. Wm. L. Johnson, D. D., Rector of Grace Church, Jamaica.*

The choir of the church added to the interest of the occasion by their singing, which was in good taste and well executed, Geo. C. Kissam, M. D., and Benj. Duryea, presiding at the organ.

The church was open in the evening of the same day, and the Rev. N. E. Smith, of Brooklyn, preached to a large and interested audience.

On Sunday, the largest congregation that has met for nearly two years, the first regular exercises took place, and the Pastor, Rev. J. B. Alliger, gave a very impressive discourse, and made many touching allusions to the particular circumstances of the church. The Rev. Mr. Spies, of Milwaukee, preached on Sabbath evening. His sermon was one of great excellence and power. Notice was given that the church would be open for Divine worship on successive Sabbath evenings, and that other ministers of distinction would preach; services commencing at 7 o'clock.—*L. I. Farmer*, Oct. 11, 1859.

1859, Oct. 19, Sunday.—" The Domine at his first service in the new church made his hymns, prayers and sermon appropriate to the occasion,

---

* 1859, Oct. 6.—Collection at dedication, morning and evening, $271.66.

His text was from Ezra 5:3: "Who hath commanded you to build this house, and to make up this wall?" He was at times quite overcome; especially when he prayed for all the building committee to be united to the visible church, and that the young might succeed to the places of their fathers. Mr. Alliger concluded to have evening services on Sundays and to invite prominent preachers from abroad to officiate. This increased the attendance."

1859, Sep. 28, Oct. 19, Nov. 30.—Union prayer meetings in the Consistory room, at 7 P. M.

Purchasers of pews,* Oct. 12, 1859. $12,230.

Nicholas Amberman.	Ludlum Frederick.	William Phraner.
Isaac Amberman,	William H. Furman.	A. Jane Powell.
Cornelius Amberman.	Maria Hegeman.	Harvey Powell.
John D. Amberman.	Daniel Hendrickson.	Rem Remsen.
John H. Bailey.	Abm. A. Hendrickson.	John Remsen.
David Baisely.	Abm. B. Hendrickson.	John Rhodes.
Remsen Bennet.	Hend'k A. Hendrickson	Stephen Ryder.
George Bennet.	Elias B. Hendrickson.	John Ryder.
Eldert Bergen.	Maria Hendrickson.	Mary Simonson.
John D. Bergen.	James A. Herriman.	William Siney.
Jacob Boerum.	Maria Johnson.	Priscilla Smith.
John N. Brinckerhoff.	Hendrick Lott.	Theodorus Snedeker.
Geo. L. Brinckerhoff.	James Lott.	John Spader.
Richard Brush.	James Lott, Fl.	Ditmars Stoothoff.
Phebe Burnet.	John S. Lott.	William C. Stoothoff.
Morris Covert,	Stephen N. Lott.	Daniel R. Suydam.
John Covert.	John B. Lott.	George Suydam.
Phebe Covert.	W. Hempie Lott.	John S. Van Nostrand.
John and Andrew De Bevoise.	Nicholas Ludlum.	Phebe and Mary Van Nostrand.
	Stephen Mills.	
James D. Ditmars.	John M. Niles.	Ann E. Van Nuyse.
Martin I. Duryea,	Nathaniel Nostrand.	Daniel S. Waters.
Samuel Eldert.	Elizabeth Onderdonk.	John T. Waters.
James A. Fleury.	Howard Pearsall.	Sidney J. Young.

Pews were rented as follows. A star is affixed to the names of those persons who afterwards became purchasers.

John Amberman.	Z. M. P. Black.	—— Colyer.
John T. Areson.	Richard Busteed.	John Covert.*
Luke Bergen.*	Conklin Carll.	Abm. De Bevoise.*

---

* Where there was no competition the pews sold mostly at their valuation. Geo. Bennet, L. Frederick, J. Van Nostrand, and George Suydam, each paid a premium of $10; E. Bergen, $15 ; D. R. Suydam, $50; and N. Ludlum, $45. The total amount of sales was $12,230. The pews not sold were offered to be rented.

Aaron A. Degrauw.*	Eliza Johnson.	Joseph O. Skillman.*
States Edwards.*	Mrs. Keeler.	Daniel Snedeker.
Nicholas R. Eldert.	Sarah R. King.	John I. Snedeker.
Daniel K. Folk.	John G. Lamberson.	Harvey G. Spalding.
Thomas H. Frederick.*	James T. Lewis.	A. M. G. Stevens.
Phebe Hagner*	George Miller.	Sarah Stoothoff.
Anna M. Ham.	Elizabeth Monfort.	Albert Stoothoff.*
Charles H. Harris.*	Mrs. Mount.	William Stoothoff.
Henry Harteau.	Mrs. Mower.	Mrs. Stoutenburgh.
Hend'k Hendrickson.	John R. Nostrand.	Mrs. Swezey.
John and Abm. Hendrickson.	Elijah H. Nostrand.	Martin Vandergaw.
	George L. Powell.*	Annie M. Van Zandt.
John Hunt	James Rogers.	Thomas Woolley.

1859, Nov. 24.—Thanksgiving was observed in church. The Methodists and Presbyterians joined with us.

1860, Feb. 1.—A union prayer meeting in the Consistory room.

1860, Feb. 5, Sunday night.—Rev. Dr. Scudder preached on missions. $80 collected.

1860, March. 17.—An association of ladies was formed to raise a fund for educating a divinity student, and to distribute tracts in Jamaica. The members were to meet and pay ten cents monthly.

1860, Apr. 19, and May 17.—Musical concert in Consistory room, by Professor Bauscher, teacher in the Female Seminary.

1860, Aug. 14.—Consistory agreed to add $200 to Mr. Alliger's salary.

1860, Aug. 16.—Nearly 100 wagons, after a parade through the main street, accompanied by a brass band from Brooklyn, set out, about 9 o'clock, for a picnic to St. Ronan's Well, Flushing. There were near 1,500 persons on the ground. The children, led by J. Henrie Young, chorister of the church, sang sweetly. Messrs. Taylor and Sprague, from New York, gave entertaining addresses. The repast was bounteous. Wm. C. Hendrickson and Jas. D. Ditmars were marshels of the day. The pastor of the church conducted the exercises on the grounds. The whole cost of the excursion was $120.

1860, Oct. 12.—Classis met in church.

1860.—Fair and festival, Christmas Eve, afternoon and evening, by the ladies, in the Consistory room, for the benefit of the church. A great variety of useful articles, including books, choice confectionery, and substantial refreshments. $408.27 realized.

1861.—About 3 o'clock, on New Year's morning, an alarm of fire was sounded. Grace Church (which had been repaired at a cost of $3,500) had caught fire from the flues of the furnace and was entirely consumed. The Episcopalians accepted the offer of the use of the Consistory room for public worship. They put a railing around the pulpit so as to administer the Lord's Supper conveniently. They had no need of Christmas greens, for it had already been festooned when we had our fair there.

1861, Jan. 4.—The National Fast Day of humiliation and prayer, in view of the distracted and dangerous condition of our country, appointed by President Buchanan and Governor Morgan, was agreed, by the Jamaica Christian Union,* to be held in the Reformed Dutch Church. The stores and principal places of business were closed during the time of religious service, and the church was well filled. Rev. Messrs. Alliger, Oakey, Henson and Huntting took part in the services.

"Friday was very generally observed as a day of fasting and prayer. Our church was crowded in the morning, and well filled in the evening. The services were very interesting. Rev. Mr. Henson (Methodist) thought our prayers should be made understandingly; and he stated the cause of the Nation's difficulties, according to the views of the *Tribune*. He asked, "What wrong have we done?" [Two ladies now got up and left the church.] Mr. Alliger replied, "It was for the sins of the *whole* Nation, it was not North nor South; but both alike guilty." M.

1861, Feb. 21.—Mr. Alliger's donation party.† He began a course of lectures on the historical books of the Bible, in the Consistory room.

1861, Feb. 18.—The anniversary of Protection Company, No. 1, was celebrated in the Consistory room, and was well

---

* This Union was organized at the time of the religious revival in 1858, and held weekly meetings. Dr. John D. Shelton was President and Wm. Phraner, Secretary.

† Donation parties, or "Ministers' Bees," were in vogue before 1814, and said to be introduced here by Dr. Schoonmaker. The donations were, instead of money, mostly the products of the farm, as flax, yarn, stockings and other gifts of small value.

attended. The exercises were opened with a prayer by Mr. Alliger. Lewis L. Fosdick, on behalf of the fair friends of the firemen, presented the company, in a neat address, with a beautiful Bible. Judge R. L. Larremore accepted the gift on behalf of the firemen, and delivered an address on "Progress."

1861, Apr. 21.—Rev. Jared W. Scudder (son of John) a missionary from India preached, on Sunday morning and evening.

<small>1861, April.—"On Sunday we had a war sermon, prayer and hymns, in our church." M.</small>

1861, June 27.—The formal opening of the Jamaica Circulating Library took place in the Consistory room, on Thursday evening, at 8 o'clock.

1861, Nov. 6.—The ladies interested in the fair for the Circulating Library, met in the Consistory room, at 2 P. M.

1861, July 30.—The Soldiers' Aid Society was formed in Jamaica.

<small>The picnic of the Reformed Dutch Sunday School, of Jamaica, took place on Thursday last, Aug. 15, at Morris' Grove. The procession left the village about 9 o'clock A. M., Wm. C. Hendrickson, marshal, who discharged his duties very creditably. Stewart's Band furnished the music. In the afternoon, an address was made by Rev. J. B. Alliger, pastor of the church.</small>

1861, Sep. 22, Sunday evening.—The Jamaica Bible Society met in the church. Though there were signs of rain, the audience was large, and was addressed by Rev. Messrs. Valentine, of Brooklyn, and Henson, of Jamaica. The choir of the church led the music in their usually effective manner. $227 collected the past year.

1861.—President Lincoln appointed Thursday, Sept. 26, as a day of humiliation, fasting and prayer; and for offering fervent supplications to Almighty God for the safety and welfare of these States, His blessing on their arms, and a speedy restoration of peace. The church was open at 10½ A. M., and Consistory room at 7½ P. M.

1861, Oct. 2.—Classis met in church, Wednesday, 2½ P. M. In the evening, Rev. John McC. Holmes preached on "The duty of the Church in regard to her institutions of learning."

1861.—On Sunday evening, Oct. 20, several of the Eighth Connecticut Regiment, with their chaplain, were at church, to listen to Rev. Dr. Scudder. $74.41 collected.

1861, Oct. 27.—Sunday afternoon, the use of the church for worship was offered to the soldiers. The spacious edifice could scarcely contain the audience. Besides 600 soldiers there was a large attendance of citizens who listened attentively to an instructive and eloquent sermon, by their Chaplain, Woolley —*L. I. Farmer.*

1861, Oct. 30, Wednesday evening.—The chaplain, Rev. J. J. Woolley, of the Eighth Connecticut Regiment, quartered in Jamaica, gave a lecture in the church, before our citizens and a part of that regiment. Over $30 was collected for a circulating library for the use of the soldiers. The chaplain thanked Messrs. Oakey and Allger for the use of their churches. —*L. I. Farmer.*

1861, Nov. 1, Friday.—The soldiers came to church to hear Rev. Jared W. Scudder.

1861, Nov. 12.—The anniversary of the Long Island Bible Society was held in the church. George Douglas gave $500.

1861, Nov. 28, Thanksgiving Day.—Rev. Mr. Alliger had a very full attendance at his church, and gave an excellent discourse. It was not a "war sermon," but replete with good sense, buoyant hopes and sound doctrines. He recognized the hand of a good Providence in all our affairs, and intended for the advancement of God's cause in the world. No matter how discouraging some things now seemed to us, they would in the end, be found to be both wise and good. We should finally be greater, happier and more prosperous than before.—*L. I. Farmer,* Dec. 3.

1861, Dec. 19.—The Tremaine family give a musical concert in the Consistory room, in aid of the Sunday school. Tickets 25 cents to be had at the stores of Wm. T. Brush and Wm. Phraner.

1861, Dec. 24 and 25.—Fair held in Consistory room in aid of Circulating Library.

1862, Apr. 10.—President Lincoln issued a proclamation, recommending to the people of the United States, that at

their next weekly assemblies, they especially acknowledge and render thanks to our Heavenly Father, who has vouchsafed signal victories to the land and naval forces engaged in suppressing an internal rebellion. On the following Sunday (Apr. 13), Mr. Alliger noticed the proclamation in appropriate words, and a *Te Deum* was sung by the choir.

1862.—A Union Army meeting will be held in the Reformed Dutch church, on next Sabbath evening, June 15, in aid of the Board of Publication for army and navy purposes. The agent of the Board, who is in constant communication with many of the chaplains in the government service, will be present, and communicate some very interesting information. Addresses may be expected by the Rev. Stephen A. Tyng, Jr., and by some Chaplain or officer recently from the army or navy. The meeting will be one of deep interest to all. All are cordially invited to attend. The Board of Publication of the Reformed Dutch Church has been very active in the distribution of religious reading, and the sick and wounded demand instant help. $57 collected.—*L. I. Farmer.*

1862, Aug. 10.—Mr. Alliger preached a sermon on "Obedience to Government."

OUR RECRUITS.—We have said before now, and we repeat, "that we feel proud of the volunteers from Jamaica." It was pleasant to see about twenty of them together in the Reformed Dutch Church, on last Sabbath evening. They cheerfully accepted an invitation from the Pastor, Rev. J. B. Alliger, to attend service; and they listened most attentively to the words of counsel and encouragement, addressed to them by one who shows a lively interest in the welfare of those, especially, who enlist from this town. There was a large audience present to give their encouragement to, and to offer their prayers for these noble men. After the service each soldier, not before supplied, was presented with a handsome copy of the New Testament and Psalms, bound in one volume; the book was cheerfully and gratefully received.—*L. I. Farmer.* Sept. 2, 1862.

1862.—John M. Johnson, of Duryea's Zouaves, died Sept. 7, in hospital, from wounds received at Manasses, Aug. 3, in his 22d year. His remains were brought to Jamaica, and the funeral appointed at the church, Oct. 3, 11 A. M., Rev. J. B. Alliger officiating, assisted by Rev. Messrs. Oakey and Huntting. It partook of a civic and military funeral. The firemen turned out in large numbers, and after the solemn service in the church, led the procession to the grave. Fifty of the Ironsides Regiment and twenty of Duryea's Zouaves were the especial escort and the latter, in two files of ten each, marched close beside the bier, acting in the capacity of pall-bearers. An unusually large audience was present though it was stormy. In the church, everything was solemn, and appropriate. The coffin was placed before the pulpit, covered with the pall and American flag. The music upon the organ and by the choir was exquisitely sweet, solemn and appropriate; and this young soldier received a fit testimony of regard and honor. The village stores were closed during the services.— *L. I. Farmer*, Oct. 7, 1862.

At a meeting of the Wardens and Vestry of Grace Church, held on the 8th of Oct., 1862, the following preamble and resolution were adopted:

To the Consistory of the Reformed Dutch Church, Jamaica, L. I.:

GENTLEMEN:—WHEREAS, the Consistory of the Reformed Dutch Church did with great liberality, and in a true christian spirit, give to the congregation of Grace Church, upon the destruction of its edifice by fire, the use of their Consistory room for the purpose of divine worship; now therefore be it

Resolved, That our best thanks and acknowledgements be, and are hereby tendered to the Consistory of the Reformed Dutch Church for the very acceptable and comfortable accommodations furnished by them to this congregation, during the period required for the rebuilding of its church edifice, and that this congregation will ever hold in grateful remembrance this act of liberality and consideration on their part.

JEREMIAH VALENTINE,
Clerk of the Vestry.

1863, March 1, Sunday evening.—On the anniversary of the Sunday School, the large church was nearly filled, the scholars occupied twenty pews. Four hymns were sung. Jas. Phraner played on the melodeon, Miss Lucy J. Ham led the music. Mr. Pardee, of New York, and Carlos A. Butler, of Jamaica, addressed the scholars.

1863, Apr. 30.—Thursday was a day of national prayer and humiliation in recognition of Divine Providence, and in supplicating the Divine Blessing on our country; for the pardon of our national sins, and restoration of our now divided and suffering country to unity and peace.* Services in church at 10½ A. M., and in Consistory room at 7½ P. M.

---

* An Irish anti-draft riot broke out in Jamaica, on the evening of July 14, 1863. Its purpose was to stop the draft which was to commence, next day. Rumors of intended violence were rife during the afternoon, and some friends of order felt disposed to arm

1863, Aug. 6.—Thursday, in compliance with the President's Proclamation, was observed in church as a day of National praise and thanksgiving to Almighty God, for his tender mercies to us in the struggle for our national liberty, and for suppressing the destroyers of our Union; and for the successive victories gained by our armies and navy.

1863, Sept. 13.—The Sunday morning service was interrupted by an alarm of fire. The barn of Mr. J. N. Brinckerhoff was consumed.

1863, Thanksgiving day, Nov. 26.—A liberal collection in church for the United States Sanitary Commission.

1863, Dec.—One of the most attractive features of the Holidays was the fair held by the ladies, in their Consistory room, Christmas eve and day. The attendance was unusually large. Substantials and luxuries were on the refreshment table; toys, books, confectionery and fancy articles of all kinds were for sale. Among the prizes drawn were an Afghan, worth $75, a sewing machine, worth $100, and other smaller articles. Over $500 was realized toward paying off the debt of the parsonage. Mrs. Aaron A. Degrauw, Mrs. M. E. Story, and Mrs. Wm. Phraner were the managers.

1864, Jan. 14.—$30.85 was collected for the Soldiers' Aid Society.

1864, Jan. 16.—Paid $432.50 for a perpetual insurance of the church, to the sum of $10,000, in Franklin Insurance Co.

1864.—The anniversary of the Sunday School was held on the evening of February 24. It was a pleasant entertainment, and the large audience in attendance seemed highly gratified. The school occupied the body

in defence of Government; but timid counsels prevailed, and the village was left to the mercy of the rioters. About dusk they began to gather together. Some one cried out: "Now for the clothing!" The mob then rushed to the building in Washington street, where the Government property was stored, with intent to destroy it. They however, contented themselves (on the entreaty of some leading democrats) with taking out some boxes of soldiers' clothing, which they broke open and piled in heaps, and then set on fire. The large pile, called "Mount Vesuvius," was about ten feet high. The woollens did not readily burn, and some was carried off by Irish women for family use. The loss was $3,446.28, and consisted of 210 knit-shirts, 80 pair stockings, 50 pair trowsers, 59 knapsacks, 400 haversacks, 389 blankets, 154 canteens, and 524 blouses. The mob next proceeded to McHugh's hotel, where they drank freely and without cost. The Provost Marshal's Office was entered and the furniture broken. The draft wheel and papers had been removed that afternoon to a place of safety; and Col. Rose, with his subordinates had fled. This draft was put off 'till Sept. 2.

of the church, and sang the hymns selected for the occasion with much spirit, having the melodeon accompaniment.

The Rev. A. W. Cornell, of Grace Church, addressed the children in a way that could not but delight and profit them. The Rev. Wm. R. Duryea, of East Williamsburgh, addressed the teachers and congregation. His speech was to the point and effective. Those in attendance seldom listened to addresses so admirably suited to the occasion as these were. About one hundred volumes of handsome and instructive books were distributed among the children. The service concluded with the Doxology by the whole congregation, the grand organ of the church accompanying.

1864, March 1.—A paper was drawn up by which the subscribers agreed to pay the sum set opposite their names (in five installments, viz: on May 1, 1864, and Jan 1, 1865, '66, '67 and '68), for paying off the debts of the church. Here follow the names.

Name	Amount	Name	Amount
Richard Brush	$500	John R. Nostrand	$75
Wm. Phraner	500	Albert Stoothoff	75
Daniel Hendrickson	300	Luke Bergen	100
Abm. De Bevoise	300	John Covert	35
James Ryder	110	Cor's. Amberman	50
Stephen Ryder	200	Mrs. St. N. Lott	100
James Lott	150	Harvey Powell	25
Isaac Amberman	150	Mrs. Mary E. B. Story	120
Ditmars Stoothoff	100	States Edwards	60
John De Bevoise	100	Remsen Bennet	75
John N. Brinckerhoff	100	Abm. A. Hendrickson	40
Hendrick A. Hendrickson	160	James Lott	100
Phebe Hegner	125	Phebe Barnet	100
Andrew De Bevoise	100	Nicholas Ludlum	100
Smith Nostrand	30	Theodorus Snedeker	100
George Bennet	100	Samuel Eldert	40
David Baiseley	50	Aaron A. Degrauw	300
Mrs. Anna M. Ham	50	Morris Covert	90
Charles H. Harris	100	Wm. C. Stoothoff	100
Martin I. Duryea	160	Ludlum Frederick	50
George Suydam	125	Hendrick Lott	50
Nicholas Amberman	90	John Amberman	10
Daniel R. Suydam	125	John Remsen	150
Joseph O. Skillman	80	Thos. H. Fredericks	75
John Van Nostrand	40	Jas. Aug. Herriman	75
John S. Van Nostrand	100		
Nathaniel Nostrand	100	Total sum	$5,947
William Nostrand	75		

1864, July 27, Wednesday evening. — Adam Chambers, the "boy preacher," preached in the Consistory room, and took up a collection for the erection of a Baptist meeting house, at Hicksville.

1864, Oct. 11.—At the annual meeting of the Jamaica Branch Bible Society, held in the lecture room of the Presbyterian Church, Mr. Henry Onderdonk, Jr., was elected president in the place of Dr. Nathan Shelton, deceased. The public anniversary of the Society will be held in the Reformed Dutch Church, on Sunday evening next, at 7½ o'clock. The meeting will be addressed by the Rev. Dr. Holdrich, secretary of the American Bible Society, and others.—*L. I. Farmer.*

1865, Feb. 6.—$50.25 was paid for a heater in the church.

1865.—The anniversary of the Sabbath School connected with the Reformed Dutch Church, of this village, was celebrated in the church on Sunday evening, Feb. 19. The building was crowded with scholars and their friends. The children sang several pieces very well; the Pastor, Rev. J. B. Alliger made a few appropriate remarks, and then Mr. Woodruff, from Brooklyn was introduced. After this address the presentation of books took place, and after singing again, the audience was dismissed, highly delighted with what they saw and heard.—*L. I. Farmer.*

FUNERAL OF LINCOLN.

1865.—The committee appointed by the citizens of this town to make arrangements for appropriate exercises on the Funeral solemnities of our late Chief Magistrate, on Wednesday, April 19, would respectfully recommend the following:

1. At 7 A. M., the bells of the different churches to be tolled in unison for one half-hour.

2. All the places of business are requested to be closed at 9 A. M., and to be kept closed during the remainder of the day, all places of business and private residences to be suitably draped in mourning.

3. By reason of the solemnity of the occasion and the deep grief of the community at the recent National calamity in the death of President Lincoln it is recommended that all public display be dispensed with, and the citizens of the town be requested to assemble at the Reformed Dutch Church, at 11½ A. M., where appropriate funeral services are to be held, such services to be under the direction of the clergy of the village.

4. That the services in the church commence precisely at 12 M., and

that the bells of the several churches be tolled for thirty minutes prior thereto.

5. The bells to be tolled for half an hour before sunset.

CARLOS A. BUTLER, Chairman.

JOHN O'DONNELL, JR., Secretary.

Last Wednesday will long be remembered by our citizens. The tolling bells, the flags at half-mast, and the houses draped in the symbols of woe, marked the deep and solemn feeling of every citizen in our midst. At seven o'clock the funeral toll of the church bells announced to all the near approach of the time to pay the last tribute of respect to the memory of the late President. At 9 o'clock all places of business were closed and remained so during the day. At half-past 11 the church bells summoned the people to the place appointed for the ceremonies of the day. And at 12 M., every part of the Reformed Dutch Church was crowded with an attentive and sorrowing congregation. Sadness brooded o'er the entire assemblage, and all felt the impressiveness of the solemn occasion that had convened them. The exercises were opened by a feeling and eloquent address by the Rev. J. B. Alliger, after which the Rev. Dr. Johnson, Rector of Grace Church, read a portion of the Episcopal burial service. Rev. Mr. Cornell, of the Episcopal Church, Rev. Mr. Farley, of the Roman Catholic Church, the Rev. Mr. Backman, of the Methodist church, and Rev. Mr. Oakey of the Presbyterian Church, delivered brief but exceedingly appropriate addresses. The Rev. Benj. Everitt, of Stroudsburgh, Penn., led the congregation in prayer.

The members of the different church choirs in the village united, and contributed much to the interest of the occasion.

The most solemn and impressive portion of the exercises was when the Rev. Mr. Alliger requested, that the vast congregation should unite in solemn, but silent prayer. And we have no doubt that all felt themselves the better for having participated in the exercises.

On Thursday, in accordance with the suggestions of Gov. Fenton, our places of business were mostly closed, and service was held in the Episcopal Church.

Several of our citizens, in addition to the emblems of mourning with which they had their residences clothed, had up inscriptions expressive of their feelings.—*L. I. Farmer*, April 25.

1865.—One of the first acts of President Johnson after assuming the duties of the office, was the appointment of the 1st day of June "as a day of humiliation and mourning," in consequence of the assassination of Abraham Lincoln, the President of the United States. Thursday next is the day; and there will be a general observance of it by the patriotic and Christian people of this land. In this village divine services will be held, beginning at half-past ten o'clock, A. M., in the Episcopal, Presbyterian, Methodist and Reformed Dutch Churches. There will be a general suspension of business on that day.—*L. I. Farmer*, May 30.

1865.—By a proclamation of the President, Thursday, Dec. 7, was observed as a day of thanksgiving to Almighty God for relieving our beloved country from the fearful scourge of civil war and from the calamities of foreign war, pestilence and famine, and for abundant crops.

1866.—The anniversary of the Sabbath School of the Reformed Dutch Church, on last Sunday evening, was an exceedingly interesting and unusually successful affair. At 7 o'clock, the hour fixed for the beginning of the exercises, the spacious church was filled to its entire capacity; seats were placed in the aisles, yet a large number were compelled to stand. The school, a large and flourishing one, was seated in the centre of the church, and occupying about twenty-four pews, directly in front of the pulpit. It was *their* anniversary, so the teachers and children had prepared themselves to sing some well selected hymns; this part was performed with spirit, to the delight of the large assemblage that listened to the sweet voices of happy children. Miss Lucy J. Ham had trained the school for these exercises, and Mrs. Story played the organ accompaniments. The speakers were Mr. Thomas Gulick, a student in the Union Theological Seminary, and son of the venerable Missionary who has been laboring about thirty-five years in the Sandwich Islands, and the Rev. Joseph T. Duryea, formerly of this village, now one of the Pastors of the Collegiate Dutch Church, New York. The first speaker, being a native of the Sandwich Islands, gave an interesting account of the habits and customs of the inhabitants, and the religious condition of the people now as compared with their condition only a generation since. The Rev. Mr. Duryea held the attention of all present in an address of considerable length, remarkable for its great simplicity, beauty and power, adapted to the understanding of the children, and wonderfully suggestive and instructive to men and women. After the address came the "presentation of books," and each scholar received a volume of profitable reading, and the date of the anniversary, neatly written in the front of the books. The Rev. Mr. Oakey, of the Presbyterian Church, conducted the devotional part of the service, and the Pastor of the church, Rev. Mr. Alliger, had charge of the exercises in general. The whole service occupied about two hours.—*L. I. Farmer*, Feb. 27, 1866.

1866.—On Sunday April 1, there was a large gathering in the Reformed Church, at the funeral of a brave soldier who never turned his back on a foe, Jacob D. Bennett, who died May 7, 1864, from a wound received at Chancellorsville. The firemen escorted the body to the church, and thence to the grave.

1866, April 17.—Classis met in the church.

1866.—A Soldier's Funeral.—The remains of Jas. Alfred Kilburn were brought from near Petersburg to his home in Jamaica. His funeral, attended by the fire department and a large concourse of citizens, took place on Sunday, April 22, at 2 P. M., in the Reformed Church which was engaged in order that those in attendance might have accommodations; and the large building was nearly filled. The services were conducted by the Rev. G. Taylor, Methodist, assisted by Rev. Mr. Alliger. The deceased fell at Fort Gregg, fighting for his country and while carrying his colors.

1866, May 6.—Collection for the German Reformed Church, Williamsburgh, $60.

1866.—Augustus Waters will give humorous and pathetic readings on the evenings of May 17 and 18, in the Consistory room. Tickets, 50 cents.*

> 1866.—The Jamaica Bible Society held its annual meeting in the Reformed Church, Sunday evening, Sept. 23, the President, Rev. P. D. Oakey, conducting the exercises. The annual report was read by Mr. James D. Ditmars. Addresses were made by Rev. Mr. Taylor, of the Methodist Episcopal Church, this village; Rev. Wm. H. Moore, of the Episcopal Church, Hempstead, and Rev. Wm. Anderson, of the Reformed Dutch Church, Newtown; and statements regarding the operations of the Society by Rev. Mr. Alliger. The audience was large and seemed deeply interested, as the addresses were very able, and all the exercises of an impressive character. Dr. G. C. Kissam presided at the organ.

1866, Oct. 22.—The Howard Mission, for support of "Little Wanderers," who sang their peculiar songs, held a meeting in the Consistory room, and took up a collection.

1866.—"A fair in the Consistory room, in aid of the Sunday School, on Christmas eve, afternoon and evening. Worsted goods, aprons, dolls, books, albums, children's toys, ice cream, oysters, cake, candies, &c., all of which will be sold at prices not exorbitant." The net proceeds were $450; and many fancy and useful articles left on hand.

---

* At the time the Consistory room was built, there was hardly any convenient room for public exhibitions or lectures, so that it was often allowed free of expense for religious and charitable purposes; otherwise it was hired out. 1864, Dec. 5.—The treasurer of the church received $27 from the Teachers' Institute, for its use; and Jan. 26, 1866, he received $30; 1867, Feb. 9, he received $25 from Dr. Sparks, for use of the room.

1867, Feb. 14.—Dr. Sparks, electric and magnetic healer, lectured in the Consistory room, to women in the afternoon, and men in the evening. Twenty-five cents admission.

1867, Feb. 17.—The Sunday School under the charge of Wm. Phraner, had its anniversary, on Sunday evening, in the church, which was crowded, Dr. G. C. Kissam presided at the organ. Addresses were made by Rev. Messrs. Alliger, Gulick, a Sandwich Islander, and Powell, a Long Islander. Each scholar was presented with a book; and especial premiums to Martha E. Phraner and Hannah Powell, for committing to memory the Heidelberg Catechism, and to Sarah Phraner, for the Hellenbroek Catechism, and to Lucy J. Ham, who, for several years, has conducted the singing, an elegant set of Smith's Bible Dictionary.—L. I. Farmer.

1867.—Mr. L. L. Allen will give a temperance lecture in the Consistory room, Thursday evening, March 7. He has letters of commendation from Lincoln, And. Johnson and Gen. Grant.—L. I. Farmer.

1867, July.—By a resolution of Consistory (Oct. 1866), a collection of $501 was taken up for church expenses.*

1867, July.—The Methodists use the Consistory room while their church is repairing and renovating.

1867, Dec. 1. Sunday evening.—Mr. Alliger's sermon to youth: "Is the young man safe?"

1867, Dec. 5.—General Synod vote to leave out the word "Dutch" from their title.

1867, Dec.—A carpet and stove (costing $151.61) were presented to Mrs. Alliger by the ladies of the church.

1868.—RELIGIOUS.—This is the "week of prayer" for the extension of Christ's Kingdom. The Church Visitation in the Reformed Church, began on Sabbath last, and religious services will be held in the church every evening this week, beginning at 7 o'clock. The first half hour will be a meeting for prayer. Rev. Mr. Ten Eyck, of Astoria officiated on Sunday, and preached two impressive sermons, to large and interested audiences. On Monday evening, preaching by Rev. C. J. Shepard, of Newtown; on Tuesday evening, sermon by Rev. Wm. H. Ten Eyck; on Wednesday evening, sermon by Rev. E. S. Fairchild, of Flushing. The public generally are invited to attend upon these services.—L. I. Farmer, Jan. 7.

---

* 1851, Jan. 1.—Five per cent was assessed on the appraised value of the pews sold, and seven and a half on those unsold in order to pay the church expenses. The pews sold in 1859 were subject to a tax of ten per cent.; those rented, to a tax of fifteen per cent.

1868.—The anniversary of the Sabbath School of the Reformed Church, was held Sunday evening, Feb. 16. The large edifice was filled with a highly intelligent audience, who were greatly interested in the proceedings. The choice collection of hymns for the occasion was admirably sung by the school. The addresses, delivered by Mr. Wm. Ferris, of Brooklyn, and the Rev. E. S. Fairchild, of Flushing, were of a superior order. Both speakers adapted their sayings to the comprehension of children, and we never saw a company of children more delighted. The presentation of books was made by the Superintendent, each scholar receiving a handsome volume.—*L. I. Farmer.*

1868.—A HAPPY PARTY.—It is not easy to surprise a Dutch Domine; but the Domine of the Reformed Church was fairly caught last week. The youth of the Sunday School had arranged for a visit at the Parsonage, and on last Wednesday evening carried out their plan. Assembling in large force at the place agreed upon, they proceeded to the residence of the Pastor, Rev. Mr. Alliger, and literally surprised his Reverence. Masters Wessell H. Bennett and Theodore J. Armstrong, heading the procession, carried a large and beautiful writing desk, well filled with all necessary articles (including a valuable gold pen), and in due form presented the same to Mr. A. The gift was kindly received, and the Minister and his family threw open their house for the enjoyment of the children, who availed themselves of the opportunity to spend a joyful evening. The party carried with them a large supply of refreshments of various kinds, and spreading a bountiful table, all present, young and old, partook of the good things, and left a large quantity behind them. The company dispersed at a reasonable hour in the best of spirits.—*L. I. Democrat,* June 9.

1868.—AS IT SHOULD BE.—During the time the repairs of the Presbyterian Church are in progress, by an arrangement made, the Presbyterian congregation will worship with the congregation of the Reformed Church. Rev. Mr. Oakey is now absent on a short vacation, and the Rev. Mr. Alliger officiates. When Mr. Oakey returns, Mr. Alliger is to take his vacation and the duties of the pulpit will be performed by the Rev. Mr. Oakey.—*L. I. Democrat,* Aug. 4.

1868.—Through the kindness of a member of his congregation, the Pastor of the Reformed Church has been enabled to take a tour of several days' duration through the charming scenery of Lakes George and Champlain, from which he has just returned, greatly benefited by this brief respite from the labors of his office.—*L. I. Democrat,* Sep. 8.

1868.—The picnic of the Reformed Church Sabbath School, on Wednesday, September 16, was an unusually pleasant and gratifying affair. Turning from old and well beaten paths, our Dutch friends determined to go to Northport, over the Long Island Railroad. A special train was chartered, of seven cars, and at 9 o'clock the company was on board, and away went the train, full of happy children, with their parents and friends. They reached Northport at 10.39, and hurried to the grove for the day's enjoyment. Baskets, boxes, melons, ice cream followed, by wagon loads, and in a beautiful spot, upon a hill covered with trees, the party spent the day in real picnic style. The band from New York, Augustus Ihl, leader, gave much choice music, and by the way, leaving Northport at 4.30 P. M., the excursionists were at Jamaica depot a few minutes after six o'clock, not the slightest mishap having occurred to mar the pleasure of the trip. Mr. Israel Carll, the owner of the ground at Northport, to his praise be it said, permitted the company to use his premises free of charge, and was so unselfish as to offer assistance in other ways freely. The cost of the excursion was $125.—*L. I. Farmer.*

1868, Sept. 13.—Collection for the church at Sayville, $60; and July 25, 1869, $31.10.

1868.—The Jamaica Bible Society met, Sunday evening, Oct. 4, in the Reformed Church. A large and intelligent audience assembled. Rev. P. D. Oakey, President, began the services; Rev. E. S. Fairchild read the Scriptures, and Rev. G. W. Pendleton offered prayer. Jas. D. Ditmars, secretary, read his report, after which Rev. Jas. Wyckoff, of Queens, and Mr. French, of Flushing, addressed the people. Two or three appropriate psalms were sung.—*L. I. Farmer.*

1869, Jan. 4-8.—This being the week of church visitation by Classis, there will be preaching in the church as follows: Monday evening, Rev. W. H. Ten Eyck, of Astoria; Tuesday evening, Rev. E. S. Fairchild, of Flushing; Wednesday evening, Rev. James Wyckoff, of Queens; Thursday evening, Rev. Cornelius L. Wells, of Flatbush; Friday evening, addresses by several clergymen.

1869.—The anniversary of the Sunday School of the Reformed Church was held on Sabbath evening, Feb. 21. The church was well filled by a large and highly pleased audience. The singing by the scholars was good, and reflected credit upon Mrs. Mary E. Story, under whose supervision this part of the entertainment was. Very interesting addresses were made by the Rev. Mr. Kip, a missionary from China, and Dr. Lansing. A very handsome and well selected assortment of books was distributed among the scholars. Misses Mattie Fleury and Emily Williamson received prizes for having recited, during the past year, the whole volume of the catechism used in the school. The school is under the superintendence of Mr. William Phraner. During the past year the number on register was 200. Two members of the school have joined the church, and one was removed by death. During the year $120 has been raised and appropriated for benevolent purposes by the scholars.— *L. I. Farmer,* Feb. 21.

1869, Mar. 17.—Paid $74.69 for slating the roof of the church.

1869. Apr. 17.—An application was made to Consistory to establish a Sunday School at East Jamaica, where are forty children. Abm. De Bevoise was appointed to organize it, next Sunday. Agreed that the salary of the pastor be raised to $1,300 and that subscription papers be circulated.

1869.—On the evening of June 17, will be exhibited in the Consistory room, Tillotson's "Grand Mirror of the Bible," illustrating 100 events in the Bible, the days of creation, &c. Twenty-five cents admission.

1869, Nov. 18, Thanksgiving.—In the Reformed Church the Rev. Mr. Alliger preached from Deut. xvi, 13. 14, 15 verses.

1869.—The meeting of the several Sabbath Schools of our village in the Consistory room of the Reformed Church, on Thursday evening, Nov. 18, was largely attended, and the interest manifested at this, the first meeting of a series which are to be held during the coming season, bespeaks the attention of all who are interested in the Sabbath School work. The meeting was conducted by Mr. William Phraner, Superintendent of the Sabbath School of the Reformed Church, who stated that the object of the meeting was to enlist the attention and sympathies of all, and especially the parents of children, in the Sabbath schools. The singing, which was an interesting feature on this occasion, was under the direction of Mr. Bernhard. The opening address was made by the Rev. Mr. Alliger, and was followed by the Rev. Mr. Thomas Cook and others, in a very pleasing and instructive manner; and most of the remarks that were made were of a practical nature, presenting a striking contrast between the religious and secular schools of the present day, and showing the importance of an increased attention by the parents, in giving to their children some religious instruction at home, and not leaving all for the Sabbath School teacher to do. The next meeting of the Jamaica Sunday School Union will be held in the lecture room of the Presbyterian Church.—*L. I. Democrat.*

1869.—The Sunday School singing meeting was held in the Reformed Church, on Monday evening, Dec. 20. Although the evening was very rainy, the storm did not prevent a goodly number from assembling and enjoying the exercises of the occasion. This meeting was a union of the Presbyterian, Reformed and Baptist schools, formed for mutual edification, and designed to awaken a deeper interest in the Sabbath School work. Mr. Phraner, the superintendent of the Reformed school, presided, and conducted the services. The hymns selected for the occasion were appropriate, and sung with spirit, Prof. Tillinghast leading the singing, and Mrs. Story presiding at the organ. Prof. T. gave an interesting Scripture lesson, in which the children and all others seemed greatly interested. Lewis L. Fosdick, and Jared Hasbrouck, Principal of Union Hall, made the chief, appropriate and impressive addresses. The next meeting will be held in the Presbyterian Church, on Monday evening, Jan. 17, 1870.—*L. I. Democrat.*

1869, Dec. 7.—Professor Tillinghast will open a singing school in the Consistory room, on the evening of Dec. 8. Twelve lessons for $1.

1870, Jan. 11–14.—In connection with the evening meetings for prayer in the church, there will be sermons by Rev. Messrs. McKelvey, Carroll and Fairchild, a visiting committee, appointed by Classis.

1870, Feb. 13.—The anniversary of the Sunday School was held in the church. Mr. Alliger, in the name of the teachers, gave Wm. Phraner, superintendent, Smith's Bible Dictionary, elegantly bound. The school had given $166 to missions the past year.

1870, March 14, Monday evening.—Children's singing meeting in the church, under the direction of Abm. De Bevoise, Superintendent of the East Jamaica Sunday School. Miss Jennie De Bevoise and Mr. George L. Powell led the music. Prayer by Rev. Mr. Alliger, and addresses by Messrs. Bernhard, Phraner and Acker and Rev. Messrs. Hill, Cook and Alliger.

1870, March 17.—A meeting was held in the Consistory room, of the friends of temperance,* humanity and truth, on Thursday evening.

1870.—Sunday evening, April 10, the East Jamaica Sunday School, in charge of Abm. De Bevoise, held their celebration in the church. Rev. Mr. Simpson, Messrs. Ditmars Jewell, and Elijah Alliger addressed the scholars, to whom books were presented.

1870, May 18, Wednesday evening.—A concert of sacred music in church, Wm. Tilinghast, conductor. Mrs. Spader,

---

* Timothy Nostrand (Sept. 7, 1829,) was chairman of the first meeting, held in Jamaica, to form a Society for the suppression of intemperance. Rev. Chas. P. McIlvaine addressed the meeting. Ardent spirits were once reckoned among the necessaries of life. While the church was being repaired, in 1815, the carpenter made daily charges of a pint of rum, 15d.; a pint of gin, 2s.; or half a pint of spirits, 1s. In 1832, drinks were poured out, at stated hours, to the workmen on the new church.

Armstrong, Story, H. U. Rider, Ella Hendrickson, Miss Mattie E. Phraner, Mr. Jas. Phraner and Mr. G. W. Allen were among the singers.

RESIGNATION OF REV. MR. ALLIGER.

1870.—We regret to learn that the Rev. Mr. Alliger tendered his resignation on Sunday, May 22. He has made many warm and devoted friends, and has labored faithfully. His salary will be paid up to Aug. 1.—*L. I. Democrat*.

1870, May 23.—Sundry members of the congregation agreed to pay the Consistory $916.33 for the benefit of our Pastor, Rev. J. B. Alliger, as a free gift.*

At a meeting of the Consistory of the Reformed Church, held on the 23d day of May, 1870, elders and deacons all present, at the church. On motion it was resolved:

WHEREAS, Our Pastor, the Rev. J. B. Alliger, has tendered his resignation to us, and we the Consistory, have consented to unite with him in an application to Classis for a dissolution of the pastoral relation subsisting between him and our church; therefore,

Resolved, That we regret that he should have felt it his duty to take this step, as we are assured that he is held in affectionate regard by the great mass of our people.

Resolved, That the severance of the tie which for nearly twenty years has bound him to us in the most intimate relation, causes us deep sorrow, and nothing but his own earnestly expressed conviction of duty would have induced us to consent to his resignation.

Resolved, That we hereby express our undiminished confidence in him, and bear testimony to his consistent christian life and fidelity as a minister of the Gospel of Jesus Christ.

Resolved, That a copy of the above resolutions be properly engrossed and transmitted to our pastor and published in the *Christian Intelligencer*.

MARTIN I. DURYEA, Sec.

Pursuant to a call of its President, the North Classis of Long Island met at the Synod's rooms, No. 34 Vesey street, New York, on Monday, the 30th day of May, 1870.

A joint application from the Rev. J. B. Alliger and the church of Jamaica, for the dissolution of the pastoral relation subsisting between

---

* The Consistory agreed (1870, Oct. 2) to pay Rev. J. B. Alliger, the sum ($539.90) claimed by him as salary due him, though they don't feel bound by any former agreement.

him and that church was laid before the Classis. After hearing from brother Alliger the reasons that influenced him to present his resignation to the Consistory, and the expression on the part of the members of Classis of their great regrets that the dissolution should take place, it was

Resolved, That the pastoral relation between Rev. J. B. Alliger and the Reformed Church of Jamaica be, and is hereby dissolved.

After a fervent prayer by the Rev. Dr. Carroll, for God's blessing on this brother and his family. The Classis adjourned.

THE REV. JOHN G. VAN SLYKE was called as pastor, Aug. 23, 1870, at a salary of $1,600 per annum with parsonage, and to be increased as the rental of the pews shall warrant.

1870, Sept. 1, Thursday.—Sunday School picnic to the Pavilion, Rockaway.

1870, Oct. 9, Sunday evening.—Jamaica Bible Society met in church.

1870.—A special meeting of the North Classis of Long Island, was held on Monday, Oct. 31, at the Synod's rooms, 34 Vesey street, New York. A call from the Reformed Church, of Jamaica, upon the Rev. J. G. Van Slyke, of Readington, New Jersey, was presented for the approval of Classis. The Classis approved the call, and Mr. Van Slyke having signified his acceptance, arrangements were made for his installation, as Pastor of the Reformed church of Jamaica. Installation to take place on Sunday afternoon, November 20.—*L. I. Democrat.*

1870.—Sunday, Nov. 6, Mr. Van Slyke* began his services here, as pastor.

INSTALLATION.—The Rev. John G. Van Slyke was installed Pastor of the Reformed Church, Jamaica, L. I., on Sabbath afternoon, Nov. 20, in presence of a large congregation. Many from other denominations with their pastors were in attendance. The introductory prayer was made by Thos. E. Vermilye, D. D.; the sermon was preached by Rev. Geo. D. Hulst, from I Cor. 1 : 17; Rev. C. J. Shepard, of Newtown, presided, read the form of installation, and proposed the constitutional questions; Dr. Vermilye then delivered the charge to the pastor, and Rev. Alex. McKelvey, of Greenpoint, the charge to the people. After singing an anthem the crowded audience received the benediction from the newly installed pastor.

On Sabbath morning, Nov. 27, the pastor preached his inaugural sermon to a large and appreciative audience, including many from other

---

* John Gurney Van Slyke was born at Coeymans 1845. Graduated at Rutgers College 1866, and at the Theological Seminary 1869. He served at Readington, N. J. till 1870 when he accepted a call to Jamaica.

denominations. His text was Ex. 17: 15, Jehovah-nissi (the Lord my banner). * The thoughts were novel, striking and pungent. Many of the people were deeply affected, and all agreed that it was a most happy effort, in which the dignity and character of the ministerial office were well set forth.

The new Pastor has been called with a singular unanimity, and with the kindest sympathies of sister denominations; and so far has realized the most sanguine expectations of the people.

1870, Dec. 11.—The teachers of the Sunday School passed resolutions of condolence, and respect for the memory of Miss Maggie Ham, their fellow teacher.*

1870, Dec. 21.—The Young Mens' Christian Association was formed in the Consistory room. E. A. Brinckerhoff, Carlos A. Butler, John M. Crane, committee.

1871, Jan. 3.—Week of prayer, Rev. Mr. Lampman lead the services in the Consistory room, Tuesday evening.

1871, Jan. 30.—Paid $6.50 for a new church record book, and $9 for a church register.

1871, Jan 31 and Feb. 6.—Donation party to Mr. Van Slyke. $500 received.

1871, Feb. 1, 2 and 7.—Classical visitation. The services consisted of prayer meetings, followed by sermons from Rev. Messrs. McKelvey, Hulst and Dr. Porter.

1871, Mar. 5.—At the anniversary of the Sunday School addresses were made by Rev. Messrs. James and Lampman, and Mr. Jared Hasbrouck. Books were presented to the scholars; and especial prizes for punctuality to Frederick Ham, Isaac De Bevoise and Marietta and Charlotte De Bevoise.

1871, April 2, Sunday evening.—The second anniversary of the East Jamaica Sunday School, of which Abm. De Bevoise is superintendent, assisted by Wm. Kirby, was held in church, and drew out an audience so large that extra seats had to be brought in. Rev. Mr. Van Slyke presided, Rev. Messrs. Hulst and Lampman made addresses. Mr. George L. Powell and Miss De Bevoise taught the singing. Fifty-four scholars were on the roll, and an average attendance of thirty-four.— *L. I. Democrat.*

---

* The teachers paid $17.80 for a wreath, anchor and twenty-eight small hand-bouquets at the funeral.

1871, May 18.—The Consistory room has been undergoing an overhauling. About $500 has been expended in making the Sunday School room pleasanter. The gallery has been fitted with sliding glass doors for an infant class-room, a new book case for the library, a new nook and elegant railing.—*L. I. Farmer.*

1871, June 4.—On Sunday fifteen persons were admitted to the church by confession, and four by certificate.

1871, June 22.—A strawberry festival of the Sunday School of the Reformed Church was held at the Town Hall, afternoon and evening. Tables furnished with ice cream, iced tea and coffee, lemonade, fruits, cakes, confectionery, flowers, fancy articles, &c. $233.06 realized.

1871, July 2.—Sunday evening, Mr. Van Slyke began his lectures on Genesis and Geology.

1871, Aug. 15.—The Reformed Church, is undergoing sundry repairs and improvements, and will be closed from September 3 to October 15. The inside is to be newly frescoed, gas-light chandeliers are to be placed in the centre of the ceiling, the side and pulpit lamps removed, &c.*— *L. I. Democrat.*

1871, Oct. 22.—Collection for relief of the Holland sufferers, in Michigan, $225.

1871, Nov. 13.—Surprize. The friends of our good Domine Van Slyke gave him money to buy a gold watch, and Nov. 20, the youth of the Sunday School gave him money to buy a chain. The young misses had provided abundant refreshments and another pleasant evening was spent at the parsonage.—*L. I. Democrat, Nov. 21.*

1871, Nov. 14.—Long Island Bible Society met in church at 7½ P. M.

1871, Nov. 30, Thanksgiving.—The places of business in the village were closed at 10 o'clock, and Presbyterians and Methodists joined in worship in the Reformed Church, where Mr. Van Slyke preached, and Messrs. Lampman and Hill took part in the services. The day was cold and windy. In the afternoon the fair of the East Jamaica Sunday School was held in the Town Hall.

---

* Paid for frescoing church, $752; repairing roof, $99; table $12.30; four reflectors, $137.50; carpenter, $660.50.

1871.—The Christmas festivities of the Sunday School were held in the Consistory room, on Saturday, December 23. Mr. E. A. Brinckerhoff addressed the children, on Christmas and the Christmas tree. The scholars thanked Mrs. B. for two beautiful tablets and scripture texts.—*L. I. Democrat.*

1871, Dec. 27.—Mr. Van Slyke's donation party. Receipts, $700.

1872, Jan. 7–14—Week of prayer.

1872, Feb. 1, Thursday evening.—The Reformed Church of Queens united with Jamaica in celebrating the Centennial of the Reformed Church in the United States. Mr. Van Slyke read the 48th Psalm, and Messrs. Chas. J. Shepard and Thos. Nichols made addresses. Closed with singing the 557th hymn.

1872, Feb. 22.—Mr. Van Slyke gave a temperance lecture in the Town Hall.

JAMAICA, Feb. 24, 1872.

To the Superintendent, Teachers and Scholars of the Reformed Dutch Sunday School:

MY DEAR FRIENDS:—If it affords you as much pleasure to receive, as it does me to give you the organ, which is now in your possession, I shall be well satisfied; and I earnestly pray that your voices may oft mingle with its tones in praise and thanksgiving unto the One who loves us and gave Himself for us. Your friend,

MRS. E. A. BRINCKERHOFF.

1872, March 3, Sunday evening.—The Sunday School had its anniversary in church. Stirring addresses were made by Messrs. Van Slyke and Lampman. A full house and fine singing.

1872, Easter.—The choir had prepared suitable anthems; but Mr. Van Slyke was too unwell to come out. No services.

1872, Aug. 6.—The Sunday School, accompanied by the Jamaica Brass Band, had their picnic at Eldert's Grove, Rockaway.*

---

* The expenses were: 6 cars, $150; music, $26; printing, $6; help, $2; for the grove and water, $5; tea, $3.24; 2 bushels peanuts, $7.40; 80 quarts ice cream, $28. Tickets sold, $198.51; ice cream, $23.65; leaving a deficit of $2.28.

1872, Oct. 30, Wednesday.—Classis met in Church.

1872, Dec. 24.—The scholars of the Sunday School met with their friends, on Tuesday afternoon, in the Consistory Room, where were singing, short addresses, and gifts to each scholar. After the fruits of the Christmas tree were shaken off, a stocking was observed on a limb, which was found to contain ten new ten-dollar bills, a gift to the school from Mrs. E. A. B.*

1872.—Centennial subscription to pay off the Church's indebtedness, being the hundredth year of the separation of the Reformed Church in America from that of Holland.

Amberman, Isaac	$125	Eldert, Aletta	50
Amberman, Nicholas	75	Fredericks, Thos. H	115
Amberman, Cornelius	56	Fredericks, James R	10
Amberman, John D	55	Frederick Ludlum	25
Baiseley, David	300	Foster, William	50
Brush, Richard	300	Griffin, Abm	25
Bennett, George	125	Gulick, Francis F	65
Bergen, Ann	120	Harris, Charles H	60
Baiseley, Michael	115	Hagner, Miss Phebe	20
Bergen, Eldert	10	Herriman, J. Augustus	290
Bailey, Cornelius Kip	50	Hendrickson, Jas. C	250
Bennet, Remsen	25	Hendrickson, Daniel	125
Baylis, David	40	Hendrickson, Susanna	60
Baylis, Charles S	25	Hendrickson, Daniel B	10
Brinckerhoff, Abm	5	Hendrickson, Maria L	10
Brinckerhoff, George L	35	Hendrickson, John S	2
Brinckerhoff, John H	50	Hendrickson, Abm. A	25
Brinckerhoff, John N	50	Hendrickson, Abm. B	25
Brinckerhoff, E. A	2,000	Hendrickson, Peter C	25
Covert, John	35	Husson, Thos. T	25
Covert, Misses M. and E	25	Johnson, Eliza	15
Champlin, Julia A	5	Johnson, A. Ditmars	10
Covert, Luke	10	Lott, Hendrick	100
De Bevoise, Abm	300	Lewis, James T	25
De Bevoise, Chas. J	200	Lott, Phebe	65
De Bevoise, Andrew	100	Lott, James	50
Degrauw, Aaron A	100	Ludlum, Nicholas	110
De Bevoise, John	50	Nostrand, William	50
Durland, William	10	Nostrand, Rem	10
Duryea, Martin I	100	Nostrand, John H	5

* Eight dollars was paid for Christmas greens to decorate the room. Flowers were displayed on the pulpit when Mr. Van Slyke preached his first sermon as pastor.

Polhemus, Theodorus	500	Stoothoff James,	25
Phraner, Wm	300	Stockholm, Harman J	100
Powell, Harvey	5	Suydam, Daniel R	60
Purdy, David J	25	Van Siclen, Garret K	250
Remsen, Abm.	110	Van Slyke, John G.	100
Rogers, Theodore	50	Van Nostrand, Phebe	60
Ryder, Stephen	110	Van Siclen John	50
Ryder, Stephen Jr	50	Van Nostrand, John S.	50
Ryder, John	20	Van Nuyse, Ann E	2
Ryder, James	10	Van Dine, John	70
Stockholm, Ann	150	Williamson, Wm. S.	220
Stoothoff, Wm. C.	100	Van Siclen, Mrs. Ida	25
Snedeker, Isaac	125	Van Siclen, James.	20
Stoothoff, Wm. W	10	Van Siclen, Ditmars	15
Stoothoff, Mrs. Sarah	10		

By the first subscription, $8,490 was raised, but this sum not being sufficient to wipe out the debt, Mr. E. A. Brinckerhoff, who had already given $2,000, offered to add another thousand, provided the congregation would make up a like sum. This was done, but we have not the names nor amount of money obtained at the second going around. A part of the original subscribers added on to their former contributions, so that on New Year's Day, 1874, the church was free of debt.

1873, Jan. 7, Tuesday.—By recommendation of the Evangelical Alliance, there will be union prayer meetings every night this week, alternately in the Consistory room and in the Presbyterian lecture room.

1873, Jan. 15.—Donation party to Mr. Van Slyke.

1873, Feb. 22—The Sunday School sent a contribution for the education of soldiers' orphans at the National Homestead, Gettysburg.

1873, Mar. 9.—The anniversary of the Sunday School was held in the church and drew together a crowded house. Rev. Dr. West and Mr. Streeter addressed the children. The death of Kitty Starr was referred to. One hundred and sixty volumes have been added to the library, and seventy-five given to another school. Each scholar was presented with a book.

1873, April 15.—Classis met in church. Services at $2\frac{1}{2}$

and 7½ P. M. Rev. G. D. Hulst preached on the "Spiritual Body." A lively discussion followed in the evening.

1873, June 11.—Sunday School convention in church.

1873, July 30.—Sunday School picnic to Garret Eldert's Grove, Rockaway.

1873, Aug. 13.—Corner stone of St. Paul's German Evangelical Church laid.

1873, Sept. 6.—The Consistory passed resolutions of condolence and respect for the memory of Wm. Phraner, treasurer, who died September 2 ; and October 13, they appointed Isaac Amberman in his stead.*

1873, Nov. 2.—Collection for sufferers at Memphis, $70.

1873, Nov. 27.—Thanksgiving in church. Union services, sermon by Rev. Mr. Van Slyke.

1873. Mrs. E. A. Brinckerhoff was at the whole expense of the Christmas tree in the Consistory room. Each scholar had a handsome box of confectionery, and the infant class had dolls and playthings too numerous to mention.—*L. I. Democrat*, Dec. 30.

1874, Feb. 22.—Anniversary of the Sunday School in church, Abm. De Bevoise superintendent. Mrs. M. E. Story had charge of the singing. Addresses by Mr. Olin and Thos. Rush, both of New York. Good and beautiful books were given to the scholars.—*L. I. Democrat*, Feb. 24.

1874, Feb. 25 and 26.—An apron and necktie fair was held in the evening, in the Town Hall, by the ladies of the Reformed Church and Sunday School, realizing $150. When a gentleman bought a necktie he had to treat some lady wearing an apron of like pattern, with ice cream or some other delicacy. This caused much sport among young and old. On the tables were refreshments, fruits and candies. Admission, ten cents.

---

* The previous treasurers were James Hendrickson, Henry Story, John Allen and Ditmars Stoothoff. Mr. Hendrickson deserved well of the church. Formerly the deacons acted as treasurers, and when, as sometimes happened, there was a small deficiency the Consistory each made it up from their own pockets. Once there was a larger deficiency than usual and Mr. H. assumed the debt. It created a sensation. It was the day of small things when a little money went a great ways, and a church member could be found who contributed only one dollar yearly toward the minister's salary.

1874, March 23.—The carpet stolen from the church March 12, was found, on the information of Edward Rothermel. It had been pawned for $16.*

<small>Edward Rothermel, indicted for burglary, with having on the night of the 12th of March, 1874, entered the Reformed Church, in the village of Jamaica, and stole therefrom sixty yards of carpet of the value of $50, was at the April Term of the Circuit Court sentenced to imprisonment at Sing Sing for three years.—*L. I. Democrat.*</small>

1874, March 15.—Sunday evening Mr. Van Slyke gave a temperance sermon, from Proverbs xx, 1, which was printed in the *L. I. Democrat*, March 24.

1874, May 13, Wednesday evening.—Professor De Launay gave a lecture in the Consistory room, on the Catacombs of Rome. No admission fee; but a collection at close of lecture.

1874, July 22, Wednesday.—Picnic of the Sunday School to Eldert's Grove, Rockaway, the best grove on the beach. A spacious hall has been engaged exclusively for this picnic. Isaac Amberman, Stephen Ryder and George L. Powell, committee; Abm. De Bevoise, superintendent.

<small>1874, Wednesday evening October 14, was the fifth anniversary of the wedding of the Rev. Mr. and Mrs. J. G. Van Slyke.† They were invited out to tea and did not return to their residence until some time in the evening, when they found their house had been taken possession of by members of the Reformed Church and a goodly number of outsiders. The clergy were represented by the Rev. Messrs. Lampman and Smith, the Rev. W. E. Davis, Manhasset, and the Rev. Mr. Hart of Locust Valley. The Domine and his wife proceeded up stairs, to lay aside hat and shawl, &c., when they found that the furniture in their bed-chamber had been changed. A splendid blackwalnut bedroom set of furniture, with mattress, &c., greeted their astonished vision; a handsome parlor stove was put in the study room, by Mr. George H. Creed; a very elegant adjustable study chair was given the Pastor and a handsome green rep chair was given Mrs. Van Slyke by John D. Amberman; Miss Briggs contributed a fine tub of beautiful flowers; Mrs. Spader gave a dish</small>

<small>* On discovery of the theft, the Consistory offered a reward of $100, on conviction of the thief, which was paid April 20, to two detectives, Holland and Short.

†The middle name of the Rev. John Garnsey Van Slyke, D. D., was originally spelled Guernsey (not Gurney); but the family now prefer and write it Garnsey.</small>

of choice flowers ornamented with clothespins; Elbert N. Remson, with an eye to business, sent a wooden meat pounder; a scripture text worked by Willie Starr and other pleasant mementos reminded the Domine that his congregation had come to celebrate his "wooden wedding." The ladies had made bountiful provision for the wants of the inner man, which was right well enjoyed by all present.—*Democrat, October* 20.

1874, November 15.—Collection for the German Reformed Church in Newtown, $10; and July 2, 1876, $26.63.

1874, December 7.—The Rev. L. H. Gerndt, pastor of St. Paul's German Evangelical Luthern church, thanks the Consistory for their christian kindness in allowing them the free use of the Consistory Room for an entire year while the congregation was being organized.

1874, December 13.—Collection for a converted Jew, $10.

1874, December 26.—On Thursday night thieves effected an entrance into the church by cutting out a small piece of glass from a window on the east side. They had evidently lit the gas to help them in their researches, as the gas was yet burning in the basement when the sexton entered the church next morning. Every door had been left open. They took the covering from the pulpit and cover of a small Sunday school organ standing in the vestibule. Three chairs were piled up by the window, and it is supposed they intended to carry them off, but were perhaps frightened away.—*L. I. Democrat.*

1874, Dec. 27.—Sunday School anniversary. Reading the Scriptures and prayer by Mr. Lampman, addresses by Rev. Messrs. Sutphen and Griffis.

1875, Jan. 31.—Mr. Van Slyke's sermon, "Beautiful Snow."

1875.—Mr. Van Slyke started for California, April 12; and gave his next sermon, Sunday, June 6, when the pulpit was decorated with flowers and the words " Welcome Home." Rev. Abm. Thompson officiated during his absence. On Wednesday evening, June 30, Mr. Van Slyke gave an account of his trip across the Continent.

1875, June 17.—The Sunday School had a strawberry festival at the Town Hall.

1875, Aug. 1.—Sunday afternoon Mr. Van Slyke gave an address to the children. The evening services were discontinued during August.

1875, Oct. 10.—Monthly services in church for children, at 3½ P. M.

1875.—Christmas festivities in the Consistory room at 3 P. M., consisting of games, refreshments, singing and addresses.

1876, Feb. 8.—The "Mite Society" gave Mrs. Van Slyke a silk dress, at her residence. The ladies had, in September, 1872, given her a gold watch.

1876, Feb.—A course of Thursday evening lectures in church was begun.

1876, Feb. 22.—There was a centennial celebration of Washington's birthday held in the Town Hall, in aid of the Sunday School. About 1,200 persons visited it, and $350 were realized. In the four corners of the room stood refreshment tables, representing the cooking of the New England, Western, Middle and Southern States, respectively. On the central tables were placed old-time relics, books, guns, swords, china-ware, household implements, shoes, buckles, &c. The lady attendants wore old-time costumes. The "Republican Court" was a sort of tableau, representing the ladies and gents of Washington's time, dressed in character. The close of the centennial tea party was followed by a promenade and dancing.

1876, March 5.—Sunday School anniversary in church. A beautiful book was presented to Miss Laura E. Brinckerhoff, organist.

1876, April 16, Easter.—Mr. Van Slyke had a sermon on "The Resurrection." In the evening were union services in church.

1876, June 3.—The Consistory appoint a committee to confer with the Presbyterian and Methodist Churches to apply to the proper Board and show the necessity of closing the liquor saloons in the village on Sundays.

1876, July 2.—It being centennial year, Mr. Van Slyke gave a historical discourse on the first Reformed Church of Jamaica, which was published in a pamphlet of 43 pages.

1876.—The Sunday evening services in church were suspended from July 9 to Sept. 3.

1876, Nov. 25.—Paid $110 for painting the church.

1876, Nov. 15.—Mr. Van Slyke reported to Consistory that he had accepted a call to Kingston, and asked them to unite with him in applying to Classis for a dissolution of the Pastoral relation.

> 1876, On Sunday evening, December 3, the Rev. Mr. Van Slyke concluded his labors and preached his farewell sermon. The church was crowded by an attentive and interested audience. No service was held in the Presbyterian Church, so that all who desired, might attend. The text chosen was the 14th verse of the 13th chapter of 2nd Corinthians: "The grace of the Lord Jesus Christ, and the love of God, and the communion of the Holy Ghost, be with you all." The sermon consisted of an able and clear exposition of the text and the doctrines involved in it, and then a brief review of the past six years and a most touching appeal to the congregation to persevere in the good work in which they were engaged.—*L. I. Democrat*, Dec. 5.

> 1876, The German Lutheran Church of this village having applied some time since to be received under the care of the North Classis of Long Island that body has decided to grant the request, upon condition that the name "Lutheran" be dropped, and that the church shall agree to conform to the customs and usages of the Reformed Church in America, as well as to receive its standard of doctrines and declare themselves willing to submit to its government.—*L. I. Farmer*, Dec. 14.

1876, Dec. 27.—The Sunday School held a sociable, in the afternoon and evening. A table was spread with cakes, sandwiches, &c. The children played games, and just before going home, each received a paper of candies and an orange.

1877, Jan. 7–14.—The week of prayer, appointed by the Evangelical Alliance.

1877, Jan. 14.—When the people came to church on Sunday they found the door locked and no fire made.* The sex-

---

* Among the sextons not named were: John Bennet, 1833; Elias B. Hendrickson, 1846; Ferdinand S. Snedeker, 1852; James S. Snedeker, 1861; Erasmus Peterson, 1866; Eldert Conklin, 1877; Benj. F. Everitt, 1879. Among the boys who blew the organ were: Isaac Simonson, Jr., and Thos. Snedeker, 1852; Isaac S. Waters, 1858; John Snedeker, 1860; Chas. Peal, 1861; Robert Ham, 1863; Thos. McGirr, 1866; Chas. Peterson, 1868; Thos. H. Carman, 1871; Fred'k Ham, 1879; Wm. Darby, 1874, Walter Brush, 1882; John A. Powell, 1884.

ton, Edward Peterson, had left for parts unknown, without giving notice.

1877.—The anniversary of the Sunday School under Abm. De Bevoise, superintendent, was held in the church, Feb. 25, and drew a large congregation together, many being obliged to stand for want of seats. Addresses were made by Rev. Wm. H. De Hart, of New York, and Mr. Bungay, of Brooklyn. Each scholar was presented with a book. Miss Ella Brush received the prize for punctual attendance, having been present at 53 sessions of the school during the year.

After the resignation of Mr. Van Slyke, Martin G. Johnson, James C. Hendrickson and Stephen Ryder were requested to look for a suitable pastor. On their recommendation the Rev. Wm. H. De Hart* was invited to preach on Sunday, Feb. 25, 1877. At night he took charge of the Sunday School anniversary services in church. Many from other churches were present. At a joint meeting of the Consistory and congregation, March 6, he was unanimously called at a salary of $1,600 per year with parsonage. Abm. De Bevoise went to New York next day and presented the call which was accepted by Mr. De Hart.

INSTALLATION.—Thursday afternoon, May 3, 1877, the Rev. Wm. H. De Hart was installed pastor of the Reformed Church in this village. The church was well filled and the exercises were of an interesting character. Around and about the pulpit was a large quantity of rare and beautiful flowers. The Rev. M. L. Haynes, of Astoria, presided. An able, eloquent and instructive sermon was preached by the Rev. O. E. Cobb, of Flushing. The charge to the pastor, full of valuable suggestions and earnest thought, was delivered by the Rev. E. S. Fairchild, of College Point, and the charge to the people was delivered by the Rev. J. G. Van Slyke, the former Pastor. Like all of Mr. Van Slyke's efforts, it was logical, well considered and effective. The new pastor starts under the most favorable auspices and we doubt not that in his hands the large and influential congregation over which he presides, will prove a power for good in our community.—*L. I. Democrat.*

1877, May 6.—Mr. De Hart preached his opening sermon :

---

* Wm. H. De Hart was born at New Brunswick, 1837; graduated at Rutgers College, 1865, and at the Theological Seminary 1868. He was at North and South Hampton, Penn., 1868-71, and in the Knox memorial chapel, N. Y., 1871-7, when he was called to Jamaica.

"Wist ye not that I must be about my Father's business." The congregation was large and well pleased.

1877, May 28, Monday.—Pleasant surprise. Rev. Mr. De Hart was visited by about forty ladies and gentlemen of the Sunday School of his former charge in New York City. They had a good time and returned in a special car, at 11 P. M., pleased to find their former pastor so pleasantly situated.

1877, Aug. 1.—There was a union picnic of the Reformed and Methodist churches, by ten steam-cars and a steam-barge to the Raritan Beach Grove. There were no evening services during August.

1877, Dec. 16.—Collection for repairing the church, $85.91.

1877, Dec. 25.—The present pulpit Bible was presented by Miss Ann Bergen. Consistory vote that the former pulpit Bible, presented by Rev. Wm. L. Johnson, D. D., be deposited with the church records and relics at the parsonage.

1878, Jan. 27.—Mr. De Hart began a series of sermons to working men. Jan.—$479.50 were expended on furniture, which is to belong to the two western parlors of the parsonage.

1878, Feb. 7.—Temperance meeting in the Town Hall, all the pastors of the village were there.

1878, Easter Day.—Mr. De Hart had an appropriate sermon, morning and evening.

1878.—The anniversary of the Sunday School of the Reformed Church was held Sunday evening, June 9, in the church which was crowded with an interested audience. The pulpit was surrounded by bright and handsome flowers, whose fragrance filled the church. The singing by the children, under the direction of Mr. E. C. Carpenter, was excellent and reflected credit upon the leader. Miss Laura E. Brinckerhoff presided at the melodeon and aided the singing by her artistic and skillful performance. The addresses of the evening were made by the Rev. Mr. Lampman and Augustus Treadwell. After this the Rev. Mr. De Hart, in behalf of the school, presented to Abraham DeBevoise, its superintendent, a handsome ebony cane with a gold head. The report of the school was read by Wm. W. Treadwell, the secretary. Books were also presented the scholars. Miss Belle Carey presided at the organ and added much to the evening's entertainment by her agreeable, pleasant music.

1878, June 16.—While the Presbyterian church is being repaired, Consistory offer them the use of our church at any convenient hour on the Lord's Day; or invite them to join with us in a series of union services, as may be mutually agreed on. The Session thanked Consistory not only for their kind invitation but for the brotherly spirit evinced therein; and conclude to attend the ordinary Sunday services of the Reformed Church.

1878, July 18.—Picnic of the Sunday School to Oriental Grove.

1878, Sept. 15.—Collection for sufferers by yellow fever, $231.32.

1878, Oct. 27, Sunday evening.—A union temperance meeting in church.

1878, Nov. 28.—Thanksgiving observed in church. Union services. Rev. Mr. Lampman preached.

> 1878.—The officers of the Reformed Church have concluded to try and make their audience room more cheerful in the evening by placing three suspended double-coned reflectors in the places of the nameless ones that have been there for several years. Those removed never gave satisfaction, but for several reasons they were allowed to remain until the present time. There will be three reflectors, one in the centre of the ceiling, containing thirty-six jets; one over the pulpit, and one over the gallery, each with twelve jets. There will also be a smaller one in the vestibule. The work is being done by J. T. Lewis, and will be completed this week.—*L. I. Farmer*, Dec. 19.

1878, Dec. 3.—The officers of the Mite Society are Mrs. Aaron A. Degrauw, president; Mrs. S. L. Spader, vice-president; Mrs. C. H. Harris, secretary, and Mrs. Stephen Ryder, treasurer, with a visiting committee of ladies.

1878, Dec. 30.—Sunday school exercises in church. Address by Rev. J. A. Davis, of Brookville.

> The Reformed Church, of this village, was decked with Christmas greens on Sunday, December 29, and presented a beautiful sight. This was in anticipation of the Sunday School festival on Monday night. Some years ago such a sight would have given offence to some over sensitive people; but now it was received with good-will and pleasure. Time works great changes and this is the era of charity and christian fellowship. Mr. De

Bevoise, the superintendent of the school deserves and was accorded great praise for his labor, skill and taste in arranging the adornments in the church.—*L. I. Democrat*, Dec. 31, 1878.

1879, February 22.—The ladies' fair in the Consistory room on Saturday, owing to the storm was continued on Monday afternoon and evening. The proceeds ($150) are to be used for fitting up the Sunday School room.

1879.—The Communion Services in the churches of our village, Sunday, March 2, were of a peculiarly interesting character. For nearly two months the Reformed and Presbyterian Churches have nightly held Union prayer meetings under the care of the pastors, the Rev. Messrs. DeHart and Lampman. These meetings were closed last Friday evening. At the Reformed church nineteen persons united with the church—four on certificate and fifteen by profession of their faith.*—*L. I. Democrat*, March 4, 1879.

On Easter day at the Reformed Church an appropriate sermon was delivered by the Pastor, Rev. Wm. H. DeHart, from the 24th chapter of St. Luke, last clause 5th verse "Why seek ye the living among the dead." The congregation was full. The display of flowers was extensive and beautiful. The music by the choir, was appropriate to the occasion celebrated.—*L. I. Democrat*, April 15, 1879.

1879.—The anniversary exercises of the Reformed Sunday School were held on Sunday evening June 8. The church was trimmed with flowers and was well filled with the friends of the children. The singing was excellent, especially the song sung by the Infant Class. Short addresses were made by the Rev. Wm. H. Phraner, Rev. Mr. Lansing, of Mohawk, N. Y., and the Rev. W. H. DeHart which were interesting. A handsome book was presented to Mr. Isaac Amberman, from his scholars, as a testimonial of their kind regards towards him as their teacher. From the report read by the Secretary, the school seems to be in a prosperous condition. The exercises closed with a song entitled "Good Night," sung by the children of the school.

1879, February 5, Wednesday.—Rev. Mr. DeHart's donation party. Stormy and bad traveling. Receipts, $170 and other presents.

1879, May 30.—The Sunday Observance Society was formed.

---

* For the Communion there are four silver cups (goblet shaped), two of which it is said were presented by Mrs. James Foster. Two were purchased by the ladies, in Mr. Allger's pastorate. The tankard and four plates are of a baser metal. A baptismal bason in a closet under the pulpit was burned with the church in 1857.

1879, July 30.—Sunday School picnic to Oriental Grove.

1879.—A garden party under charge of the ladies of the Reformed Church, will take place at the Judd mansion and grounds, now owned by A. A. Degrauw, Jr., on Wednesday, October 1, afternoon and evening. Games of croquet, archery, &c., will be provided on the lawn which will be illuminated in the evening. Ice cream, lemonade and other refreshments will be served in the parlors of the mansion. Supper from 6 to 10. P. M.—Admission to the grounds, ten cents. If stormy, the party will occur the first fair day.

Our friends of the Reformed Church Sunday School are making some notable improvements in the Consistory room, on Union avenue, adding class rooms, painting the walls, putting two large windows on each side near the front of the building, and otherwise improving the building, both inside and out. Chairs are to occupy the place of the old wooden settees. The sessions of the school are held in the Church during the progress of the work. The cost of repairs was $1,200—*L. I. Democrat*, September 16, 1879.

1879, October 27.—Additional subscriptions for painting and repairing the Consistory Room.

Martin G. Johnson	$25	Nostrand & Remson	$10
Peter C. Hendrickson	25	Hendrick Lott	10
Stephen Ryder	10	Miss Phebe Hagner	5
Harman J. Stockholm	10	James Van Sielen	10
Rev. W. H. DeHart	25	James R. Fredericks	5
Isaac Amberman	25	Abm. Griffin	5
Cornelius K. Bailey	10	William C. Stoothoff	5
Charles H. Harris	10	John H. Brinckerhoff	10
Martin I. Duryea	10	George L. Brinckerhoff	5
Abraham DeBevoise	25	John Ryder	5
Ditmars Eldert	10	Isaac Snedeker	5
James C. Hendrickson	25	George L. Powell	5
Daniel Hendrickson	10	Susan Hendrickson	10
Thomas H. Fredericks	10	Phebe Lott	10
Miss Ann Bergen	10	Wm. S. Williamson	20
George Bennett	25	Total	$385

1879, December 30.—Christmas exercises by the scholars and teachers of the Sunday School, this evening. Speaking recitations, singing and distributing Christmas gifts.—All are welcome.

1879, December 31. Mr. DeHart, at the Watch-night services in the Methodist Church, preached from Psalms cxix, 59, 60.

1880, Jan. 6–10.—Week of prayer. The union services, (Tuesday evening in the Consistory room), were continued another week.

1880, Feb. 17.—Mr. De Hart lectured on "Water and the gases of which it is composed," for the benefit of the Methodist Church.

1880, April 20, Tuesday.—Classis met in the church and had their refection at the parsonage.

1880, Easter Day.—The pastor, Rev. Mr. De Hart gave an appropriate sermon. The pulpit was surrounded with beautiful potted flowers.* The choir under the leadership of Mr. James Phraner rendered a graceful Easter carol. In consequence of the storm the evening services were omitted.—*L. I. Democrat*, March 30.

REFORMED CHURCH.

1880, May 2.—The Rev. Mr. De Hart on Sunday May 2, announced to his congregation, that just three years had passed since he was called to be their pastor, and during that time 72 persons had united with the church, 26 members had been removed by death, and 4 dismissed; 34 persons had been baptised; he had officiated at 26 weddings and 40 funerals. During this time he had made more than 700 calls. There are 141 families connected with the church, and a membership of 287. He then took his text from II Corinthians, v, 20, "In Christ's stead." He said in substance: "when one man fails another is appointed to take his place. The Great Head of the church has appointed others to take up his work and carry it on, and the christian minister is to go to the *Book* as the only place containing the word of life for the instruction of his people; there the only way of salvation is made known. He does not stand in the pulpit to discuss the political aspects of the day, nor to tell men how to do their daily business. Christ preached against the sins of the people, so must the minister, he is to preach 'In Christ's stead,' and in doing so he preaches with authority, and here is where the pulpit differs from the platform, the latter being only the authority of men. It is also the duty of the people to hear, and to ascertain by searching the Word, if the preacher is really preaching 'In Christ's stead.'" At the close of the sermon the pastor said his heart over-flowed with gratitude and thanksgiving for spiritual and temporal blessings he had enjoyed during his

---

* Flowers (it is said) were first displayed on the pulpit, Nov. 6, 1870.

pastorate, and asked forgiveness for anything he had said or done where men differed; but not for any word spoken in Christ's stead, as his minister and in his name, and hoped that the blessings of the past would continue in the future. L.

1880, The Sunday School connected with the Reformed Church, held its anniversary, Sunday evening, June 13. The church was more than crowded, and a large number were unable to obtain admittance. Mr. J. B. Everitt, gratuitously loaned the use of his camp stools, but even then all were not seated. The exercises consisting of speaking, singing and the presentation of books, were of an interesting character. From the report of the Secretary, the school is now in a prosperous condition, Mr. E. C. Carpenter, the school's musical director,* deserves credit for the musical part of the programme. Addresses were made by the pastor of the church, Rev. William H. De Hart, and others. Miss Laura E. Brinckerhoff presided at the organ.—*Democrat*.

1880, July 21.—The Sunday School joined with that of East Jamaica in a picnic to Harbor Hill.

1880, October 19.—The funeral of Rev. Julius Hones was held in church, services in English and German.†

1880, December 29.—Sunday School festival in the Consistory Room.

1881, Jan. 4.—Week of prayer. Union services, Friday and Saturday in the Consistory room.

1881.—The ladies of the Reformed Church, Jamaica, will hold a festival and bazaar for the benefit of the Sunday School connected with said church, in the Town Hall, on Monday evening, Feb. 21, 1881, and Tuesday afternoon and evening, Feb. 22, when a large variety of useful and fancy articles, confectionery and fruits of various kinds will be offered for sale. Also lemonade and ice cream of all flavors. A bountiful supper will be provided for all who may give them a call. Supper fifty cents; admission, ten cents. Profits, $260.

1881.—WELL ATTENDED.—We learn that the praise meeting held in the Reformed Church, this village, Sunday evening, Feb. 20, was well attended and interesting in every respect.—*L. I. Democrat*, Feb. 22.

---

* Among the choristers were: Thomas Bradler, 1839; Abraham Duryea and John C. Metcalf 1853; Lendall F. Pratt, 1857; James Heurte Young, 1860; William Tillinghast 1871; William L. Tomlins, 1872; S. H. Newbury, 1875; E. C. Carpenter, 1877; Richard H. Baggot, 1879; William F. Wyckoff, 1882.

† 1881, March 1.—Rev. Henry Frech was called to be pastor of St. Paul's German Reformed Church.

1881, Easter Day.—The interior of the Reformed Church, was most splendidly decorated with flowers and evergreens, a memento for the Easter exercises. The pastor, Rev. Wm. H. De Hart, preached an able sermon.—*L. I. Democrat*, April 19.

1881.—Last Sunday being Pentecost or Whit Sunday, the attendance at our several places of worship was larger than usual, for the day was bright and cheery. In the Reformed Church the Lord's Supper was celebrated and three persons added to the communion. At the preparatory services on Saturday four infants, first borns, were christened, and on Sunday, before the administration of the Sacrament, two persons were baptized.—*L. I. Democrat*, June 7.

1881.—As Sunday evening, June 12, was a most delightful and pleasant one, the people from this village and also from abroad vizited the Reformed Sunday School anniversary, in large numbers. Long before the time to commence, the church was crowded with people; many being compelled to stand in the aisles and at the back part of the church unable to obtain a seat. The vestibule was also crowded with anxious ones looking in vain for a seat. Nearly everybody late visited the gallery but returned as there were no vacant seats to be found, even there. The Rev. Lewis Lampman, of the Presbyterian Church, filled the place of the pastor, Rev. Mr. De Hart, who was detained home through illness. He made a short opening address and then the Rev. Thos. Stephenson, of the Methodist Episcopal Church, made a fervent prayer. The singing by the school was delightful, under the training of Miss Jennie Spader, who also lead the singing. Miss Laura E. Brinckerhoff presiding at the organ, brought out some sweet music to sing by. Miss Fannie Ryder sang a solo, entitled "He leadeth me home." Mr. Lampman then introduced the Rev. Mr. Stephenson who made an able and appropriate address to both old and young. The secretary, Mr. Wm. W. Treadwell, read the annual report which showed the school to be in a prosperous condition, with 162 scholars and teachers, and a balance of over $200 in the treasury, over all expenses. The report showed that two of the members have been present during every session of the year. The school may well feel proud of their leader (the superintendent) Mr. Abraham De Bevoise, who always has and yet takes a great interest in the welfare of the smaller ones. After a short address by the Rev. Mr. Lampman, who spoke especially to the boys, on "Dogs." "Boys, I once owned a dog," said he, "but finding that he was a thief, a liar, and a murderer, I was compelled to kill him." The little boys seemed to pay a strict attention to all that was said concerning "the dogs." Next came the distribution of books to the scholars and teachers. Mrs. Chas. H. Harris was surprised by her scholars and presented with two beautifully bound and printed volumes entitled "Life and Works of Christ," by Dr. C. Geikie, as a slight token of their appreciation of her services as a teacher. The floral display was grand, not only just around the pulpit, but all around the church, were hung handsome baskets of choice plants, which filled the building with rich perfume. On each side of the pulpit was placed a handsome cross and an anchor, made of flowers. Camp stools were placed in the aisles and given to those wishing to change their position, a short time after the services commenced, by the sexton, Mr. Benjamin F. Everitt.—*L. I. Democrat.*

1881.—The largest excursion from Jamaica this season, was that of the Reformed Sunday School, on Wednesday August 10 to Starin's Glen Island. Six passenger cars, all well filled, left the depot in this village for Hunter's Point, where the commodious barge "Arthur" lay in wait to convey the excursionists to their destination. Glen Island reached, the children found many things to amuse themselves with, while the older ones roamed about finding pleasure on every hand. The committee in charge deserves much credit for the manner in which everything passed off. We learn that 800 tickets were sold and about $85 was cleared over and above expenses. The sail down the bay was delightful.—*L. I. Democrat,* Aug. 16, 1881.

1881.—Thursday, September 8, by authority of the Governor's proclamation, was observed as a day of prayer for President Garfield's recovery from his wounds. In the evening a union service was held in the Consistory room, which was largely attended.

1881, Sept. 26, Monday.—Mr. De Hart spoke in the Presbyterian Church, which was draped in mourning on the occasion of President Garfield's death.

1881, Nov. 24.—Thanksgiving Day was appropriately celebrated in our village. Union services were held in the Reformed Church in the morning, in which the members of the Methodist, Reformed and Presbyterian congregations united. The Rev. Messrs. De Hart, Lampman and Stevenson took part in the services. The sermon preached by the Rev. Mr. Lampman, was an earnest, able and practical one. The collection taken up was for the benefit of the Howard (colored) Orphan Asylum, of Brooklyn.

1881, Dec. 28.—The children of the Sunday School had a Christmas tree and games in the Consistory room, and baskets of candies to carry home.

1882, Jan. 1-7.—The Presbyterian, Reformed and Methodist Churches of the village observed the week of prayer by union services. During the week two prayer meetings were held in the lecture room of each church, the pastors leading them in turn. The exercises were interesting, and the attendance good. On Sunday evening the three churches celebrated the Lord's Supper together, in the Reformed Church, and although the evening was very unpleasant there was a good attendance. The opening exercises were conducted by Rev. Lewis Lampman. Rev. Thos. Stephenson addressed the congregation. He referred to the pleasant circumstances under which they met as brethren in Christ; that although differing in some matters, yet they were showing to the world their virtual unity by coming together at the Lord's table. In closing he spoke briefly of the nature of the service in which they were about to engage. Rev. W. H. De Hart administered the bread. Before doing so, he read a portion of the Liturgy of the Reformed Church, the congregation uniting in repeating the Apostles' Creed. Rev. Lewis Lampman administered the wine, and delivered the closing address. The officers of the churches assisted in the distribution of the elements, four officers having been selected from each church for the performance of this duty.—*L. I. Democrat*, Jan. 10, 1882.

1882, Jan. 8, Sunday morning.—Anniversary of the Missionary Society of the Reformed Church, Mr. De Hart preached on missions.

1882, Jan. 12.—CLASSICAL VISITATIONS.—The first of a series of visitations by committees from the North Classis of Long Island to the churches connected with that body, was made to the Reformed Church of our village, on Tuesday evening, January 10. The visiting committee consisted of Rev. Charles J. Shepard and Elder H. S. Vanderveer, of Newtown, and Rev. James B. Wilson, of Jericho. The audience was large, considering the unpleasant evening, and the services were deeply interesting. Rev. William H. Phraner offered the invocation, and Rev. Andrew Hageman, of Queens, the prayer. Rev's. Wilson and Shepard delivered earnest and impressive addresses, which were listened to with close attention by the congregation.—*L. I. Farmer*.

1882, Feb. 2.—Rev. Wm. E. Griffis, of Schenectady gave a lecture in the Consistory room, entitled : "The Dutch have taken Holland."

1882.—On Wednesday evening, March 1, in spite of the bad weather, a large company of the congregation and friends of the Rev. W. H. De Hart made him their annual visit. A very enjoyable evening was spent. Besides hearty congratulations and expressions of good will, the faithful pastor received various tokens of esteem, together with about $230 in money, to which will doubtless be added the remembrances of many prevented by the weather and other circumstances from attending.—*L. I. Democrat.*

1882, May 2 and 3.—Particular Synod met in church, forty or fifty delegates present.* Rev. David Cole, D. D., preached, Tuesday evening; and on Wednesday P. M. the sacrament of the Lord's Supper was celebrated.

1882, June 11.—Anniversary of the Sunday School, in church. Addresses by Rev. Mr. Williams, of Jamaica, and Jeremiah Johnson, of Brooklyn. There was a profusion of floral decorations. Each scholar received a prize book.

1882, June 25, Sunday evening.—Anniversary of Sunday Observance Society, was held in church. Union services. Rev. Messrs. Williams, Lampman and D. Hart spoke. Singing by the united choirs.

1882, July 20.—Sunday School picnic to Glen Island Grove. Music, ice cream and other refreshments on the barge. Six hundred persons went; $100 cleared.

1882, Nov. 22.—A very pleasant and agreeable evening was spent at the recent visit of the congregation and friends of Rev. Wm. H. De Hart, pastor of the Reformed Church, on Wednesday evening, November 22. As a token of regard for the pastor, donations of about $300 were presented him.—*L. I. Democrat.*

1882, Nov. 30.—Thanksgiving.

On Sunday last, six new members were added to the Reformed Church. A children's service will be held on the afternoon of the first Sunday in each month, at the Reformed Church. At such times the ordinary evening services will be omitted.—*Jamaica Standard*, Dec. 9.

The Reformed Sunday School will hold their Christmas festival in the Consistory room, on the evening of Wednesday, December 27.—*L. I. Democrat.*

1883, Jan. 7-14.—The week of prayer which began yesterday is one of the marked evidences of the progress and unity of the Christian faith. Its first general observance began in 1860, and was proposed by a Presbyterian Missionary in India. Since then, the week of prayer is an event looked for with deep interest in every land upon the face of the globe, where the Christian religion has a foothold. Originally started for the purpose of interesting Christians in the heathen lands, it has developed into a most successful agency of destroying sectarianism, and binding in closer union all who believe in the Christian religion. The week fol-

---

* Alonzo B. Pettit served eighty-five meals to the members of Synod at 50 cents each.

lowing the first Sunday in January, summons the whole Christian family to one common altar of prayer. Services will be held this evening in the Presbyterian lecture room, on Wednesday and Thursday evenings in the Consistory room, and on Friday and Saturday evenings in the Methodist lecture room.—*L. I. Democrat.*

1883, Feb. 6.—The Rev. W. H. De Hart is delivering on Tuesday evenings, in the Consistory room, a course of lectures on "Bible Lands," illustrated by colored diagrams. The subject for this evening is " Egypt and the Bible."—*L. I. Democrat.*

1883.—The ladies of the Reformed Church of Jamaica, will hold a bazaar in the Town Hall, on Wednesday afternoon and evening, February 21, and on Thursday afternoon and evening, February 22. When a variety of useful and fancy articles, fruits and confectionery of various kinds, will be offered for sale. Also lemonade and ice cream of all flavors. A bountiful supper will be provided for all who may favor us with a call. Supper, 50 cents; admission, 10 cents.—*L. I. Democrat.*

1883.—The fair or bazaar of the Reformed Church held at the Town Hall, on Wednesday and Thursday last was one of the most successful ever held in the village. The ice grotto where lemonade was sold, presented a very pretty appearance, imitating ice and snow with great fidelity. The "Old Lady who Lived in a Shoe," was well represented. The "Japanese Tea Party," where the pretty cups and saucers were sold with the cup of tea, was a new idea to us. Among the prettiest articles at the tables was a banner painted by Miss Maggie Fleury. A beautiful banner, contributed by Mrs. Van Wickel was purchased and given to the Rev. Mr. De Hart. A pair of panel pictures on plush by the same lady, was purchased and presented to Mr. Abraham De Bevoise, the Superintendent of the Sunday School. The chair made of polished horns, the property of Mr. Stephen Ryder, was on exhibition, but was not for sale. The ice cream department was waited upon by ladies in Quaker dresses. There were no lotteries, drawings or chance games. Everything was sold at reasonable prices. In place of the usual "grab bag" a "bran pie" was substituted, in which small articles were imbedded in bran, and for a trifling fee were fished out by the customers. The confectionery stand was well patronized, and added materially to the profits of the fair. The recipe and cook book, "Mites of Help," containing valuable and original recipes, brought in $278.36. The gross receipts were $1,078.25. Expenses $224.05, leaving a net profit of $854.20, with some books remaining to be sold.—*L. I. Democrat.*

1883, March 25, Easter Day.—At the Reformed Church, there was a large display of cut and potted flowers. The attendance was good, and the Pastor, Rev. Wm. H. De Hart preached a sermon appropriate to

Easter. The singing was a prominent feature. Miss Jennie Spader sang a solo.—*L. I. Democrat.*

1883, April 11.—Miss Ann Bergen paid $285.50, a donation, for cost of horse sheds in rear of the Consistory room.

1883.—The anniversary exercises of the Reformed Sunday School, took place at the church on Sunday evening, June 17. The singing by the school was excellent. The address of the evening was made by the Rev. Mr. De Hart, his subject being "Light," which he illustrated by candles of various sizes, explaining how one candle couldn't give more light than another, also showing various objects which obstructed light and darkened men's minds, such as a whiskey bottle, trade dollar, etc. The church was tastefully decorated with flowers, and the exercises listened to by a crowded house. $15.84 was collected.—*L. I. Democrat.*

1883, July 24.—Rev. Mr. De Hart preached his ante-vacation sermon last Sunday. He goes to Pennsylvania. During August the church is to be closed for repairs. It is to be painted and a new carpet added.

1883.—On Sunday, September 2, the Reformed Church was opened for the first time since it had been cleaned, carpeted and renovated. Rev. Mr. De Hart celebrated the communion and five members were added to the church. A new and elegant pulpit,* of solid black-walnut, the affectionate gift of bereaved parents, has superseded the old one, bearing the inscription:

"In Memoriam,

MORRIS FOSDICK DEGRAUW."

The platform was tastefully decorated with flowers. On the stand beside the minister was a beautiful cross made up also of flowers. The pews have been carpeted and painted of a darker color and are much improved in appearance. The carpet is of comely and pleasing pattern and in keeping with the grave simplicity of the church. A burglar alarm has also been introduced.—*L. I. Democrat.*

---

*This memorial pulpit was presented to the church by Mr. and Mrs. Aaron A. Degrauw. The cornice is richly carved with a series of Gothic arches filled in with the ivy vine, under which runs a row of knobs. The cornice is supported in front by coupled columns with carved capitals, standing in the corners. At either end of In Memoriam is the Trinity leaf. The centre panel is elaborately carved, with Alpha and Omega, the first and last letters of the Greek alphabet, (see Rev. xxii; 13) intertwined with the Passion flower vine full of open and half open blossoms. The spandrils of the arch are filled with foliage. The arch itself is filled at intervals with carved ball flowers. The base is heavily moulded to agree with the projection of the cornice. On a brass plate inserted in the top of the pulpit is the following inscription:

In memory of
Morris Fosdick Degrauw,
Son of Aaron A. and Mary E. S. Degrauw,
Died, January 25th, 1878.
Aged 10 years.

The four hundreth Lutheran anniversary was observed on Sunday in the Reformed Church. On the pulpit was a profusion of flowers and a picture of the great Reformer. Rev. Mr. De Hart gave an outline of Luther's life and labors, which was listened to with marked attention. One of Luther's noble hymns was sung. In the evening there was a union meeting of the Germans and Dutch in the Reformed Church, when both pastors officiated to an audience that would have been larger but for the stormy weather.—*L. I. Democrat*, Nov. 13, 1883.

1884, Jan. 7-12.—The week of prayer, will be observed by the Presbyterian, Reformed, and Methodist Churches. Last evening the first meeting was held in the lecture room of the Methodist Church, and the meeting this evening will be held in the same place. To-morrow and Thursday evening the services will be held in the Presbyterian lecture room. On Friday and Saturday evenings, in the Consistory room. Services commence at half-past seven. The services will be under the direction of the Pastors of the three churches represented.—*L. I. Democrat*.

1884, March 12.—A Young Men's Association was formed.

1884.—The anniversary of the Sunday School connected with the Reformed Church, was held on Sunday evening, June 8. The church was crowded and the exercises listened to with much interest. The singing of the school was excellent, and showed careful training. The duet by Misses Nellie and Jennie Spader and solo by Carrie Everitt were well rendered. Addresses were delivered by Rev. Mr. Lampman, and the pastor, Rev. Mr. De Hart. The report of the secretary showed the school to be in good condition, financially as well as in membership.—*L. I. Farmer*.

1884, June 8.—Collection for the Sunday School, $44.10.

1884, Aug. 7.—The new building now being erected at East Jamaica, for the Reformed Sunday School, is enclosed and rapidly nearing completion.* It will have a seating capacity for 450 people, and will cost about $2,500. Horse sheds have been built in the rear of the grounds, and post holes begun for a handsome picket fence around the entire plot. It will be completed and ready for services, in November.—*L. I. Farmer*.

Rev. Wm. H. De Hart preached a discourse on the Third Commandment last Sunday evening. Mr. De Hart has undertaken a very interesting

---

* Thos. T. and Josephine Husson (April 22, 1884), for one dollar, conveyed to the Reformed Church, a lot 50 by 100 feet, for a Sunday School.—*Queens County Records*, book 633, 73.

series of discourses on the Commandments and has ably illustrated those which he has already given.—*L. I. Farmer*, Oct. 2, 1884.

1884, Oct. 1.—Married in church in presence of a large assembly (among whom were the Rev. Messrs. Stocking and Rice) by the Rev. Wm. H. De Hart, Wm. F. Wyckoff, chorister, to Nellie Spader, organist. The ushers were J. L. Wyckoff, E. E. Dayton, A. G. Henderson and J. H. J. Stewart. As the newly married couple were returning down the aisle flowers were showered upon them from the gallery. They passed from the door to their carriage on the east side of the church over a carpet and under an awning.

The ladies of the East Jamaica Sunday School will hold a pink bazaar and festival, at the new school building, East Jamaica, on Wednesday, October 8th, afternoon and evening. There will be for sale fancy goods, useful and ornamental; ice cream and refreshments of all kinds. Supper, 50 cents; admission, 10 cents. Conveyances will leave this village, corner of Fulton street and Union avenue (Beers & Cornell's), at 3, 5 and 7 o'clock P. M.; returning, leave 4.30, 6.30 and 9.30 o'clock P. M. If the weather on the above date should prove stormy, the festival will be continued the next day. Proceeds for the benefit of the school. $410.50 were realized.—*L. I. Farmer*.

1884.— A Quaker tea party will be given by the "Steady Gleaners," of the Reformed Church on the evening of Thursday, October 16, in the Sunday School room. Over $70 were realized.

Names (not elsewhere mentioned) of those who have been pew-holders for a longer or shorter time since 1851.

Abrams, David.	Cobleigh, Daniel.	Foster, Wm. A.
Adrain, Margaret.	Cortelyou, Mrs.	Gilbert, Dr. C. E.
Allen, John.	Creed, B. Hendrickson.	Gillet, Mrs.
Allen, Wm.	Davis, Wm. D.	Gunter, Mr. H. H.
Badger, A. H.	Decker, Lucas E.	Hall, Mrs.
Beach, J. M.	Dellert, George	Hannas, Andrew J.
Bergen, David.	Douglass, Burdett.	Hardcastle, Lewis.
Bergen, G. S.	Durland, Smith.	Hasbrouck, Jared.
Briggs, Jeremiah.	Doughty, Benj. W.	Hendrickson, Smith
Brinckerhoff, John L.	Duryea, Jacob M.	Herricks, Wm.
Brush, Wm. T.	Eldert, J. H.	Hoople, Wm. H.
Campbell, John A.	Everitt, Conrad	Hoyt, George
Carpenter, John.	Elmore, James H.	Hyatt, Thos. D.
Champlin, Mrs. Julia A.	Foote, Mr.	Jenkins, Mrs.

---

* "The form for the confirmation of marriage before the church," as given in our Liturgy is not binding on the minister. By request of the bride, Mr. Alliger, June 18, 1867, at the marriage in church of Charles H. Harris and Florence Hall, used "The form of solemnization of matrimony," contained in the Book of Common Prayer. Mr. De Hart used the form drawn up by Rev. Dr. Bethune.

FIRST REFORMED DUTCH CHURCH.

Kendrick, Wm.
Keteltas, Mrs. Rebecca.
Ketcham, E. B.
Kissam, Dr. Geo. C.
Kolyer, John D.
Lawrence, Thos.
Lott, Dow S.
Lott, James H.
Loudon, George
Loux, A. J.
Lowe, Beauman,
Lowerre, Sam. W.
Marshall, George.
Mills, Jesse.
Miller, Jacob.
Miller, Thomas.
Miller, Sarah.
Miller, Misses.
Monfort, John.
Monfort, Henry A.
Morris, Mrs. E. K.
Nostrand, George.
Nostrand, John W.
Nichols, Lemuel.
Noyes, O. H. P.
Quinby, Daniel O.
Pettit, Theodore H.
Powell, Mrs. John
Powell, Mrs. Samuel.
Powell, Mrs. Joseph.
Reeve, Jeduthan.
Reeve, David S.
Roe, Henry [his sons].
Ryder, James.*
Schaeffer, Mrs.
Sealey, Samuel J.
Simonson, D. H.
Smith, Geo. R.
Smith, Abm. H.
Spader, John L.
Sneleker, George.
Starr, Henry W.
Stebbins, Horatio N.
Stimpson, Mr.
Story, Henry.
Sturdevant, John J.
Suydam, Hendrick.
Sweet, Nathaniel*
Talmage, D. M.
Terry, Mr.
Thompson, Mr.
Tompkins, Thos.
Tompkins, Mrs. Hannah
Tyson, Stephen.
Van Brunt, Tunis.
Van Dergaw, Cornelius.
Van Gaasbeek, J. H. J.
Van Rensselaer, Mrs.
Van Sielen, Ditmars.
Van Wicklen, Garret.
Waldo, Lewis T.
Weart, Mrs.
Whitehead, Mrs.
Whitson, I. Youngs.
Whitson, Mrs.
Williamson, Stephen.
Williamson, Wm. T.
Williamson, Peter S.
Wyckoff, Rev. Jacob S.

The present order of worship in the Reformed Church:

Prelude on the organ, as the minister enters.
Invocation.
Salutation.†
Reading the Ten Commandments.
The choir chant: "Lord, have mercy upon us, and write all these Thy laws in our hearts, we beseech Thee."
Reading first Scripture Lesson.
The choir sing: "Glory be to the Father, and to the Son, and to the Holy Ghost; as it was in the beginning, is now, and ever shall be; world without end; Amen, Amen.
Reading second Scripture Lesson.
Singing by the congregation.
Prayer before sermon.
Singing by the congregation.
Sermon.
Prayer after sermon.
Collection.
Singing and Doxology by the congregation.
Benediction.
Postlude on the organ.

* James (not John) Ryder and Nathaniel Sweet bought their pews, October, 12, 1859.
† The salutation is sometimes omitted.

ADDITIONAL.

At the burning of the church (page 117) the Domine was in the belfry doing his best with pails of water, carried up the steeple stairs by the boys. The bell rang till the last moment, when it fell with a crash into the basement, where it was found all melted.

The laying of the corner-stone (page 122) consisted in putting a zinc box with its contents in a hole, ten inches square and six inches deep, hewed out of the stone, and then a slab laid over it; after which a heavy stone was laid on that. The brick walls were about four feet above the stone foundation. There was a large gathering of ladies, mostly, who sat on seats arranged over a floor of loose boards. A stage was erected for the speakers, with a canvas covering, under which sat the ministers, Consistory and building committee. The choir sat on a bench by the stage, and sang first: "Let Zion and her sons rejoice," and at the close of the addresses sang: "Behold the sure foundation Stone."

1859, Oct. 16.—On the Sunday after the sale of the pews, it was interesting to see the people seeking to find their new seats. The Domine's text was: "They [the brethren] came to meet us as far as Appii Forum."

The new bell, costing about $500, was brought from New York on a cart with apparatus to hoist it to its place. It was suspended from a frame screwed to the floor so as not to shake the tower. It tolled for the first time on Sunday, September 4, 1859, at the funeral of Wm. H. Stoothoff, a lad who lost his life by a fall in his father's barn.

1871, Feb. 22. Consistory agree to adopt the "Hymns of the Church." When it was first introduced (April 9) it was intended that the choir should come down stairs and spread themselves among the people and so have congregational singing. The change had no success.

On page 29, for "two ministers" read "the new minister;" and on page 120, for "Wardens," read "Trustees."

FIRST REFORMED DUTCH CHURCH.

SUBSCRIBERS' NAMES FOR A HALF YEAR'S SALARY TO DOMINE SCHOONMAKER. 1830.

	£	s.		£	s.
Abm. Hendrickson	1	4	George Lowden		4
James Hendrickson	1	8	John Oakley		12
Daniel Hendrickson		8	Abm. Golder		4
Aury Remsen, Sr.,		16	David Abrahams		6
John Bennet, weaver		8	Rem Remsen		6
Wm. Hendrickson		4	Thomas Brush		—
John J. Bennet		12	William Martin		2
Bernardus Bennet, Sr		8	George Bennet		4
Bernardus Bennet, Jr		6	John Rhodes, blacksmith		4
James Bogart		8	Ruth Golder		3
Ann Bergen		5	John D. Ditmis		16
Gilbert S. Bergen		4	Isaac Bennet's widow		4
Lucas Bergen		4	Mr. Benson		16
Widow Higbie		4	John Wiggins		4
Melancton Carpenter		4	Remsen Golder		2
Nicholas Wyckoff	1	4	John Golder		3
Oldfield Bergen		8	Charles Fosdick		4
Timothy Rhodes		12	Wait S. Everitt		16
Benj'n Rhodes		12	Cornelius Amberman		3
Mrs. Cortelyou		8	Hendrick Hendrickson		4
John Hegeman		10	John Remsen		4
Nelly Hegeman		2	Nathaniel Nostrand		6
Derick Remsen		8	Rem Nostrand		6
George Rhodes		4	Stephen Mills		4
Abm. D. Remsen		4	Abm. Hendrickson		8
John Van Nostrand		12	Margretie Smith		2
John S. Van Nostrand		4	John W. Messenger		8

Early in 1832, when the church was becoming too small to seat the increasing congregation comfortably, a meeting was called to consider the propriety of erecting a new edifice, its size, location, &c., and papers were put in circulation to see what encouragement there would be to the undertaking. Most of these papers are now lost. The subscription money went toward the purchase of a pew, and if over the appraised value, it was accounted as a donation to the church. Contributions were made by some whose names do not appear as pew holders, viz: Chas. Fosdick, $10; Catharine Hoogland, $5; Ann Hackett, $4; Margaret Hendrickson, milliner, $25; John Jones, $5; Mrs. Simonson, $15; John Wiggins, $13; Isaac Skirm, $5. Other names are on the records, as Mrs. Corrie, James H. Lodge, Samuel Powell, Abm. D. Snedeker, John Simonson, county clerk; Daniel Smith, Henry and Aury Van Arsdale, Wm. Rhodes, Frederick Smith, Johannes Wyckoff's heirs, Capt Cornelius

Eldert, Mrs. Harmpe Conklin, Aletta Brinckerhoff. In 1841, Henry Roe took Mrs. Van Lew's seat and in 1844, Mr. Hurry took Peter P. Larremore's seat. On page 95, Colden and Peter Bartow should be Peter Coleman Bartow; and on page 153, December 26, should be Feb. 26.

Leonard Cooper, of Booklyn, was paid $15 for a plan and specification of the church.

When the old church was taken down, the materials were sold at auction in 128 lots named variously, lumber, timber, boards, shingles, plates, posts, sills, roof, stairs, doors, pews, shutters, sashes, box, iron, hinges, stove pipe, hooks, nails, &c. The sounding board sold for $43\frac{3}{4}$ cts.; the communion table for 75 cents; the four poplar trees for 50 cents each; the bell axle, 6 cents. The bell was sold to Meneely and $390 paid for a new one. Nothing is said of the vane.

As the old church was repaired at different times, alterations were made. The bell-rope was carried from the centre to the west side of the church. The benches of 1785, were superseded by pews as the congregation increased.

The children have destroyed so many of their fathers' Dutch books that we can hardly guess what their reading consisted in. Doubtless they had but few books, and those mostly religious. Newspapers must have been scarce indeed, for none were printed in New York before 1725, and that weekly.

SUBSCRIPTION LIST FOR 1857, A HALF YEAR'S SALARY.*

Wait S. Everitt	$3 50	Widow Gretie Smith	50
Cornelius Amberman	1 00	George Nostrand	50
James Hendrickson	6 00	Henry Simonson	1 00
Dow I. Ditmis	1 50	Widow Sarah Bennet	50
John I. Bennet	3 00	Widow Remsen	50
Bernardus Bennet, Jr	1 50	Jeffrey Smith	50
John Rhodes	75	Wm. Golder	50
Aury Remsen, Sr	3 00	Sarah Skinner	25
Aury Remsen, Jr	1 00	Daniel Smith	1 00
John Remsen	1 00	Hendrick Hendrickson	1 00
Daniel Hendrickson	2 50	Abm. Hendrickson	50
William Hendrickson	1 00	James S. Remsen	50
John Bennet, Sr.	2 00	Oldfield Hendrickson	50
Abm. Hendrickson, Sr	3 00	Remsen Bennet	—
Hendrick A. Hendrickson	1 00	Cornelius Bennet	25
Nathaniel Nostrand	1 50	Henry Story	10 00
Rem Nostrand	1 50	Sarah Ann Bennet	50
Stephen Mills	1 00	Steven Nostrand	50
Abm. B. Hendrickson	3 60	John Bennet, Plains	50
The rest torn off.			

* The pews (1844) were not sold subject to a tax, but the Minister's salary was raised by voluntary contributions.

APPENDIX.

APPENDIX.

THE VILLAGE SUNDAY SCHOOL.

When the Village Sunday School was commenced is not known. The minute book begins July 10, 1831. The Rev. John Mulligan, principal of Union Hall Academy, opened the session with prayer. There were present seven male and seven female teachers, twenty-eight male and twenty-two female scholars.

Isaac Simonson seems to have become superintendent December, 1832, and ended his services December 29, 1833. Henry Onderdonk, Jr. was superintendent from June 15, 1834, to October 5, 1834. After this it is probable the school was suspended for a time. When it was resumed James D. Ditmars became superintendent. He was succeeded by William Phraner, who occupied the position until his death in the fall of 1873. January 15, 1874, Abraham DeBevoise was chosen to take charge of the school and has occupied his position until the present time.

The school first held its sessions in the old octagon church, afterward in the basement of the new church. After that building was destroyed by fire, the present Consistory Room was erected, and the school has been held there since.

The Consistory Room was built on Union avenue, upon ground donated by the owners, Richard Brush and John A. King. February 28, 1858, Richard Brush, John T. Waters, John N. Brinckerhoff, Isaac Amberman and Stephen L. Spader were appointed by the Consistory as the building committee. Under their supervision the building was soon completed.

In the Spring of 1871, about five hundred dollars were expended in making the room more convenient for the Sunday

School. Besides other improvements, the gallery was extended and furnished with glass doors in front, so that it might be used for the infant class; a new book case was provided for the library, and a portion of the room under the gallery was partitioned off by a railing for the use of the librarians. In the fall of 1879, the room was still further improved at a cost of about twelve hundred dollars. A cornice was put around the walls of the room, the walls and wood-work were newly painted, the library was removed from the front to the rear of the room, under the gallery on either side of the entrance a Bible class room was made with sliding-doors between each and the main room, all the rooms were carpeted, chairs took the place of wooden settees, cornices and lambrequins were placed over the windows, the pulpit platform was lowered and a new walnut desk purchased. These and other improvements gave a beautiful and comfortable room, not only well adapted for the accommodation of the school, but for other purposes for which it was desired to use it.

Collections are taken in the classes every Sunday. These are gathered quarterly. One-half of them are for the expenses of the School, and the other half are divided between the four Boards of our church—Foreign Missions, Domestic Missions, Education, and Publication. For instance, the collections for one quarter are for the Board of Foreign Missions, the next quarter for the school, the next for the Board of Domestic Missions, the next for the School, &c.

The International series of lessons are studied. In addition to these, as a Catechism, "the Compendium of the Christian Religion" is taught. On the latter the Pastor examines the scholars the last Sunday of each month. Just before the anniversary in the Spring, those scholars who present themselves, are examined separately on all the lessons of the International series studied from the first of the previous October. Those who pass this examination receive an extra reward at the anniversary.

The following officers were chosen at the annual meeting, held January, 1884: For Superintendent, Abraham DeBevoise;

Assistant Superintendent, Isaac Amberman; Secretary, David L. Hardenbrook; Assistant Secretary, J. Elmer Ryder; Librarian, Charles C. DeBevoise; Assistant Librarians, Aaron A. Degrauw, Jr., William W. Treadwell, William E. Remsen; Treasurer, Stephen Ryder.

There are connected with the school, officers and teachers, 28; scholars, 128; total, 156.

EAST JAMAICA SUNDAY SCHOOL.

An application was made, April 17, 1869, to the Consistory for the establishment of a Sunday School at East Jamaica. The following persons were appointed as a committee to organize the school: Rev. J. B. Alliger, Abraham DeBevoise, Horatio N. Stebbins and George L. Powell.

The school was organized April 18, 1869, with the following officers: Superintendent, Abraham DeBevoise; Secretary, William Kirby; Treasurer, Francis Lott. May 23, Alfred M. Morrell was elected Librarian. July 11, William Kirby was made Assistant Superintendent, and George L. Powell Secretary in his place. Besides these officers there were connected with the school at its beginning the following teachers: Mrs. Van Allen, Lydia Rapelye, Catharine Lott, Charles J. DeBevoise, Oakley Ketcham, Harman J. Stockholm.

Abraham DeBevoise continued Superintendent for about two years when he was succeeded by George L. Powell. The latter held the office until 1873. William Kirby succeeded him and remained in the office for three years. After this George L. Powell was again elected and still continues as Superintendent.

The officers of the school at present are: Superintendent, George L. Powell; Assistant Superintendent, Abraham J. DeBevoise; Secretary, Charles T. DeBevoise; Librarian, Samuel Colton; Assistant Librarian, Charles Stockholm; Treasurer, Daniel H. Carpenter. The school numbers, officers and teachers, 16; scholars, 52.

The first anniversary of the school was held in the church April 10, 1870. The second was held in the same place April 2, 1871. The other anniversaries have been held in the public school house, where the school met until Dec. 7, 1884.

The school was called a Union School, but as it had been organized under the direction of the Consistory of the church, and as with a few exceptions those connected with it belonged to either the Reformed Church at Queens or to our own church, at a joint meeting of a committee of the school and the Consistory of the church, held March 17, 1884, the following resolution was adopted :

Resolved, That the Consistory propose to the East Jamaica Union Sunday School to take it under our care, and to receive it as one of the Sunday schools of our church, provided the officers and teachers of said school agree to such an arrangement.

The officers and teachers accepted the proposition, and at a meeting of the Consistory held March 26, 1884, the school was formally received under the care of the Consistory, its name to be, "The East Jamaica Sunday School of the First Reformed Church of Jamaica."

It being desirable to have a building especially adapted to the use of the school and other religious purposes, it was determined to erect a chapel. Mr. Thomas T. Husson donated to the Consistory for the purpose a lot of ground fifty by one hundred feet, to which he afterward added the gift of a bell for the tower of the building. The school had accumulated a building fund of about five hundred dollars, to which were added subscriptions from friends sufficient to warrant the commencement of the chapel. Abraham J. DeBevoise, Samuel G. Cozine and Samuel Colton were appointed the building committee. The contract was awarded to Francis F. Gulick. October 8, the building was so far completed, that the ladies held a fair in it for the purpose of raising funds for furnishing the room. About four hundred dollars were realized. On Sunday afternoon, December 14, 1884, the opening exercises were held in the new chapel. The Pastor presided. Addresses were delivered by Rev. Lewis

Lampman of the Presbyterian Church, Jamaica; Rev. Andrew Hageman, of the Reformed Church at Queens; Rev. Henry B. Hibben, of the U. S. Navy, and Rev. Henry Frech, of St. Paul's Reformed Church, Jamaica. The last address was in German. The singing was rendered by the school, the congregation uniting in some of the hymns. A quartette was also sung by Mary Estelle Powell, Ida A. Bergen, George L. Powell and James Phraner.

The school thus established in its new home it is hoped has a bright and useful future before it.

THE MITE SOCIETY.

The Mite Society was organized September, 1873. The object of the society is to furnish an organized medium, to the ladies of the congregation, for charitable operations, likewise to promote inter-communion and social intercourse between the members of the church and congregation.

The first officers were, for President, Mrs. Aaron A. Degrauw; for Vice-President, Mrs. J. Garnsey Van Slyke; for Treasurer, Mrs. Stephen Ryder; for Secretary, Miss Mattie E. Phraner. Since the organization of the society there have been a few changes in the officers. Mrs. William Foster succeeded Mrs. J. Garnsey Van Slyke as Vice President, and she in turn was succeeded by Mrs. Stephen L. Spader. Mrs. Charles H. Harris is now Secretary.

Besides other ways in which the object of the society has been carried out; money and garments have been distributed to the needy in our village, many social gatherings have been held, the Sunday school room has been furnished, and recently the church has been carpeted.

THE MISSIONARY SOCIETY.

This society was organized October 1, 1878. Its object and character are shown by the following extracts from its Constitution:

The object of the society shall be the promotion of the spirit of Christian missions, and the raising of funds for the dissemination of the

Gospel among the spiritually destitute, both in our own country and in foreign lands. The society shall be regarded as auxiliary to the missionary boards of our Reformed Church.

Any person whose name is placed upon a collector's book and who makes a monthly contribution to the society shall be a member of the same.

The whole congregation is divided into districts, each district having a collector and comprising four or five families.

The collectors shall solicit contributions for the society; keep a record of the regular monthly contributors; collect each month the amount subscribed, and hand the same to the Treasurer at the regular meeting of the executive committee.

The money collected by the society, the necessary expenses of the society being deducted, shall be divided equally between foreign and Domestic missions. The portion for Domestic missions shall be given to the Board of Domestic Missions. Two-thirds of the portion for Foreign missions shall be given to the Board of Foreign Missions and one-third to the Woman's Board of Foreign Missions of the Reformed Church.

The anniversary of the society shall be held on the second Sabbath morning in January. On this occasion an address or addresses shall be delivered and the report of the Secretary and of the Treasurer for the past year read.

The Pastor shall preside at the anniversary of the society; and is requested to deliver an address or sermon relating to the subject of missions before the society on the second Sabbath of April, July and October, or as near as convenient to these times. On these occasions he is also requested to read the quarterly report of the Treasurer.

At the organization of the society the following officers were chosen: President, Mrs. Aaron A. Degrauw; Vice-President, Mrs. Wm. H. DeHart; Secretary, Mrs. James A. Fleury; Treasurer, Mrs. Stephen L. Spader.

The following were chosen for 1884: President, Mrs. Wm. H. DeHart; Vice-President, Mrs. Jacob S. Wyckoff; Secretary, Miss Mattie E. Phraner; Treasurer, Mrs. Stephen L. Spader; Collectors, Mrs. Elbert N. Remsen, Mrs. James M. Oakley, Mrs. Henry L. Nostrand, Mrs. Stephen Ryder, Mrs. George Durland, Mrs. Ditmars Eldert, Mrs. John L. Pentecost, Mrs. Jacob S. Wyckoff, Mrs. John G. V. A. Duryea, Mrs. Stephen Ryder, Jamaica South; Mrs. John Hendrickson, Mrs. Andrew J. Van Sielen, Mrs. David L. Brinckerhoff, Miss Mary H. Bergen, Miss Anna A. Griffin, Miss Mary A. Brinckerhoff,

Miss Mary E. Ludlum, Miss Sarah DeBevoise, Miss Mary E. DeBevoise, Miss Jennie H. Spader, Miss Susan A. Higbie, Miss Anna C. Hendrickson, Miss Ada Carpenter.

The result of the efforts of the society may be seen to some extent by the increase in the contributions to Foreign and Domestic missions since its organization. Contributions from the church for the six years immediately preceding the organization of the society:

For Foreign Missions	$410 33
For Domestic Missions	307 88
Total	$718 21
Average each year for both causes	119 70

Contributions for the six years since the organization of the society:

For Foreign Missions	$1,032 93
For Domestic Missions	981 45
Total	$2,014 38
Average each year for both causes	335 73

That is, the society has been a means of increasing the contributions of the church to missions very near threefold.

THE STEADY GLEANERS.

This society was organized by a company of young ladies April 1, 1884, under the direction of Miss H. Louise Stevens, at a meeting held at her home.

The object of the society is the promotion of the missionary spirit, and the collection of money for missionary purposes. "In order that the members may assist each other in learning about missions they agree to ask questions and give such bits of information as may be useful in accomplishing the desired end."

The officers of the society are: President, Mary Estelle Powell; Vice-President, Annie L. Pentecost; Treasurer, Susan Ann Hoyt; Secretary, Anna Wyckoff, Assistant Secretary, Jennie Miller.

On Thursday Evening, October 16, 1884, the society gave a "Quaker tea party" in the Consistory Room. It was a very pleasant entertainment and well patronized. The proceeds amounted to $71.98. The society decided to spend about twenty-five dollars of this sum for books upon missionary topics, for the use of the members of the society, and others who might desire to read them, the books to be placed in the Sunday school library.

On October 22, 1884, it was determined to prepare a box of clothing and other articles for one of our missionaries at the West. This box was started on the way to its destination December 13, with the expectation that it would reach the person for whom it was intended by Christmas.

YOUNG MEN'S ASSOCIATION.

The Young Men's Association of the First Reformed Church, of Jamaica, was organized March 12, 1884. The object of this association is to unite its members in efforts to promote their religious, intellectual and social welfare, and to further the temporal and spiritual interests of the church.

The regular business meetings are appointed for the first Wednesday evening of each month.

Under the direction of the association, prayer meetings are held, social gatherings promoted, lectures delivered, &c.

The present officers are: President, Rev. Wm. H. De Hart; 1st Vice-President, Benj. F. Everitt, 2d Vice-President, Wm. W. Treadwell; Secretary, David L. Hardenbrook; Assistant Secretary, Charles A. Ryder; Treasurer, Wm. F. Wyckoff. Devotional Committee, Wm. W. Treadwell, Benj. F. Everitt, and Andrew Stockholm. Membership Committee, Andrew J. Van Sielen, Charles C. DeBevoise and Benj. F. Everitt. Entertainment Committee, Wm. F. Wyckoff, Samuel E. Cozine, David L. Hardenbrook, Samuel Burger and Wm. W. Treadwell. Reception Committee, John L. Wyckoff, John T. Suydam, Gilbert S. Bergen, G. Elmer Van Sielen, Andrew J. Van Sielen, Wm. H. DeHart, Wm. W. Treadwell, and Abm. DeBevoise.

LIST OF THE

PASTORS, ELDERS AND DEACONS, AND MEMBERS,

OF

THE FIRST REFORMED DUTCH CHURCH,

OF

JAMAICA, L. I.

NOTE.—The Consistory in the early history of the church do not appear to have kept an account of their proceedings. The Baptisms are regularly recorded from 1702-1742; after this there are interruptions until 1785. Marriages are not recorded until 1802. Although there are some papers and fragmentary minutes bearing dates previous to 1785, yet it is not until this year that the minutes appear to have been systematically kept. There are no books or papers to be found by which the officers and members of the church previous to 1785 may be to any extent known.

The list of the Pastors contains the names of all, as far as known, who have officiated regularly in the church from its commencement until the present time, together with the dates of their ministrations. The list of Elders and Deacons and members, with the exceptions hereafter noticed is complete for one hundred years, 1785-1884.

PASTORS.

1705. VINCENTIUS ANTONIDES. 1744.
[Also over the churches of Bushwick, Flatbush, Flatlands, Brooklyn, New Utrecht and Gravesend.]

1740. JOHANNES HENDRICUS GOETSCHIUS. 1748.

1754. THOMAS ROMEYN. 1760.

1760. ABRAHAM KETELTAS (Supply). 1762.
[He preached in English, Dutch or French. The church desired him as a Pastor, but the Classis of Amsterdam were not satisfied with his views of the Divinity of Christ, and refused their assent.—*Corwin's Manual.*]

1766. HERMANUS LANCELOT BOELEN. 1772.

1775. SOLOMON FROELIGH. 1776.

1785. RYNIER VAN NEST. 1797.

1794. ZACHARIAS H. KUYPERS (COOPER). 1824.
[All the above, excepting Vincentius Antonides, were also over the churches of Newtown, Success and Oyster Bay.]

1802. JACOB SCHOONMAKER. 1850.
[Also over the church of Newtown from 1802-1849.]

1835. GARRET J. GARRETSON. 1849.
[Also over the Church of Newtown.]

1850. JOHN B. ALLIGER. 1870.

1870. JOHN GARNSEY VAN SLYKE. 1876.

1877. WILLIAM HENRY DEHART.

[Van Basten appears to have supplied Jamaica, Newtown, Success and Oyster Bay, 1739-1740, but doubtful whether he was ever settled.]

CHURCH OFFICERS.

	Elders.	*Deacons.*
1785.	Ares Remsen,	Cornelius Monfort,
	Jacob Lott,	Isaac Amerman,
	Isaac Lefferts,	Jost Van Brunt,
	Peter Monfort.	Stephanus Lott.
1786.	Garret Noorstrand,	Jacob Adrianse,
	Abram Ditmars.	Johannis Duryea.
1788.	Jeremias Van Derbelt,	Isaac Brinckerhoff,
	Stephen Lott.	Hendrick Hendrickson.
1789.	Jeremiah Remsen,	Martin Jansen,
	Jost Van Brunt.	Elbert Hoogland.
1790.	Isaac Lefferts,	William Golder,
	Peter Monfort.	Johannis Lott.
1791.	Isaac Amberman,	Johannis Duryea,
	Abram Ditmars,	Hendrick Hendrickson.
1792.	Jeremias Remsen,	Roelef Duryea,
	Jeremiah Van Derbelt.	Elbert Hoogland.
1793.	Johannis Duryea,	Johannis H. Lott,
	Hendrick Hendrickson.	Isaac Amerman.
1794.	William Bennet,	Jan Williamson,
	Isaac Brinckerhoff.	Rem Snedeker.
1795.	Jost Van Brunt,	Jan Amerman,
	Abram Ditmars.	Johannis Lott.
1796.	Stephen Lott,	Abram Lott,
	Elbert Hoogland.	Isaac Hendrickson.
1797.	William Golder,	Jan Williamson,
	Martin Jansen.	Isaac Amerman.
1798.	Roelef Duryea,	Rem Snedeker,
	Johannis Duryea.	Johannis H. Lott.
1799.	Hendrick Hendrickson,	John Lott, Jr.,
	Isaac Brinckerhoff.	John Amberman.
1800.	William Bennet,	Johannis H. Lott,
	Abraham Ditmars.	Rem Snedeker.
1801	Jost Van Brunt,	Isaac Hendrickson,
	Albert Hoogland.	Isaac Amberman.
1802.	Stephen Lott,	Hendrick Emmons,
	Hendrick Hendrickson.	Hendrick Lott.
1803.	John Williamson,	Rem Remsen,
	Isaac Brinckerhoff.	Albert Snedeker.
1804.	Rem Snedeker,	Johannis S. Lott,
	Hendrick Hendrickson.	Hendrick S. Lott,
1805.	Albert Hoogland,	Isaac Hendrickson,
	John Duryea.	Abraham Hendrickson.
1806.	Isaac Amberman,	Johannis H. Lott,
	Johannes S. Lott.	Hendrick Emmons.

APPENDIX.

	Elders.	*Deacons.*
1807.	Albert Hoogland, John Duryea.	Isaac Hendrickson, Rem Remsen.
1808.	Hendrick Hendrickson, Rem Snedeker.	Aaron Duryea, Nicholas Ryder.
1809.	Isaac Brinckerhoff, Abraham Ditmars.	Aury Snedeker, John Duryea, Jr.
1810.	Johannis S. Lott, Hendrick Hendrickson.	Hendrick S. Lott, Hendrick Brinckerhoff.
1811.	Isaac Hendrickson, John Duryea.	Bernardus Bennet, John Duryea, Jr.
1812.	Rem Remsen, Rem Snedeker.	Aaron Duryea, Johannis H. Eldert.
1813.	Abraham Ditmars, Albert Hoogland.	Bernardus Lamberson, Nicholas Ryder.
1814.	Hendrick S. Lott, Abraham Hendrickson.	Hendrick Brinckerhoff, Barney V. D. Suydam.
1815.	Aaron Duryea, John Duryea.	James Van Sielen, James Hendrickson.
1816.	Rem Snedeker, Isaac Amberman.	John Bergen, Abraham Hegeman.
1817.	Nicholas Ryder, Hendrick Brinckerhoff.	John Bennet, Johannis Lott.
1818.	Hendrick S. Lott, James Hendrickson.	Johannis H. Eldert, John Bennet.
1819.	Aaron Duryea, John I. Duryea.	George Johnson, Aury Remsen.
1820.	Rem Snedeker, Abraham Hendrickson.	
1821.	Hendrick Brinckerhoff, Nicholas Ryder.	Hendrick Hendrickson, James Van Sielen.
1822.	Hendrick S. Lott, James Hendrickson.	Bernardus Bennet, George Johnson.
1823.	John Bergen, John Duryea.	Abraham Hendrickson, Johannis J. Lott.
1824.	Abraham Hendrickson, Nicholas Ryder.	Isaac Amberman, William Stoothoff.
1825.	Hendrick Brinckerhoff, Johannis Lott.	John Amberman, James Van Sielen.
1826.	Hendrick S. Lott, James Hendrickson.	John I. Bennet, Abraham Hegeman.
1827.	John Bergen, James Van Sielen.	Abraham I. Hendrickson, John A. Ditmars.
1828.	Nicholas Ryder, John Van Nostrand.	Hendrick Hendrickson, William Stoothoff.

APPENDIX.

	Elders.	*Deacons.*
1829.	Johannis I. Lott, Abraham I. Hendrickson.	Timothy Rhodes, Jost Lott.
1830.	Hendrick S. Lott, James Hendrickson.	John Simonson, Theodorus Snedeker.
1831.	George Johnson, Timothy Rhodes.	John I. Bennet, Luke Covert.
1832.	Nicholas Ryder, James Hedrickson.	Albert A. Amberman, Abraham Hegeman.
1833.	John Van Nostrand, John A. Ditmars.	Abraham B. Hendrickson, John Bennet.
1834.	John I. Bennet, William Stoothoff.	John W. Stoothoff, Theodorus Snedeker.
1835.	James Van Sielen, Timothy Rhodes.	Bernardus Bennet, Nathaniel Nostrand.
1836.	John Bennet, Abraham Hegeman.	David Baiseley, Jonathan Burnet.
1837.	Johannis Lott, Benjamin Rhodes.	John Amberman, Melancton Carpenter.
1838.	James Hendrickson, Theodorus Snedeker.	Isaac Simonson, Peter Lott.
1839.	George Johnson, John Van Nostrand.	John Simonson, Smith E. Hendrickson.
1840.	Abraham Smith, John I. Bennet.	Jonathan Burnet, Abraham Hendrickson, Jr.
1841.	David Baiseley, Timothy Rhodes.	Isaac Simonson, Benjamin Hegeman.
1842.	Abraham Hegeman, John Bennett	James Ryder, Nathaniel Nostrand.
1843.	James Van Sielen, John Van Nostrand.	Nicholas Emmons, Smith E. Hendrickson.
1844.	Theodorus Snedeker, Bernardus Bennett.	Peter Lott, Abraham A. Hendrickson, Abraham Ayres, one year in place of Smith E. Hendrickson, removed from cong'n.
1845.	Johannis Lott, Timothy Rhodes.	Daniel Hendrickson, James D. Ditmars.
1846.	Abraham Hegeman, Nathaniel Nostrand.	Aury Remsen, Isaac Simonson.
1847.	George Johnson, Benjamin Hegeman.	John Amberman, Sr., James D. Ditmars.
1848.	Peter Lott, Daniel Hendrickson.	William Phraner, John Skidmore VanNostrand
1849.	Benjamin Hegeman, David Baiseley.	Henry Story, Stephen N. Lott.

APPENDIX.

	Elders.	Deacons.
1850.	Theodorus Snedeker, Abraham A. Hendrickson.	Stephen H. Lott, George Rhodes.
1851.	E. W. Van Voorhis, John S. Van Nostrand.	John Allen, Ditmars Stoothoff, Nicholas Amberman in place of John Allen, removed from congregation.
1852.	Henry Story, Stephen N. Lott.	Stephen Ryder, George Rhodes.
1853.	Samuel W. Loweree, Daniel Hendrickson.	Remsen Bennet, Isaac Amberman.
1854.	Stephen H. Lott, Nathaniel Nostrand.	James D. Ditmars, John Rhodes.
1855.	E. W. Van Voorhis, David Baiseley.	Ditmars Stoothoff, William Phraner.
1856.*	Theodorus Snedeker, George Rhodes.	James D. Ditmars, William Nostrand.†
1857.	Daniel Hendrickson, Stephen Ryder.	Isaac Amberman, Remsen Bennet.
1858.	John S. Van Nostrand, Theodorus Snedeker.	Ditmars Stoothoff, William Phraner†
1859.	David Baiseley, Abraham A. Hendrickson.	James D. Ditmars, Hendrick A. Hendrickson.
1860.	Stephen N. Lott, William Phraner.	William Stoothoff, Joseph O. Skillman.
1861.	Abraham A. Hendrickson, Nathaniel Nostrand.	John Rhodes†
1862.	Stephen Ryder, Remsen Bennet.	James Lott. John H. Van Nostrand† Harman J. Stockholm†
1863.	James D. Ditmars, Daniel Hendrickson.	
1864.	Theodorus Snedeker,	John DeBevoise, William Nostrand.†
1865.	Richard Brush, Abraham DeBevoise.	James Ryder,
1866.	John S. Van Nostrand, John N. Brinckerhoff.	Charles J. DeBevoise, Abraham H. Smith
1867.	Hendrick A. Hendrickson, Isaac Amberman.	James C. Hendrickson, Michael Baiseley.

* A portion of the records having been lost, the list from 1856-1865 is made up from other sources. The year in which some of the Elders, who served during this period, were chosen to office may have been one year earlier or later than here given but the names of all are correct, having been obtained from the minutes of the North Classis of Long Island. In the list of Deacons there are several vacancies which could not be supplied. A few names have been inserted of persons, who it is supposed served during a portion of this period. These names are designated by †.

	Elders.	*Deacons.*
1868,	Abraham A. Hendrickson, Henry Onderdonk, Jr.	James H. Stoothoff, Thomas H. Fredericks.
1869,	William Stoothoff, Abraham DeBevoise.	Martin I. Duryea, Abraham Remsen.
1870,	John S. Van Nostrand, Richard Brush,	Hendrick Lott, Ditmars Eldert.
1871,	John N. Brinckerhoff, Martin I. Duryea,	Michael Baiseley, James C. Hendrickson.
1872,	Charles J. DeBevoise, Isaac Amberman.	Elbert A. Brinckerhoff, Stephen Ryder.
1873,	Isaac Snedeker, William Phraner.	Harman J. Stockholm, David Baylis.
1874,	James C. Hendrickson, Stephen Ryder, Isaac Amberman, for one year in place of William Phraner, deceased.	Charles H. Harris, Elbert N. Remsen.
1875,	John N. Brinckerhoff, Isaac Snedeker.	Harman J. Stockholm, George L. Powell.
1876,	John Van Siclen, James C. Hendrickson.	James R. Fredericks, George Bennet.
1877,	Michael Baiseley, Abraham DeBevoise.	John H. Van Nostrand, George L. Powell.
1878,	Martin G. Johnson, Stephen Ryder.	William W. Treadwell, Peter C. Hendrickson.
1879,	Isaac Amberman, Martin I. Duryea.	Ditmars Eldert, Harman J. Stockholm.
1880,	James C. Hendrickson, Abraham DeBevoise.	Elijah H. Nostrand, John A. Hegeman.
1881,	Martin G. Johnson, Isaac Bennet.	Thomas H. Fredericks, James H. Stoothoff.
1882,	Abraham Schenck Bergen, George Higbie.	Charles C. DeBevoise, Andrew J. Van Siclen.
1883,	Isaac Snedeker, John A. Hegeman.	David Baylis, Thomas H. Fredericks.
1884,	Samuel G. Cozine, Francis F. Gulick.	John Hendrickson, Ditmars Eldert.

APPENDIX.

CHURCH MEMBERS.

[w. indicates wife, wid. widow, a bracket husband and wife, c. joined on certificate.]

1786,	Isaac Brinckerhoff,
May 19,	{ Hendrick Hendrickson,
	} Mrs. Hen'k Hendrickson,
	Ida Van Deventer, wid. of Garret Stryker.
	{ Johan Duryea, c.
	} Mrs. Johan Duryea,
	Isaac Rykman, c.
	Jeremiah Van Derbelt, c.
1788,	William Golder,
April 20,	Elbert Hoogland,
	Maria Brinckerhoff, w. of Cornelius Monfort,
1789,	{ Johannes Lott,
Nov. 20,	} Nelly Suydam,
1791,	{ Johannes Lott,
Dec. 16,	} Margareta Van Nuys,
	{ Rem Snedeker,
	} Maria Van Derveer,
	Roeleph Duryea,
	Isaac Amerman, Jr.,
	Jan Amerman, Jr.,
	Phebe Scidmore, w. of Wm. Golder,
	Gertye Van Siclo, w. of Abram Lott,
1793,	{ Jan Williamson,
Nov. 1,	} Ariaentye Suydam,
1795,	{ Femmetye Monfort, wid.
June 5.	of Wm. Monfort,
	{ Isaac Hendrickson,
	} Sarah Monfort,
	Jacob Brinckerhoff,
1798,	{ Femmetye Springsteen,
Nov. 9,	w. of Is'c Hendrickson
1801,	Annatie Bennet, w. of
May 29,	Isaac Brinckerhoff,
	{ David Sprong,
	} Eva Van Lew,
	{ Elbert Snedeker,
	} Maria Rapelye,
	Nelly Van Lew, wid. of John Van Lew,
	Altie Bloodgood, wid. of Cornelius Monfort,
	Tunes Bergen,
	{ Rem Remsen,
	} Annatie Bennet,
	Antie Brinckerhoff, w. of Jan Amberman,
	Elizabeth Oakley, wid. of John Nostrand,
1801,	{ Abraham Van Arsdale,
May. 20,	{ Lametie Amberman,
	Abr'ham H. Hendrickson
	Cornelia Duryea, w. of Jost Van Brunt, Jr.,
	{ Hendrick Emmons,
	} Sarah Bergen,
	{ Garret Snedeker,
	} Johanah Bogert,
	Femetie Rapelye, wid. of Martin Johnson,
	Hendrick Lott,
	Sarah Onderdonk, wid. of Abraham Brinckerhoff
	{ Johannes Brinckerhoff,
	} Rebecca Lott,
	Aaron Duryea,
1803,	Peter Antonides, c.
Oct. 15,	
Oct. 16,	Aury Snedeker,
	Femetie Covert, w. of Garret Van Wickelen,
1807,	John Seidmore,
Feb. 21,	Jane Seidmore,
	Maria Wolf, w. of Thos. Smith, Jr.,
May 14,	{ Nicholas Rider,
	} Hannah Lane,
1808,	{ John Duryea,
Nov. 10,	} Phebe Johnson,
	{ Hendrick Brinckerhoff,
	} Sarah Snedeker,
	Elizabeth Barkelow, c.,
1809,	{ Bernardus Bennet,
Nov. 9,	{ Charity Amberman,
	Sarah Vooris, w. of Isaac Bennet,
1810,	Mrs. Letitia Mills,
May 3,	Mrs. Ann Bergen,
Nov. 8,	Hendrick Poulis, c.,
	Harriet Nostrand, c., w. of Peter Kuypers,
1811.	Phebe Lott, wid. of Stephen Lott, Jr ,
May 2,	
Nov. 7,	Derick Amberman,
	Bernardus Lambertson,
	Phebe Boorem, w. of Isaac Amberman,
1812,	Johannis H. Eldort,
April,	Phebe Remsen,
	Sarah Amberman, w. of Bernardus Lambertson,

1813, April 22, Phebe Sprong, wid. of John Suydam,
Barnet VanDeventer Suydam,

1814, April 22, James Hendrickson,
Elizabeth Oakley, w. of Wm. Willis,
Gersina Brower, w. of Daniel Selover,
Patty Kean, w. of Wm. Raymond,
Elizabeth Snedeker,
Adriana Snedeker,

May 8, { James Van Sielen, e.,
Ida Kouwenhoven, e.,

Nov. 11, Sarah Rosevelt, w. of Dr. Hitchcock,
Jane Duryea, wid. of Mr. Caton,

1815, April 20, { Abraham Hegeman,
Ann Lott,

Nov. 10, Jane Willis, w. of Albert Hoogland,

1816, April 18, { John Bergen,
John H. Lott,
Abigail Bergen,
Sarah Higbie, w. of Aury Remsen,
Sarah Ammerman,

1816, Nov. 9, { John Bennet,
Mary Rhodes,
John Bennet,
Harriet Bennet,
Daniel Selover,
Letitia Ryder, w. of Rem Remsen,
Margaret Watts,

1817, April 5, Aury Remsen,
George Johnson,
Charity Boerum, w. of Wm. Hendrickson,
Elizabeth Ludlum, w. of Abraham Hendrickson
Hannah Higbie, w. of Hend'k Hendrickson,
Ida Ryder, w. of Peter Antonides,

May 1, Wilhelmus Stoothoff,
Bernardus Bennet,
Elizabeth Lott, w. of Simeon Marsten,
Elizabeth Mills, w. of Bernardus Bennet,
Catharine Demott, w. of Joseph Hendrickson,
Maria Hendrickson, w. of John Bergen,
Ann Dyckman, w. of Richard Covert,

1817, May 1, Catharine Oldfield, w. of James Hendrickson,
Miriam Oldfield, w. of John Bergen,
Elizabeth Bennet,
Aletta Brinckerhoff,

Oct. 24, Sarah Van Winkle, e., w. or wid. of John Slusser,
Hendrick Hendrickson,
Isaac Amberman,
William Hendrickson,
John Amberman,
Hannah Mills, w. of Isaac Amberman,
Abigail Golder, w. of Melancton Carpenter,
Ann Remsen, wid. of John Bennet,
Willempe Schenck, w. of George Lott,
Phebe Bergen, wid. of Abraham Hendrickson,
Maria Lott,
Elizabeth Hendrickson,
Allete Hendrickson,

1818, —— Williamson, e.,
Nov. 5, Derick Covert,

1819, Tennis Covert,
April 30, Abraham Hendrickson,
Jane Amerman,
Sarah Nostrand,
Elsie Demott, w. of Oldfield Bergen,
Margaret Smith, e., w. of John Amerman,

Oct. 21, Sarah Lawrence, w. of Peter Cortelyou,
Catharine Bennum, wid. of Elias Hendrickson,
Ruth Ludlum, wid. of Abraham Golder,

1820, April 14, Charity Antonides, wid. of David Abrams,
Catharine Wyckoff, wid. of Derick Covert,
Maria Snedeker,

Nov. 10, Moicha Ryder, w. of Eldert Eldert,
Margaret Amerman, w. of George Duryea,
{ Cornelius Suydam, e.,
Ida Rapelye, e.,

1821, April 27, George Duryea,
Maria Van Arsdale, w. of Derick Amerman,

1822, April 22, Ida Lott, w. of Uriah Hendrickson,
Elsie Westervelt, w. of Mr. Robertson, e.,

APPENDIX.

1822, Oct. 25,	Elizabeth Remsen, wid, of Peter Nostrand,	1828, April 18,	Sarah Skidmore, w. of Henry Van Arsdalen, Nelly Hegeman, c.,
1823, Oct. 24,	Catharine Nostrand, w. of Aury Higbie,	Nov. 28,	Theodorus Snedeker, Timothy Rhodes,* Margaret Bennet,* Jane Snedeker, Martha Golder, w. of John B. Golder,
1825, April 29,	Maria Golder, John Van Nostrand, c., Fanny Nostrand, c.,		
1826, April 28,	John A. Ditmars, George I. Lott, Maria Voorhees, Peggy Bennet, Margaret Hendrickson, Nauche Bennet, w. of Hendrick Hendrickson, Cynthia Simonson, w. of Nicholas Williamson, Elizabeth Smith, w. of Jeffrey Smith, Sally Smith, w. of Henry Mills,	1829, May 1,	Luke Covert, Patience Smith, Catalina Ditmars, wid. of Samuel Eldert, Sally Nostrand, w. of James Bogart, Phebe Covert,
		Oct. 15,	Albert A. Ammerman, Ellen Peterson, Mary Morrell, wid. of Jonathan Morrell, John W. Stoothoff,
Oct. 14,	Hend'k A. Hendrickson, Sarah Hendrickson, c., Smith E. Hendrickson, Susan Rider, Sarah Bennet, w. of Rem Remsen, Elizabeth Bennet, w. of Garret Nostrand, Phebe Van Nostrand,	1830, April 30,	Margaret Hendrickson, c., w. of Jacob Ryder,
		July 31,	Catharine Onderdonk, c. w. of Dow I. Ditmis,
		1831, April 29,	Cornelius Amerman, Albert Nostrand, Sarah Bennet, w. of Andreas Nostrand, Nelly Skidmore, w. of John Nostrand, Catharine Brush, w. of Stephen Henderson, Nelly Lott, Sarah Ann Bennet,
1827, April 6,	Isaac Skirin, Margaret Storm, Nicholas Amberman, Sarah Golder, Henry Simonson, Isaac Simonson, Geerche Bennet, w. of William Martin, Ann Bennet, wid. of Peter Stoothoff, Agnes Snedeker, wid of John Waters, Sarah Ann Simonson,		
		Oct. 15,	Abraham Snedeker, Sarah Brinckerhoff, Peter Nostrand, Margaret Lott, George Nostrand, John Rhodes, Nelly Watts, w. of Nathaniel Nostrand, Margaret Nostrand, Nelly Lott, Rich'd L. Schoonmaker, c
1827, Oct. 14,	Hannah Skidmore, w. of John Simonson, Mary Lott,		
1828, April 18,	John Van Arsdalen, Nicholas Simonson, Rebecca Mills, Abraham B. Hendrickson Phebe Golder, Alletta Smith, w. of William Stoothoff, Jane Stoothoff, Catharine Hendrickson, Phebe Smith, w. of Wait Everitt, Hetty Morrel, Charity Van Arsdalen, Susannah Hegeman,	1832, May 11,	Nathaniel Nostrand, Johanna Hendrickson, Moicha Ryder, c., w. of Eldert Eldert,
		May 12,	Catharine Paynter, w. of William Totten, Elsie Smith, c., w. of Nathaniel Nostrand, Eliza Ludlow, c., w. of Peter P. Larremore,
		Nov. 9,	Phebe Freeman, c., w. of Richard Ammerman,

* Date uncertain

APPENDIX.

1833,
Feb. 3, Ann Stoothoff, c. wid. of James Higbie,
April 26, Margaret Terhune, wid. of John Wyckoff,
Maria H. Onderdonk, c. w. of H. Onderdonk, Jr
Sally Murray, w. of Morris Covert,
Nelly Jones (colored),
Oct. 25, Charity Remsen,
Leah Simonson, c. wid. of Leonard Seaman,
Hannah Ambler Weed, c. w. William Seaman,
Margaret Seaman, c.,
Jane Elizabeth Seaman, c

1834,
April 25, Elizabeth Van Brunt, w. of Nicholas Wyckoff,
Phebe Suydam, wid. of Dominicus Snedeker,
Mary Smith, c., w. of Nicholas Amberman,
Catharine Wyckoff, c., w. of William Bennet,
Oct. 23, Phebe Sprong, w. of Stephen H. Lott,
Lemmata Van Arsdalen, w. of John Nostrand,

1835,
April 24, Peter Stoothoff,
Oct. 10, Cornelia E. Hendrickson
Winifred Hendrickson, w. of Abraham Bergen,
Mary Mills, w. of Remsen Golder,
Jonathan Burnett, c.
{ Abraham Smith, c.,
{ Deborah Hulst, c.,

1836,
April 8, Maria Bennet, w. of Hendrick L. Van Wicklen,
Melancton Carpenter,
Peter Lott,
{ David Baiseley, c.,
{ Sarah Powell, c.,
{ Isaac Bogart, c.,
{ Mary Monfort, c.,
Hannah Bogart, c.,
Ann Bogart, c., wid. of Samuel Dusenberry,
Aug. 13, { John N. Brinckerhoff,
{ Mary M. Adrain,
Magdalen Lott,
Dec. 2, Ann Maria Thompson, w. of Thomas Brownell,
{ Henry Story, c.,
{ Eliza Bond, c.,
Jane Elizabeth Wright, c., w. of Abraham Brinckerhoff,

1837,
April 8, Alletta Wailey, wid. of Robert Allen,
Catharine Bogie, w. of Samuel Corrie,
James (Jacobus) Ryder, c
Aug. 11, Ann Lott, w. of John Spader,
1838,
Aury Van Arsdalen,
April 6, Maria Hendrickson, w. of Cornelius Bennet,
Ann Jenkins, c., w. of Garret Nostrand,
Aug. 10, Nelly Suydam, w. of Anselm H. Conklin,
{ William Palmer, c.,
{ Mrs. William Palmer, c.
1839,
Benjamin Hegeman,
May 30, John Amberman,
{ Ab'm A. Hendrickson, Jr.
{ Elizabeth Carpenter,
Adriana Hendrickson,
Sarah Rhodes, w. of Abm Duryea Remsen.
Margaret Smith, w., of James (Jacobus) Ryder
Sarah McKee, w. of John B. Bennet,
Abigail Jane Lott,
Sarah Elizabeth Van Nostrand,
Ruth Bennet,
Sarah Ann Bennet, w. of Rem Nostrand,
Susannah R. Areson, w. of John Simonson,
Phebe Hendrickson, w. of Nathaniel Nostrand,
Jane Locy, c., w. of Daniel Snedeker,
Sept. 5, Daniel Simonson,
Anna Simonson,
Maria Wyckoff, w. of William Van Dine,
Dec. 13, Phebe Hagner,
1840,
Hannah A. Higbie, w. of Joseph Simonson,
Aug. 7, Cor'lia E. Hendrickson, c.
1841,
James Whightman, c.,
April 3, Ann Mary Daggart, c.,
Sept. 3, George Crane, c.,
1842,
Jan. 20, Martha Seaman,
April 1, Elizabeth Nostrand, w. of Wm. Golder,
Marietta Rodgers, w. of Talman Waters,
Elizabeth Crane, c., w. of George Crane,
Margaret Adrain, c.,

APPENDIX.

1842, Sept. 16, Palmyra Pettit, w. of Peter Amberman.
James Ditmars, Jr.,
Priscilla Hendrickson, wid. of Daniel Smith.

1843, Feb. 3, Nicholas Emmons,
Abraham Ayres,
Magdalen W. Van Lew,
Johanna W. Van Siclen, w. of Wm. H. Woolley,
Sarah Bergen,
Phebe Maria Bergen,
Sarah Monfort, w. of John Allen.

May 13, Anne Simonson, wid. of Isaac Amberman,
Elizabeth Hendrickson, w. of Peter Remsen,
Catharine Baiseley, w. of Nicholas Emmons,

Aug. 18, John H. Bailey, c.,
Eliza Ann Kip, c.,

Nov. 23, Eleanor Clem, c., w. of Isaac Ludlam,

1844,
May 24, Maria Suydam, wid. of Matthew T. Van Zandt,

Aug. 30, Rebecca Creed,
Sarah Wyckoff, c., w. of Wm. C. Stoothoff,
Helen Van Pelt, c., wid. of Barent Wyckoff,

Dec. 6, Daniel Hendrickson,
Hannah Cortelyou,
William L. Hendrickson,
Maria Bennett,
Bernardus Bennett, Jr.,
Elizabeth Mary Hendrickson,
Elizabeth Luyster, wid. of Garret Monfort,
Ann Bergen,
Sophia Platt, w. of John L. Brinckerhoff,
Sarah Wood (colored),

1845, April 4, Abraham D. Remsen,
George Rhodes,
Elizabeth Hicks,
Eleanor Remsen, w. of Nathaniel Sweet,
Mary Wright, w. of Hendrick Remsen,
Catharine Remsen,

July 18, John S. Van Nostrand,
Ellen Maria VanDerveer, w. of Wm. Phraner,

1846, Jan. 16, Harriet Coe, c., w. of Stephen Tyson,
Judith Mills Golder,

April 10, James Bogart,

1846, April 10, Mary Jane Van Siclen, w. of John Amberman,

July 18, Eliza Adraine, c., w. of Rev. Peter S. Williamson,

1847, Jan. 15, John Covert,
Cornelius Amberman,
Jane Bennett, w. of Harvey Powell,
Ruth Ann Golder,
Catharine Bennett,
Charity Ann Simonson,

July 30, Isaac Amberman,
Phebe Higbie, c.,

Oct. 22, William Phraner,
Sarah Ann Amberman,

1848, John Allen,
Jan. 28, Alletta Ann Allen,
Oliver Lawrence,

April 7, Stephen N. Ryder,
Stephen N. Lott.
Cornelia Van Derveer,
Cataline Eldert, w. of H. S. Lott.
Catharine Stoothoff, w. of Nicholas Eldert,
Hannah Maria Seaman,
Susan Simonson, wid. of John Van Wicklen,
Maria J. Suydam, c., w. of Gilbert Bergen,

July 27, Alletta Ann Higbie,
Elizabeth Higbie,

Oct. 20, Maria Van Wicklen,
Cornelia Van Siclen,
Gitty Ann Van Siclen,
Hannah Hall,
E. W. Van Voorhis, c.,
Maria L. Barker, c.,

1849, Jan. 26, Maria Marsten, wid. of Albert Amberman,
Margaret Marsten, wid. of John Powell,
Mary Eliz. Brinckerhoff,
Mary Ann Manley, c., w. of Zebulon Mount,
Mary Jarvis (Wright), c., w. of Johannes Lott,

April 13, Ann Ryder, w. of Stephen Ryder,
Harriet K. Mills,

July 27, Ditmars Stoothoff,
Annie Maria Van Zandt,
John Thompson, c.,
Elizabeth Louge,

Oct. 19, Stephen H. Lott,
Maria Duryea, w. of Benjamin Hegeman,
Ellen Jessup, wid. of Bergen Simonson,

APPENDIX.

Date	Name	Date	Name
1849,	John Lott Simonson,	1858,	Sarah M. Amberman,
Oct. 19,	Elizabeth Amberman,	June 20,	Nathaniel Sweet,
1850,	Phebe Hulst, c., w. of		Mary Valentine, w. of
Jan. 25,	Ditmars Stoothoff,		Cornelius Amberman,
May 3,	Deborah Duryea, wid. of Isaac Bowne,		Elizabeth Luyster, c. wid. of Garret Montfort,
	Ida Sprong, w. of Jacob M. Duryea,		Elizabeth Montfort, James A. Fleury,
	Ida Ann Sprong, w. of William Foster,		Henry Onderdonk, Jr., Elizabeth Onderdonk,
July 2.	Ferdinand Van Wicklen,		Sarah Ann Hendrickson,
Aug. 2,	Margaret T. Storm, wid. of Ferd'nd VanWicklen		w. of J. S. Van Nostrand,
	Morris Covert,	Sept.	Joseph O. Skillman,
	Ida Jane Eldert,	Dec.	Sarah Stoothoff, c., w. of William Stoothoff,
	John Allen, c., Sarah Monfort, c.,		Catharine Maria Hendrickson,
1851,	Sally Ann Carpenter, w. of George Bennet,	1859,	Anna Maria Gorman, w. of Henry C. Ham,
Sept. 5. Dec. 5,	Phebe Eldert, w. of Martin R. Van Siclen,	March.	Catalina Johnson, w. of Eldert Bergen,
	Samuel W. Loweree, c., Rebecca Frazee, c.,	June,	Helen M. G. Stovens, c., Louise H. I. Stovens, c.,
	Margaret J. Amberman,		Abigail Ives Stevens, c.,
1852,	Mary Ditmars,		Sarah J. Simonson,
June 5.	Sarah Ann Tompkins, w. of Daniel S. Waters,	Dec.	James Stoothoff, Mary Catharine Stoothoff
	Elmira Stoothoff,		Eliza Ann Durland,
	Mary Golder, c.,		Caroline Durland, w. of
	John Suydam, c., Elizabeth Snedeker, c.,		Thomas Hyatt
Dec. 4,	Rem Remsen, Nathaniel Nostrand,	1860,	Caroline Myckle, c., w. of William Phraner,
* 1853,	Elizabeth Ditmars, w. of	March,	James Lott, c.,
March 5,	Martin I. Johnson, Phebe Johnson,		Catharine M Gulick, c., Ann Louise S. Lott, c.,
Sept.	Ann Eliza Brinckerhoff, c., wid. Jeromus Van Nuyse,	Dec. 1861, Dec.	Mary A. Brinckerhoff, Jane Catharine Stoothoff Cornelia A. Lamberson,
1854,	William Nostrand, Sarah Ann Amberman,	1862,	Mary H. Lamberson, Abraham De Bevoise, c.
	Rachel S. Amberman,		Anna Maria Covert, c.,
1856,	Jacob S. Amberman, Mary E. Amberman,		John De Bevoise, Malvina Way,
	William Stoothoff, c.,	1863,	Sarah Huntting,
	Catharine Pool, c.,	March,	Mary Agnes Waters,
	Ida Jane Stoothoff, c.,	June,	Anna A. Ham,
1856, March,	Abigail Tompkins, w. of Jacob Phraner,		Elizabeth Waters, Florence Hall,
1858,	Julia Ann Stoutenburgh, w. of Jesse Champlin,		Andrew DeBevoise, Abigail Nostrand,
	Julia Champlin, w. of James Ryder,		Walter Rapelye, Mary A. Hendrickson,

*On account of the loss of church records, the list from 1853 to 1870 is made up from private memoranda and the recollection of individuals. Dates so far as known are given. The names of those members, the time of whose admission into the church is not ascertained, are placed in alphabetical order. The list without doubt for this period is very imperfect, many names being necessarily omitted.

APPENDIX. 197

1863, Sept.	Phebe E. Reeve, c., w. of John H. VanNostrand,
Dec.	John H. Van Nostrand, James Ryder,
1864,	Richard Brush,
	{ William T. Brush,
	{ Sarah E. Smith,
	Catharine Hendrickson, wid. of James Hendrickson,
	Susan Mills, w. of Hendrick A. Hendrickson,
	Kate Simonson,
	Ella Simonson,
	{ Albert Stoothoff,
	{ Sarah Murray,
March,	Mary Ruth Phraner,
June,	Abigail C. Nostrand,
Mar, 1865,	Arabella P. Stoothoff,
June,	{ Martin I. Duryea,
	{ Elizabeth Van Alst,
Dec.	Martha Ellen Phraner, Alice Champlin,
1866,	{ Thomas H. Fredericks,
June,	{ Sarah M. Amberman,
	Sarah Elizabeth Rhodes,
	Ditmars Eldert,
	John Eldert,
	Mary Catharine Eldert,
	Phebe Eldert,
	{ Michael Baiseley,
	{ Sarah Jane Smith,
	{ James C. Hendrickson,
	{ Matilda R. Van Siclen,
	Samuel Hendrickson,
	Hend'k A. Hendrickson,
	Matilda J. Hendrickson,
	Phebe A. Ammerman,
Sept.	Sarah Mills,
1867,	Annie D. DeBevoise,
	Margaret Amelia Nostrand,
	Anna Nostrand,
	Rem Nostrand,
	{ Ludlum Fredericks,
Dec.	{ Elizabeth Smith,
Mar.1868,	Abraham Remsen,
	{ George L. Powell,
	{ Mary E. Bennet,
	Elijah Alliger,
1869,	{ Hendrick Lott,
	{ Caroline Way,
April,	Luther F. Stevens,
June,	Mary R. Briggs,
1870,	Eliza Valentine (Seaman) w. of Nicholas Amberman,
	Ida Davis, w. of Elijah Alliger,

Frances T. Duyckinck, w. of Rev. John B. Alliger,
Aletta Rhodes, w. of John Areson, Jr.,
{ John D. Ammerman,
{ Mary Jane Van Siclen,
Hannah Bennet, c.,
Mary H. Hicks, w. of George Bennet,
{ Remsen Bennet,
{ Phebe Frederick,
Mrs. Phebe Burnett,
Ellen G. Tuthill, w. of Richard Brush,
Dorcas Champlin,
Kate Covert,
Maggie Covert,
Sarah Smith, w. of John Covert,
Sarah Hendrickson, w. William Covert,
Elsie Ann Davis,
Kate Davis,
{ Charles J. DeBevoise,
{ Jane K. Stockholm,
Elizabeth Elmira DeBevoise,
David Ditmars,
Maria Ditmis,
Abraham Duryea,
Benjamin Duryea,
Jennie DeBevoise, w. of John G. V. A. Duryea,
Theresa Ebert,
Catharine A. Baiseley, w. of Nicholas Emmons
Henry Fleury,
Lucy J. Ham,
Margaret E. Ham,
{ Andrew J. Hannas,
{ Mrs. Andrew J. Hannas,
{ Jared Hasbrouck,
{ Mrs. Jared Hasbrouck,
Elizabeth Martin, w. of Stephen Henderson,
Catharine ———— w. of James Hendrickson,
Mrs. Elias B. Hendrickson,
Joanna ————, w. of Jacob Hendrickson,
John S. Hendrickson,
Hendrick Hendrickson,
Mary Hendrickson,
Mary Granger, w. of Daniel B. Hendrickson,
Emma Jane Lott,

APPENDIX.

	Sarah Van Nostrand, w. of Nicholas Ludlum,	1871, June 4,	John Van Sielen, Elizabeth J. Remsen, Harman J. Stockholm, c. Maria Gertrude Lott,
	Mrs. John Nostrand, William H. Phraner, Sarah Jane Savage, w. of Erasmus Peterson, Abigail Jane Lott, wid. of Joseph Powell, Emmeline Hendrickson, w. of Abraham Remsen John Rhodes, Sarah A. Bennet, Stephen Ryder, Stephen Ryder, Magdalene Van Wicklen, Abby Simonson, J. Augustus Simonson, Isaac Simonson, Mrs. Isaac Simonson, Abraham H. Smith, Alice Smith, Mrs. George Smith, Mrs. Frank Smith, Isaac Snedeker, Cornelia Eldert, Ann Lott, wid. of Andrew Stockholm, Elizabeth Pawling, c., w. of Wm. P. Stoutenburgh Isaac T. Waters,		Serena L. Smith, wid. of Stephen L Spader, Eliza Ann Whitson, w. of Abraham A. Hendrickson. John D. Amerman, c., Mary B. Disbrow, c., w. of George W. Hoyt, Gertrude Lott, c., w. of James Van Sielen,
		Dec. 2,	Emily Vermilye, c., w. of Elbert A. Brinckerhoff,
		Dec. 3,	James Aug. Herriman,
		1872, Mar. 2,	Sarah Frances Ludlum, Margaret Fleury, Mrs. Emmeline Duryea, w. of Wm. Stoothoff, Phebe Duryea, w. of Isaac R. Snedeker, Matilda Hegeman, w. of Garret K. Van Sielen, Mrs. Frances A. Hewlett, c., w. of John Ryder,
		June 1,	Early Granger, John Remsen, William Stoothoff, Ellen Foster,
*1870, Dec. 17,	Aletta A. Griffin, Mary Esther Young, c., wid. of Cornelius Nostrand, Mary Amerman, c., w. of Rev. J. G. Van Slyke, Ellen Mulford, c., wid. of Daniel Amerman, Francis F. Gulick, c., Helen Tasker, c.,	Sept. 1,	William C. Stoothoff, Jane Eliza Lott, w. of Abraham DeBevoise, Jr David Baylis, c.,
		1873, Mar. 1,	Martha J. Doughty, Elbert N. Remsen, Kate S. Nostrand,
		May 31,	Abraham Griffin, Sarah Van Sielen, c., w. of Garret Griffin, Ann Van Nuyse, c., w. of Stephen Voris, Susan Rebecca Voris, c., Phebe Maria Voris, c.,
1871, Mar. 4,	Sarah E. Phraner, Hester Ann Durland, w. of James M. Oakley, Phebe Durland, w. of A. Ditmars Johnson,		
May 21,	Sarah Caroline Baylis,		
June 3,	Aletta J. Durland, w. of Abraham Griffin,	Sept. 7,	Abigail W. Kouwenhoven c., w. of Jas. R. Fredericks,
June 4,	Mary Magdalene Bennett Sarah Ham, Sarah Catharine Van Nostrand, Charlotte T. Husson, Emily Williamson, A. Ditmars Johnson, Charles H. Harris, William W. Treadwell,	1874, June 7,	Arabella Stoothoff, c., w. of Benj. S. Waters, Laura Edwards, c., w. of John H. Brinckerhoff, Carrie Maria Bergen,
		Sept. 5,	Mary E. S. Willets, w. of A. A. Degrauw, Mrs. H. W. Starr.

* Here the church records begin again.

APPENDIX. 199

1874,	Letty Murray, c., w. of Theodore H. Pettit,	1877, June 2,	David Schuyler Reeves, c Jane Stoothoff, c.,
Sept. 5,		Sept. 1,	George Higbie, c.,
Dec. 5,	James Remsen Fredericks,		Amelia Nostrand, c.,
	Aletta Ann Fredericks, wid. of John Higbie,		Susan A. Higbie, c., Abby Higbie, c.,
	Catharine Gertrude Gulick,		Ella B. Higbie, c.,
		Dec. 1,	John H.J. VanGaasbeck,c
	Lizzie Augusta DeBevoise		Catharine Westbrook, c.,
	Hester E. DeBevoise,		Elijah H. Nostrand, c.,
	Sarah W. DeBevoise,		Jane Higbie, c.,
	Anna J. DeBevoise,		Daniel Cobleigh, c.,
	Nicholas Lott, c.,		Mary L. Wiswell, c.,
	Elizabeth B. Gilbert, c.,		Anna Duryea,
1875,	Jane L. Smith, w. of Edgar Whitson,	1878, Mar. 2,	Cornelia A. Schenck, w. of Abraham VanSiclen,
Mar. 6,			
	Emma Whitson,		Aletta Duryea, w. of Townsend Albertson,
	Lizzie Jones,		
	Theodore Lott,		Sarah Emma Stoothoff,
	Sarah Carman, c., w. of Chas. A. Hendrickson,		Jennie H. Spader, Alice Ann Amberman,
	Mary Frances Averill, c.		Annie Westbrook Van Gaasbeck, c.,
June 27,	George Bennet,		
	Abraham James Hendrickson,	June 1,	Abraham S. Bergen, c., Maria Snydam, c.,
	Josephine T. Husson,		Gilbert S. Bergen, c.,
	Marietta Lott,		Ida Ann Bergen, c.,
	Caroline Amanda Lott,		Magdalene Bergen, c.,
	Harriet Louise Stevens, c		Annie Bergen, c.,
	Mary Eliz'beth Stevens, c		James Spice, c.,
Dec. 5,	Anna R. Gulick,		Catharine J. VanTassel, c
Dec. 17,	Hiram D. Shultis,		Sarah H. Forman, c., w. of Rev. Jacob S. Wyckoff,
1876,	Brewster W. Baylis,		
Mar. 4,	W. F. Traphagen,		
	Samuel Colton,		Mary E. Fredericks, c., w. of Joseph West,
	Maria Augusta Lott,		
	Charlotte F. Lott,		Charles C. DeBevoise,
June 3,	Eveline Ham,		Anna S. Van Siclen,
	Elizabeth Fleury,		Phebe Young, w. of Geo. Durland,
	Mary Aletta Powell,		
	William L. Fredericks,		Eloise DeBevoise,
	Peter C. Hendrickson,		Emily Baiseley, w. of William S. Williamson,
	Jane B. Collison,		
	John Hendrickson,	Aug. 31,	Sarah Baiseley,
	Mary Collison.	Nov. 30,	Maria Catharine Skillman
	Martin G. Johnson, c.,	1879,	Georgie Ella Hendrickson,
	Margaret T. Nostrand, c	Feb. 27,	
	Cornelia C. Van Siclen, c. w. of George Nostrand		Ida Kouwenhoven Van Siclen,
	Ann Van Siclen, c., wid. of George Hoogland,		Harriet Ella Van Siclen, Annie Livingstone Pentecost,
	Mary E. Hoogland, c.,		
	Ida Anna Foster,		Mary Estelle Powell,
Sept. 2,	John L. Pentecost,		Ella Louise Darby,
	Maria Sutherby, c.,		Isaac Bennet, c.,
1877,	Janette Rich, c., w. of Rev. Wm. H. DeHart,		Sarah Pettitt, c.,
June 2.		Mar. 1,	George Byron Loux,
	Phebe W. Van Derveer,c. w. of Henry L. Nostrand		Margaret Hendrickson Bergen.

APPENDIX.

1879,
Mar. 1, Joanna Agatha Voris,
Amanda Mal'na Edwards w. of Joshua W. Battee
Sarah Ann Denton, w. of Elijah Raynor,
{ William Edmund Tilton,
Adelia Ann Baldwin,
John Henry Ammerman,
Mary Lotus Clark,
Emma Platt Tappan, e., w. of Henry A. Monfort,
Mary Stillwell Pool, e.,

May 31, Agnes Conklin Fredericks
Aletta Ma'lda Fredericks
Catharine Voris,
Phebe J. Smedes, e., w. of John A. Campbell,

Sept. 5, Mary Eliz'th Fredericks,
Nov. 19, Ida Kouwenhoven Skillman,
Dec. 6, { John Aug'tus Hegeman, e
Phebe Louisa Eldert,
Benj. Franklin Everitt,
Mary Eliza Baylis,
Alexander H. Collison,
Jean Wylie Miller,
Marietta Lidsey Miller,
Jane Maria Gulick,

1880,
Mar. 6, Stephen Lott,
Helena Pettigrew Miller, w. of Geo. T. Van Deverg,

June 5, { Samuel G. Cozine, e.,
Lucy Ann White, e.,
Samuel Edmund Cozine, e

1881,
Mar. 5, Andrew James Van Sielen
Ida Jane Stoothoff,
June 4, Anna Cortelyou Hendrickson,
Adelaide Josephine Clark wid. of John Henry Conklin,
Elizabeth Clark Conklin,

Sept. 3, Ellen Augusta Brush,
Ella Van Brunt Remsen,
Elizabeth Rapelye, wid. of Richard H. Garretson,

1882,
Mar. 5, Charles Sterling Wyckoff
Walter Way DeBevoise,

1882,
Mar. 5, Florence Isabella Van Sielen Miller,
June 3, C. L. Martin, e., w. of E. K. Morris,
Abram Ella Bergen,
Sept. 2, Sarah Augusta Smith,
Dec. 2, Susan Ann Hoyt,
Maud Kissam,
Laurestine Johnson,
Elvira Campbell,
Sarah Jane Miller,
Robert Ham, e.,

1883,
Mar. 3, Elias Hendrickson, e.,
June 2, Phebe Furman Starkey,
Ida Reeve Van Nostrand
{ Daniel H. Carpenter, e.,
Catharine Johnson, e.,
Sept. 1, Aletta Stoothoff, wid. of Samuel Eldert,
{ John J. Davies, e.,
Emily Hall, e.,
Thomas W. Nadal, e.,
Mary Ann Higbie, e.,
Dec. 1, Charity B. Nostrand, e., wid. of Abraham Ammerman,
Sarah K. Volckman, e. w. of Edwin Johanknecht
Mary Emma DeBevoise,
Anna Lilian Davies,
Annie Statesir Wyckoff,
Harriet Elizabeth Crossman, w. of William A. Warnock,
Mary Conklin,

1884,
Mar. 1, Erwin Skidmore VanNostrand,
Emma Louise DeBevoise
Emma C. Smith, e., w. of John Hausmann,
May 31, Isaac Rapelye Snedeker,
Lulu White Cozine,
David Langdon Hardenbrook,
Andrew Stockholm, e.,
Clara F. R. Bills, e.,
Sept. 6, William Forman Wyckoff
Cornelia Spador, e.

APPENDIX. 201

OCCUPANTS OF PEWS, 1884.

1. Deacons,
6. Joshua W. Battee,
7. John H. Brinckerhoff,
8. Howard Pearsall,
10. Mrs. Jeromus Van Nuyse,
11. Garret K. Van Sielen,
    Andrew Stockholm,
12. Ditmars Eldert,
13. Martin H. Van Sielen,
14. Henry Johnson,
15. Mrs. Stephen L. Spader,
16. William Durland,
    James M. Oakley,
18. Hendrick Lott,
19. Oliver H. Ryder,
20. Mrs. Joseph Powell,
21. William W. Treadwell,
22. Mrs. George Hoogland,
23. John L. Pentecost,
24. John Covert,
30. George Miller,
31. George L. Powell,
32. Luther F. Stevens,
33. Harvey Powell,
34. John J. Davies,
35. Garret Griffin,
36. Bailey Brothers,
37. J. H. Eldert,
38. George S. Van Wickel,
39. Martin I. Duryea,
    John G. V. A. Duryea,
40. Franklin James Lott,
41. Mrs. Stephen Lott,
42. Daniel H. Carpenter,
43. William W. Stoothoff,
44. Mrs. Samuel Eldert,
45. Mrs. Eldert Bergen,
46. Mrs. Daniel R. Suydam,
    John T. Suydam,
47. Isaac Snedeker,
    Isaac R. Snedeker,
48. Henry L. Nostrand,
49. Mrs. William Stoothoff,
51. William Foster,
52. Ludlum Fredericks,
    Thomas H. Fredericks,
53. Nicholas Auberman,
54. Daniel Hendrickson,
    Peter C. Hendrickson,
55. James C. Hendrickson,
    James Van Sielen,
56. Mrs. Harman J. Stockholm,
    Charles Lott,
57. Mrs. Jacobus Ryder,
    James Ryder,
58. Stephen Ryder,
59. Pastor's Pew,
60. For Strangers,
61. James A. Fleury,
62. George L. Brinckerhoff,
63. Samuel G. Cozine,
    Samuel E. Cozine,
64. James R. Fredericks,
    John A. Hegeman,
65. John Hausmann,
66. John W. Van Dine,
    Stephen Lott,
67. James Stoothoff,
68. Lucy J. Ham,
    Elizabeth Montfort,
74. Jacob Schoonmaker Amberman,
75. Abraham Stoothoff,
77. David Bavlis,
78. George Higbie,
79. Henry Onderdonk, Jr.,
80. Abraham A. Hendrickson,
    John Hendrickson,
81. Mrs. Jacob S. Wyckoff,
82. Charles J. DeBevoise,
    Mrs. Andrew Stockholm,
83. Joseph W. Conklin,
84. Michael Baiseley,
    Thomas Baiseley,
85. Aaron A. Degrauw,
86. Abraham DeBevoise,
    Charles C. DeBevoise,
87. Mrs. John Remsen,
    Abraham Remsen,
88. James Lott,
    Alexander H. Collison,
89. Charles A. Hendrickson,
90. Martin G. Johnson,
91. David J. Purdy,
92. Isaac Bennet,
    Ruth Bennet,
94. David L. Brinckerhoff,
95. Mrs. John H. Van Nostrand,
    Phebe Van Nostrand,
96. George Bennet,
97. Charles H. Harris,
98. James Phraner,
100. Benjamin F. Everitt,
101. William S. Williamson,
102. George Durland,
103. Andrew DeBevoise,
     George DeBevoise,

104. Isaac Amberman,
105. Nicholas Ludlum,
106. Mrs. Hendrick A. Hendrickson,
    Jaques V. B. Voris,
107. Thomas T. Husson,
    Samuel Colton,
108. Mrs. William L. Hendrickson
109. Francis F. Gulick,
110. Francis F. Gulick,
111. Abraham S. Bergen,
112. Cornelius Amberman,
119. John D. Ammerman,
118. Charles Conklin,
120. Ann Bergen,
121. Dr. Thomas Nadal,
122. Abraham H. Smith,
123. Isaac C. Remsen,
124. Thomas T. Husson,
125. Abraham D. Rhodes,
126. Nicholas Lott,
127. Stephen Ryder,
128. John DeBevoise,
129. William A. Warnock,
130. Elbert N. Remsen,
131. Richard Brush,
    William T. Brush,
132. Isaac Rapelye,
    Phebe Hagner,
    Mrs. Richard Garretson,
133. Mrs. Jacob Phraner,
134. Elijah H. Nostrand,
135. Edwin Johanknecht,
139. William Voris,
142. Elders.

ANNUAL STATISTICAL REPORT

To the North Classis of Long Island, April 16, 1894.

Number of Families		165
Communicants,	Received on Confession	10
	Received on Certificate	9
	Dismissed,	5
	Died	5
	Total now in Communion	289
Baptized,	Infants	15
	Adult	1
Number of Catechumens		75
Sunday Schools,	Number of Schools	2
	Total Enrollment	229
Contributions,	Religious and Benevolent Purposes	$ 514 13
	Congregational Purposes	3,582 86

INDEX.

A

	PAGE.		PAGE.
Academy	74	Anderson, Wm.	138
Alliger, J. B.	103, 145	Antonides, V.	7, 67
Alms-chest	49, 53, 62, 84, 99	Apron and Neck-tie Fair	151
Altar	19, 94, 98	Arondeus, J	44, 48
Amberman, D	65	Ascension Day	27
Anabaptists	23, 135		

B

Baird	11, 14, 21, 113	Bier	91, 107
Baldwin, Eli	92, 94	Billeting	65
Bands	60, 107, 109	Boel Henricus	41, 44, 67
Baptism	41, 70	Boelen, H. L.	54
Bason	70, 124, 159	Bostwick, David	42
Bazaar	162, 167, 170	Bouquets	146
Bell	20, 47, 52, 172	Bread	77
Bell-ringer	75, 83, 90	Breeches	56
Benneway, Peter	56	Brinckerhoff, E. A.	146, 149, 150, 151
Bergen Miss Ann	157, 168	Brinckerhoff, Aletta	99
Bible	71, 75, 157	Broadhead, Jacob	103, 105
Bible Society	107, 135, 141		

C

Campbell, W. H.	167	Classical Visitation	141, 146, 165
Candidate	58, 84	Classis	98, 130
Candles	91	Clock	98
Carpet	91, 101, 114, 152, 168	Coetus	34
Carroll, J. H.	143, 145	Clowes, S	17
Catechism	27, 78, 88, 108, 139	Coal	91
Cemeteries	33	Cobb, O. E.	157
Centennial	148, 154	Cockefer, John	5, 13
Chairs	48	Cole, David	166
Chambers, T. W	105, 135	Collections	17, 79, 106
Chandeliers	101, 115	Communion	70, 159
Choir	96, 108, 129, 172	Conferentie	50, 55
Cholera	87, 101	Consistory Room	121, 122, 128, 138, 147, 160
Chorister	91, 162	Cooper, Z. H	75
Christmas	27	Coppers	19, 55, 83
Christmas Tree	148, 164	Corner-stone	81, 91, 122, 172
Christening	70, 163	Crane, Elias W	96
Christian Union	128	Creed	6, 121, 165, 170
Church Masters	12, 20, 50	Cuyler, T. L	116, 123
Circle	13		

D

	PAGE.		PAGE.
Deacons, List of	186	Donation Party,	104, 106, 128, 166
Dedication	87, 93, 124	Dort, Synod of	19, 25
Deeds	15, 36, 79, 87, 94, 169	Doxology	123, 171
Degrauw, A. A.	36, 127, 168	Draft Riot	132
Delfart, Wm. H	156	Drisius, Samuel	7
Demarest, James	96	Dubois Walter	67
DeRonde, L.	47, 60	Duryea,	84, 90, 116, 124, 131, 137
Disbanding	87	Dutch,	6, 73, 75, 100, 113, 139
Domine	41	Dwight, M. W.	96

E

Easter	27, 86, 163, 167	Evangelical Alliance	150
Elders, List of	186	Evangelical Union	113
East Jamaica	142, 117, 170, 177	Examination	47, 59
Ellmendorf, Anthony	125, 108	Excursion	115, 166

F

Fairchild, E. S	156	Fly	53, 105
Fair	94, 102, 104, 106, 115, 159	Foresinger	83
Fast,	61, 73, 85, 87, 93, 99, 101, 113, 121, 128	Fourth of July	96, 98, 114
		Fragment Society	91
Ferris, Wm	140	Freeman, B	7, 67
Filkin, Henry	15	Frelinghuysen,	35, 37, 47, 67
Fire	115, 117, 128, 133, 172	Froeligh, Sol.	58, 60, 69, 85
Firemen	115, 128, 131	Funerals,	69, 72, 102, 107, 111, 114, 131, 135, 138, 162.
Firewood	9, 109		
Flowers	167	Furnace	116, 118

G

Gallery	105, 106	Goetschius, J. H	35, 43, 68
Ganon	10, 14	Gown	60, 107, 109
Garden Party	160	Grace Church,	8, 108, 119, 128, 132
Garretson, G. J	95, 100	Griffis Wm. E	153, 165
Gas	125, 117, 153, 158,	Gunther, C. G	112

H

Hageman, And	165	Himrod, John S	125
Hall, B. R	119	Holmes, John McC	130
Hammond, J. W	125	Horse Sheds	19, 168, 169
Haynes, M. L.	156	Hulst, G. D	146, 151
Heermance, H	76, 98	Humphreys	21
Hendrickson, Abm	97	Husson, Thos. T	169
Hessian fly	73	Hymns of the Church	75, 172

I

Incorporation	86	Induction	49, 54
Independence	96, 98, 125	Installation	59, 96, 104, 145, 156
Indians	8, 67, 85, 101		

INDEX.

J

	PAGE.		PAGE.
Jackson, John F	79	Jews	109, 153
Jamaica	9	Johnson, W. L.	94, 108, 115, 125, 136
Janeway, J. J	92		

K

Keteltas, Abm	53, 60, 171	Knob	30, 168
King, John A	105, 117, 123	Kissam, G. C	125, 171
Kip	13, 14, 141	Kuypers, Z. H	60, 75, 88

L

Lampman, Lewis	169	Liturgy	19, 165
Lamps	104, 115	Livingston, J. H	76
Lansing, John A	159, 141	Lord's Supper	25, 54, 70, 163, 166
Lead	20, 21	Lowe, Peter	76
Lefferts, Isaac	23, 63	Lupardus, Wm	7
Legacies	97, 99	Lutheran	155, 169

M

Macdonald, J. M	98, 99	Members of the Church	191
McKelvey, Alex'r	143, 145	Methodists	120, 139
Mandeville	34, 107, 122	Missionary Society,	79, 85, 93, 113, 165, 179
Manice, D. F	122		
Marriage	51, 70, 113, 170	Mite Society	154, 158, 179
Marselus, N. J	107	Mulligan, John	89
Mastodon	122	Music	96, 104
Melodeon	122		

N

Necessary	90	Nichols, Thos	148
Newtown	26, 32, 79, 87, 100	Noll	91, 98
New Years	27, 57, 104, 116		

O

Oakey, P. D	111, 140	Organist	113
Ordination	76	Oysterbay	26, 30, 46, 79, 88
Organ	104, 132		

P

Paas	27, 57	Pinxter	27, 57
Pall	72, 91	Plates	19, 90
Parsonage	35, 49, 79, 87, 111, 112	Polhemus	5, 149
Pastors, List of	185	Poor	20, 56
Pentecost	163	Porter, E. S	105, 117, 116
Pews, Occupants of	94, 103, 124, 126, 139, 201	Prayer Meetings	62, 106, 124
		Preparatory Service	27, 109
Pewter	70	Presbyterian Church,	81, 100, 116, 158
Phraner, Wm. H	165		
Picnic	122, 160, 166	Priest, Albert	112

P

Primer 71	Psalm Book 18, 75
Proponent 81	Pulpit 18, 90, 109, 117, 168, 172
Psalm-board 18	

Q

Quadragenian 97	Queens 115, 121, 148
Quakers 23, 65	

R

Rates 52	Riot 133
Religion .. 71, 86, 87, 88, 91, 97, 121	Ritzema, Johannes 44
Revolutionary Incidents 61	Romeyn, Thos 45, 53, 68
Ring 43	Rubell, J. C 50, 62, 64, 68

S

Sabbath 9, 99	Soldiers 130
Salary, ... 27, 72, 84, 109, 113, 115, 120, 127, 145, 173	Spies 125
	Statistical Report, 1884 203
Sand 56, 90, 91	Steady Gleaners 181
Sashes 58	Steeple 21
Sayres, G. H 99, 107	Simpson, Edward P 113
Schol, Cordwainer 34	Stoves 19, 90, 106, 116
Schoonmaker .. 62, 68, 78, 107, 173	Strawberry Festival 147, 153
Scudder 99, 127, 129, 130	Strong 96, 105, 107
Seat 20, 91	Stryker, Peter 76
Seats 17, 119	St. Roman's Well, 115, 116, 122, 127
Seraphine 102	Success 26, 31, 50, 76, 87
Sexton 105, 155	Sunday 9, 71, 99
Sewing Society 101, 106, 112	Sunday Observance 166
Shepard, C. J 139, 145, 165	Sunday School, Village 89, 106, 115, 139, 163, 175
Sherlock 22	
Shinneall, R. C 89	Sunday School, East 142, 147, 170, Jamaica 177
Singing 47, 83, 84, 96	
Smith, N. E 111, 125	Surprise Party 140, 152
Slaves 41, 54, 64, 79	Sutphen, David S 153
Sociable 155	Sweeping 56, 84
Soldiers' Aid Society 129, 133	

T

Taxes 114	Thanksgiving, 27, 54, 131, 133, 137, 164
Tea 63	
Te Deum 131	Thieves 152, 153
Temperance 87, 98, 139, 143, 148, 151, 157, 158	Thompson, Abm 153
	Treasurers 151
Ten Eyck, Wm. H 139	Trustees 81

U

Union Hall 74, 109, 119, 123	Union Services, 114, 121, 124, 126, 127, 164, 166

V

	PAGE.		PAGE.
Vacation	140, 168	Van Sinderen, U	14, 17, 64, 68
Van Buren, John M.	122	Van Slyke, J. G	145, 156
Van Doren, Isaac	84	Van Zandt, A. B	123
Van Nest	58, 73, 77, 124	Verbryck, Samuel	49
Van Santvoord, Cor's	67	Vermilye, Thos. E	124, 145

W

Wampum	19	Williamson, Peter D	106, 107
Ward, John W.	105	Wilson, James B.	165
Week of Prayer	139, 146, 161, 168, 169	Wine	57, 77, 90
Wells, C. L.	144	Wolf	21
West, Jacob	125, 150	Wood	84, 90, 109
Westbrook, Cor's D.	92	Woolsey, Benj.	15, 17, 42
Whitehead, Daniel	6	Wolver Hollow	26, 88, 89
Whit Sunday	27, 163	Wyckoff	141, 171

Y

Y. M. C. Association ....146 | Young Men's Association......182

Z

Zouaves 131

OTHER CONTRIBUTIONS TO LOCAL HISTORY,

BY HENRY ONDERDONK, Jr.

Revolutionary Incidents of Queens County	1846
" " " " second series	1881
Letters to J. F. Cooper on the capture and death of General Woodhull (cuttings from the *Home Journal*,)*	1848
Revolutionary Incidents of Suffolk and Kings Counties, Battle of Long Island and British Prisons and Prison Ships	1849
Genealogy of the Onderdonk Family (in Riker's Newtown)	1852
Queens County in Olden Times, first series	1865
" " " " second series, ready for the press	——
Suffolk County in Olden Times, Newspaper Cuttings*	1865
Kings County in Olden Times, Newspaper Cuttings*	1866
Bibliography of Long Island (in Furman's Antiquities,)	1866
Reformed Dutch Churches and Ministers on Long Island, (cuttings from the *Christian Intelligencer*,)*	1866
Ancient Agriculture, Stock-breeding and Manufactures in Hempstead (in Report of Queens County Agricultural Society)	1867
Governor Stuyvesant and the Quakers (cuttings from the *Christian Intelligencer*,)*.	1868
Rise and Growth of the Society of Friends on Long Island and in New York City (in American His. Record,)	1872
Jamaica Centennial, July 4th, Newspaper Cuttings*	1876
Letters on School and College Life, Newspaper Cuttings*	1876-8
Annals of Hempstead, and Rise and Growth of Friends	1878
Roslyn in Olden Times, Newspaper Cuttings*	1879
Induction of Rev. Wm. Vesey (in N. Y. Churchman)*	1879
Antiquities of the Parish Church, Jamaica	1880
Antiquities of the Parish Church, Hempstead	1880
Criticisms on Thos. Jones' His. of N. Y. (in Mag. of Amer. His.	1880
Prize History of Queens Co. Agricultural Society	1882
History of the Turf in Queens county	1882

*These cuttings may be seen in the Astor and some other Libraries.

www.ingramcontent.com/pod-product-compliance
Lightning Source LLC
Chambersburg PA
CBHW031737230426
43669CB00007B/383